DISSENT

FROM THE

CREED

DISSENT
FROM THE
CREED

HERESIES
Past and
Present

RICHARD M. HOGAN

Our Sunday Visitor Publishing Division
Our Sunday Visitor, Inc.
Huntington, Indiana 46750

Nihil Obstat
Rev. George A. Welzbacher
Censor Librorum

Imprimatur
Most Rev. Harry J. Flynn, D.D.
Archbishop of St. Paul and Minneapolis
February 22, 2001

The Nihil Obstat and Imprimatur are official declarations that a book or pamphlet is free of doctrinal or moral error. No implication is contained therein that those who have granted the Nihil Obstat or Imprimatur agree with the contents, opinions, or statements expressed.

Scripture verses used in this work, for which the publisher and author are grateful, are taken from the Catholic edition of the *Revised Standard Version Bible*, © 1965 and 1966 by the Division of Christian Education of the National Council of the Churches of Christ in the U.S.A., and are used by permission of the copyright holder; all rights reserved. Every reasonable effort has been made to determine copyright holders of excerpted materials. If any copyrighted materials have been inadvertently used in this work without proper credit being given in one form or another, please notify Our Sunday Visitor in writing so that future printings of this work may be corrected accordingly.

ISBN: 0-87973-408-6
LCCCN: 00-140016

Cover design by Monica Haneline
PRINTED IN THE UNITED STATES OF AMERICA

Table of Contents

Preface

I WAS VERY PLEASED WHEN MICHAEL DUBRUIEL OF OUR SUNDAY VISITOR Publishing called me over a year ago to discuss a new book. After a few conversations, he suggested the topic of this volume, which coincided with my own interests.

Church history is indeed the history of the continued presence of Christ in the world. The history of its teaching is an autobiography of Christ's knowledge, of what is known and believed by the mystical Christ, the Church. There is no question that the history of the Church is a sacred science, a sacred study of the mind of the Church, i.e., the mind of the mystical Christ.

I have thought for some time that Church history might be divided into doctrine and morals (prophetic office of Christ), prayer and worship (priestly office of Christ), and internal organization as well as relationships with governments (kingly office of Christ), each treated chronologically. This study of the heresies proposed against Church teaching is not, of course, a complete history of doctrine, but it does consider an important aspect of the story of the Church's participation in Christ's prophetic office.

The importance of these ideas is seen in even clearer light when it is realized that many of the proponents of these heresies proposed their ideas as possible solutions to genuine doctrinal problems, e.g., the difficulty of the Trinity or that of the Incarnation. Many, but certainly not all, of those who proposed heresies were attempting to resolve difficulties, not, at least at the beginning, to introduce false teaching into the Church.

While I was pleased to take up this project and am delighted that it will see the light of day, I did not conceive it, nor write it, as original historical research. With the possible exceptions of the commentary about the crisis following the Second Vatican Council and the content of the last chapter, the material presented has been taken from secondary sources. What is offered is a convenient survey of most of the heresies presented against the teaching of the Church. (It would be hard — not to say impossible — to catalog each and every idea diverging from Catholic teaching in twenty centuries.)

As a survey, it summarizes the salient points of each of the heresies, explains their origins, touches on the major events associated with the heresies, assesses their place in history, and describes their impact on the Church. Sometimes the decline of the heresies is noted. In other cases, the continued existence of the heretical idea is briefly sketched.

One might well suggest, with all the books published on this topic and related ones, that this work seems superfluous. However, it does bring the stories of all the prominent heresies together in one place in English. Further, it adds to previous works some of the benefits of more recent scholarship. It seems to me that it could be used in a course on heresies and/or as a reference book for those who want to be able to find information on a particular heresy quickly. Obviously, there will be those who are interested in the topic and want the full story. It is my hope that they will find this volume a useful tool and an interesting discussion of the history of heretical ideas.

Since the book was conceived for the non-specialist, I have not included the usual scholarly apparatus, e.g., footnotes, bibliography, etc. I have relied heavily on Hubert Jedin's and John Dolan's (editors) ten-volume *History of the Church* as well as other general discussions of Church history. From time to time, more specialized studies have been consulted: e.g., Jean Danielou and Henri Marrou, *The First Six Hundred Years*.

The preliminary remarks section begins with a description of the world at the time of Christ. This information is important because in the early years of Christianity some heresies took their ideas from the prevailing culture or were reactions to that culture. To understand these heresies, it is important to have some understanding of the world as it existed when Christ lived and the Church was born. Further, in order to understand heresy — an opposition to a teaching that the Church proposes as a matter of faith for all to believe — one must understand something of Church teaching, its sources, and its authority. Therefore, the second topic in the preliminary remarks is a brief outline of Revelation, Scripture, Tradition, and the development of doctrine, and how these relate to one another in the life of the Church. This section concludes with a definition of heresy and the differences between heresy and schism, as well as an outline of the remaining chapters.

I sincerely hope that all those who read the book will find in it hope for the Church. There is no question that the Church, having survived all the doctrinal crises recorded in these pages, will last to the end of time!

May God bless all those who read these words!

(REV.) RICHARD M. HOGAN
ST. PAUL, MINNESOTA
AUGUST 25, 2000

Acknowledgments

AN AUTHOR IS INDEBTED TO MANY, MANY PEOPLE, AND I CAN ONLY MENTION a few of those important in this endeavor. First of all, I must thank all my teachers and all those who have studied and taught the history of the Church and especially the history of doctrine through their publications. I want to thank all those who have taught me, especially the history faculties of the University of St. Thomas (1969-1973) and the history faculty of the University of Minnesota (1974-1978). Two of my teachers were of special importance: Dr. William Delehanty (St. Thomas) and Dr. Bernard S. Bachrach (University of Minnesota). Of course, all those who have published in this area have been of immense aid, and this book could not have been done without their work. I also want to thank the two pastors at St. John's in St. Paul, where I lived during the preparation of this work, Rev. Joseph Fink and Rev. Thomas Pingatore. Without their consideration and that of all their staffs, this work (and many other things in the last years) would have been impossible. I am also grateful to the trustees of the parish for their generosity and hospitality while I worked on this volume.

I also must pay a debt of gratitude to the Rev. Frank Pavone, International Director of Priests For Life, who allowed me some free time from my duties with Priests For Life to do the necessary writing, as did the Rev. Daniel McCaffrey of the Natural Family Planning Outreach Office of the Archdiocese of Oklahoma City, who also graciously allowed me the time necessary to complete the work after I accepted a position with his apostolate. Together with Fr. McCaffrey, a note of thanks is due to Mr. John Fitzgerald, a benefactor of the Natural Family Planning Outreach office, who has financed the position I accepted with Fr. McCaffrey's apostolate. His support during the last stages of the work on this book was essential.

A note of thanks is owed to many personal friends who listened (often) to my rather dull recitations of heresies and their history in the last year or so. Despite my frequent verbal dissertations, they still invited me to suppers, dinners, and other events. I am grateful to each and every one of them.

One of my very good friends, Mr. Harold Hughesdon, offered to prepare the index and I am most grateful. I need also to record a note of thanks to my own family: to my uncle, the Rev. Richard J. Schuler, and to my mother, Jeanne, for their unswerving support.

Every priest working on a project such as this one benefits from the support of the Church, and I am no exception. I want to thank my own Archbishop, the Most Rev. Harry Flynn of the Archdiocese of St. Paul and Minneapolis, for his pastoral care and for his devotion to the true teaching of the Church. I would not be a member of the Church, let alone a priest, or know or love the Church as I do without the work of Archbishop Flynn, his predecessors, the auxiliary bishops, and all the priests, deacons, sisters, brothers, and lay people of the Archdiocese of St. Paul and Minneapolis. I am especially grateful to Archbishop Flynn for the *Imprimatur* and to the Rev. George Welzbacher for the *Nihil Obstat*.

Finally, no author can neglect the editors. I am very grateful for the suggestion of this book and for the shepherding of the book through the publishing process. Without my editors, Michael Dubruiel and John Laughlin, this work would not exist.

Abbreviations

CCC: *Catechism of the Catholic Church.* 2nd ed.

CIC: Code of Canon Law

DV: *Dei Verbum,* Dogmatic Constitution on Divine Revelation, Second Vatican Council

GS: *Gaudium et Spes,* Pastoral Constitution on the Church in the Modern World, Second Vatican Council

LG: *Lumen Gentium,* Dogmatic Constitution on the Church, Second Vatican Council

Preliminary Remarks

"In those days a decree went out from Caesar Augustus that all the world should be enrolled. This was the first enrollment, when Quirinius was governor of Syria. And all went to be enrolled, each to his own city. And Joseph also went up from Galilee, from the city of Nazareth, to Judea, to the city of David which is called Bethlehem, because he was of the house and lineage of David, to be enrolled with Mary, his betrothed, who was with child. And while they were there, the time came for her to be delivered. And she gave birth to her first-born son." (See Luke 2:1-7.)

I. The World of Christ's Birth

The well-known words from Luke's Gospel, read each Christmas by Christians everywhere, record the story of Christ's birth. The Son of God, "God from God and light from light" (see the Nicene Creed), was born at a particular time and at a particular place and thereby entered human history. The Lord was born in the "fullness of time," at the time and place willed by the Father.

Christian historians have remarked often that the date, time, and place of the birth of the King of Peace was particularly appropriate and fitting. He was born when the Roman legions were maintaining the *pax romana*, the Roman peace, across the entire Empire. During Christ's entire life, the known civilized world was at peace. Further, the known world was united through the political and economic structure of the Roman Empire.

While there were many peoples, nations, and ethnic groups with many different languages, there was still a dominant culture prevalent in the Empire. The Mediterranean, which the Romans called *mare nostrum* (literally, "our sea"), symbolized this Roman unity because all the countries washed by its waters were united under imperial Rome. The Roman system of roads, unmatched until modern times, was the backbone of the Empire because it facilitated travel and communications. Without this system of roads, the early missionary journeys of the Church would have been very difficult and would have taken much, much longer.

From a religious point of view, Christ was born into a culture rejecting previous systems of belief. Most, if not all, of the educated classes had long since abandoned a belief in the Graeco-Roman gods. An attempt had been made, as the Empire moved eastward and encountered Greek culture, to adopt the Greek gods. Temples to the Greek gods were erected even in Rome. However, by the time of Christ, belief in either the Roman gods or the Greek gods had been largely abandoned.

Octavian (27 B.C.-A.D. 14), who reformed the old Roman Republic into the Empire and became the first Emperor, attempted to introduce a cult of the Emperors, making the ruler into a god. This attempt was partially a political one. He wanted to cement the loyalty of all the peoples of the Empire to him and of course to his successors, who like him would become gods as they rose to power. Since the cult of the Emperors was primarily a political statement, rather than a system of religious beliefs and practices, it failed to meet the religious needs of many people. There were many at the time who were looking for a religious system that would answer the fundamental questions of life, such as "Why is there not a resurrection from the dead for human beings as there is for plants, which die and then in the next year come back to life?"

One attempt to answer the need for a religious set of beliefs and practices involved the eastern mystery cults arising from the cultures of Egypt, Syria, Asia Minor, and Iran. Egypt contributed the cult of Isis and Osiris. From Syria came the worship and practices centered around the fertility goddess Cybele. Asia Minor had a similar belief structure, calling its goddess Atargatis and her consort Adonis. Iran gave the Roman world the well-known cult of Mithras. All these mystery cults had some elements in common, one of which was a hint at a future life beyond the grave. Further, most of the mystery cults attracted more men than women. The worship practices of some cults were derived from their belief in a female goddess of nature, were very emotionally charged, and appealed to the most base senses.

The result was that members of these cults were engaging in unseemly behavior (from the Jewish or Christian point of view) under the cover of religion. This state of affairs led to a religious superficiality which was little better than that of people who had not joined the cults.

The popular religion, as opposed to the imperial cult or the mystery religions, was a combination of astrology, magic, interpretation of dreams, and a very strong belief in miracles. Many of the less educated members of society embraced this popular religion. The educated and cultured classes often turned toward the philosophers, the Stoics and others, to answer any religious questions which rose in their minds from time to time.

The Jewish people, of course, did not accept the Roman gods or the popular religion or the mystery cults. Their religion contrasted markedly with all those represented in the Roman world. However, Christ was born in Bethlehem in Judea and was known to be of the house and family of David. Further, the earliest beginnings of the Church were within the Jewish world. Therefore, in considering the culture surrounding the foundation of the Church, it is important to examine the situation of the Jews in the Roman Empire.

Jewish settlements in cities throughout the Mediterranean were founded in the sixth century before Christ. King Nebuchadnezzar of Babylon, who conquered Judea in 586 B.C., exiled the leading citizens of Judea to Babylon, where they remained for fifty years. Even though Cyrus allowed the Jews to return to their homeland in 536 B.C., some did not go back to Jerusalem. Instead, they settled in many different towns in the eastern Mediterranean. Therefore, when Christ was born, there were Jewish settlements throughout the eastern Roman Empire as well as in Palestine.

Judea was under Roman influence and supervised by the Roman governor of Syria when Christ was born. But there was a Jewish king. (This was King Herod, who is mentioned in the infancy narratives of the Gospel.)

In A.D. 6, some years after the birth of Christ, the Jews requested that they be given their own Roman governor. At this time, Judea became a Roman province, but the Jews retained some of their own governmental institutions. For example, the Sanhedrin (a religious court) and the kingship (held by Herod at the time of Christ's birth) continued. These institutions were restricted by the powers of the Roman governor. As we know from the Gospels, at the time of Christ's death the Roman governor in Judea was Pontius Pilate and a sentence of capital punishment was reserved to him.

The Jews were granted a special status by the Romans. Rome generally insisted, as did most ancient city-states, that conquered peoples accept and worship Roman gods. This was not so much a religious obligation as a political one. The acceptance of the Roman gods was an acceptance of

Roman governmental authority. While the Jews were willing to accept the authority of Rome, they absolutely refused to worship the Roman gods. (The Jews would only worship the one true God.)

The Romans, always very practical, exempted the Jews from this obligation. The Jews were also exempted from military service. The Romans made these exceptions because the Jews were not numerous (and so the exceptions meant little from the imperial vantage point of the Romans), because the attempt to force the Jews to acknowledge the Roman gods and do military service would have been futile (the Jews would have resisted even to the point of extermination), and because the Jews did not try to make converts to their religion (and so the exceptions would remain limited to a relatively small population).

Nevertheless, the Jews living in Palestine became increasingly unhappy with Roman rule, even though in A.D. 6 they had invited the Romans to rule them. Roman taxation weighed very heavily on them. There are many references to tax collectors in the New Testament. (For example, see Luke 5:30; Luke 18:9-14; Luke 19:1-10.)

They also hated the Roman government because it was against their religion to be ruled by Gentiles, non-Jews. The ethnic and national loyalty of the Jewish people to their own system of government was for them a religious obligation. They formed God's kingdom on earth. In their minds, this kingdom was both a political and religious reality. According to their faith, it was nearly impossible for them to be loyal to a non-Jew who did not share their religion, because the kingdom of God on earth was identical with the Jewish state.

Consequently, they constantly dreamed of a political leader who would restore the glories of the Jewish kingdom as it had been under David. In fact, the term *Messiah* (Christ or anointed one), given to Jesus, had the connotation of a political leader. The Lord had to show even His own disciples that His mission was not a political one. In A.D. 66, the opposition of the Jews to Roman rule exploded. A Jewish political-religious party called the Zealots led a revolt against the Romans. Roman officials and a Roman garrison were driven out of Jerusalem.

Vespasian, not yet Emperor, was entrusted with the reconquest of Judea. In late A.D. 67 and A.D. 68, he conquered the fortresses and cities of Judea, except Jerusalem. After becoming Emperor, he entrusted the siege of Jerusalem to Titus. Titus began the attack on Jerusalem in A.D.70.

The Romans took the city and destroyed the Temple. (The only remaining part of the Temple is the Western or Wailing Wall, which can be visited in Jerusalem even today.) Judea was given a Roman legate (a Roman ambassador) and the Jews were dissolved as a political community. They no longer had their own leaders. However, their exemptions from the worship of the Roman gods and from military service continued, on the condition that they each paid two denarii (about 40 cents) to the Emperor every year. This was a kind of license fee. In effect they purchased a license from the Emperor every year that allowed them to be recognized as Jews.

The Jews outside Judea enjoyed the same exemptions as those in Judea. They were not subject to military service and were exempt from the worship of the Roman gods. This caused some troubles with their neighbors in the same towns, but they enjoyed the protection of the Emperor.

Understanding the Jewish history of this period is important for grasping the very early development of Christianity.

II. The Birth of the Christian Church

While Jesus was on earth, He taught His Apostles by word and example. After He ascended into heaven, the Apostles remained secluded in the upper room. Between the Ascension and Pentecost (ten days), the Apostles did not publicly teach. They were afraid to teach. They feared that the Jewish authorities would do to them what they had done to the Lord. They did do one thing. They chose Matthias to replace Judas. However, after the tongues of fire (a manifestation of the Holy Spirit) appeared to them at Pentecost, they began to teach.

Pentecost is described by St. Luke in the Acts of the Apostles: "And suddenly a sound came from heaven like the rush of a mighty wind, and it filled all the house where they were sitting. And there appeared to them tongues as of fire, distributed and resting on each one of them. And they were filled with the Holy Spirit and began to speak in other tongues, as the Spirit gave them utterance." (See Acts 2:2-4.)

Pentecost was an outward sign of the gift of the Holy Spirit on the Apostles. In fact, the Apostles had received the Holy Spirit earlier. On Easter Sunday night, Jesus said to the Apostles, "Receive the Holy Spirit." (See John 20:22.) As Pope John Paul II has said, Pentecost constitutes the definitive manifestation of what had already been accomplished in the . . . upper room on Easter Sunday." (See Pope John Paul II, *Dominum et Vivificantem* , "The Lord and Giver of Life," no. 25.)

Even though the Holy Spirit had been given to the Apostles on Easter Sunday evening, Pentecost is still a most significant event in the history of the Church. Pentecost is not only an outward sign of the gift of the Holy Spirit, it also marked a genuine change in how the Spirit worked in the world. After Pentecost, the Apostles felt full of strength and felt capable of carrying out the mission of the Church. Pentecost marks an outward sign of the gift of the Holy Spirit, already accomplished, but beyond that it marks the beginning of the Holy Spirit's perceptible guidance of the Church. Pentecost is the birthday of the Church.

After the tongues of fire appeared about the Apostles' heads, they left the upper room and began to preach the Gospel. Peter announced that Jesus was sent by God the Father (as is proven through the signs and wonders Jesus worked), that Jesus died for sins, rose from the dead, and was glorified by His Father in heaven. Peter also proclaimed that Jesus would come to judge the living and the dead. The proper response to the announcement of this good news was to be baptized. There were three thousand who accepted Baptism on that day. Ever since that first Pentecost, the Church has enjoyed the guidance of the Holy Spirit in its proclamation of the Gospel.

III. Revelation and the Teaching Authority of the Church

Under the guidance of the Holy Spirit, the Catholic Church teaches a defined set of beliefs. Catholics, through their Baptism, commit themselves to these beliefs and also to all that the Church proposes to them to be believed as contained in divine Revelation.

Revelation is what God has told us about Himself through His words and through His deeds. It is what Christ said and did because He, as God the Son, the second Person of the Blessed Trinity, revealed fully the mystery of God. (See CCC, no. 73.) He said as much in response to a remark Philip, one of the Apostles, made. Philip said to him, "Lord, show us the Father, and we shall be satisfied." Jesus said to him, "Have I been with you so long, and yet you do not know Me, Philip? He who has seen Me has seen the Father; how can you say, 'Show us the Father'?" (See John 14:8-9.)

Revelation is found in the Scriptures and in Tradition. In this sense, Tradition does not mean a custom or practice, like the custom (which is said to be traditional) of having turkey on Thanksgiving. The word Tradition comes from the Latin *tradere*, which means to hand on. In other words, Tradition is what is communicated from one person to another, particularly from persons of one generation to people of the next generation.

Tradition refers to what the Apostles handed on to their successors "by the spoken word of their preaching, by the example they gave, by the institutions they established, what they themselves had received." (See DV, no. 7, and CCC, no. 76.)

Christ revealed the mystery of God fully and He entrusted this Revelation to His Apostles, who handed it on by their preaching, their example, and the institutions they established. "Tradition transmits in its entirety the Word of God which has been entrusted to the apostles by Christ the Lord and the Holy Spirit." (See DV, no. 9, and CCC, no. 81.)

Since Tradition is the Word of God "in its entirety," Scripture, which is also the Word of God, is the fruit of Tradition. The Apostles transmitted Revelation not only orally, but also in written form through the New Testament. In other words, the New Testament is the first written statement of the Gospel, the first written statement of Tradition. "Sacred Scripture is the speech of God as it is put down in writing under the breath of the Holy Spirit." (See DV, no. 9, and CCC, no. 81.)

Although the New Testament is the fruit of the fullness of Christ's Revelation, the Church recognizes the truths made known in the Old Testament. In the light of what has been revealed through Christ — through the fullness of Revelation found in the New Testament and in Tradition — the Church sees in the Old Testament that "the mystery of our salvation is present in a hidden way." (See DV, no. 15, and CCC, no. 122.) The books of the Old Testament are venerated as truly the Word of God "even though they contain matters imperfect and provisional." (See DV, no. 15, and CCC, no. 122.)

It is interesting that there is a scriptural foundation for the Catholic belief in Tradition. St. John says in the last verse of his Gospel that "There are also many other things which Jesus did; were every one of them to be written, I suppose that the world itself could not contain the books that would be written." (See John 21:25.) In other words, John is saying that not everything Christ said and did is found in Scripture. These other sayings and acts of Christ are the content of Tradition.

The Second Vatican Council summarizes the relationship between Scripture and Tradition: "Sacred Tradition and Sacred Scripture, then, are bound closely together, and communicate one with the other. For both of them, flowing out from the same divine well-spring [Christ], come together in some fashion to form one thing, and move towards the same goal." (See DV, no. 9, and CCC, no. 80.)

The source of Revelation is Christ. He surrounded Himself with the Apostles and disciples. The Apostles and those whom they closely associated with them through the laying on of hands with prayer to the Holy Spirit were given the awesome task of communicating what they had seen and heard to the world. They did this through writing (Scripture) and through their teaching and preaching (Tradition).

Tradition continues in the Church through the successors of the Apostles, the bishops. "The Apostles left bishops as their successors . . . [and] gave them 'their own position of teaching authority' . . . . The apostolic preaching [Tradition] which is expressed in a special way in the inspired books, was to be preserved in a continuous line of succession until the end of time." (See DV, nos. 7, 8, and CCC, no. 77.)

Tradition is found in everything the Church is and does. "The Church, in her doctrine, life and worship perpetuates and transmits to every generation all that she herself is, all that she believes." (See DV, no. 8, and CCC, no. 98.) Tradition is found in the creeds, in the decrees of the councils of the Church, in the writings of the early Church Fathers, and in the Church's lived-out faith, both in practice and liturgy.

Tradition is the Church's continuing and constant effort to restate the Revelation of Christ, and this task is the life-blood of the Church. The New Testament was the first written statement of Revelation, and once the books of the New Testament were accepted by the Church together with those of the Old Testament, the Scriptures became part of Tradition — part of the living heritage of the Church.

Other written statements of Revelation followed, such as the creeds. Each of these statements, once accepted by the Church, became part of Tradition — that is, each of these statements, with Scripture enjoying a preeminence, became a source of additional written and oral expressions of Revelation. And so the Church is a vibrant, living organism constantly renewing its teaching without ever changing the content of Revelation.

Given the value of the Revelation of Christ and the extraordinary effort Christ made to give us this precious gift (nothing less than the Incarnation), it is impossible to believe that God would not provide — both for the transmission of these truths (which He did through Scripture and Tradition) and for a proper and certain interpretation of these truths.

When a story is told to one person and that person repeats it to a third individual and the third person repeats it to a fourth and so on, by the time it reaches the thirtieth person the story has been completely altered to the point that the first person hardly recognizes his or her own tale.

If there were no authentic interpretation of Revelation which is sure and certain, God's Revelation, told to one person after another throughout the centuries (not just to thirty people, but literally to millions of people) would have been totally distorted and unrecognizable. It is inconceivable that God, Who went to such effort to give us this Revelation, would allow such corruption of His own Word. Even the written word does not prevent misinterpretations. Consider how many different opinions there are on passages in Shakespeare or Milton. In our own day, we have also seen the many varied possibilities of meanings people see in the Scriptures.

God, of course, did not allow His Word to be corrupted. He gave us the Church which, through the Pope and the bishops in union with the Pope, authentically interpret Revelation found in Scripture and Tradition. " 'The task of giving an authentic interpretation of the Word of God, whether in its written form or in the form of Tradition, has been entrusted to the living, teaching office of the Church alone. Its authority in this matter is exercised in the name of Jesus Christ.' (See DV, no. 10.) This means that the task of interpretation has been entrusted to the bishops in communion with the successor of Peter, the bishop of Rome." (See CCC, no. 85.) The Pope and the bishops in union with him constitute the Magisterium or teaching authority of the Church. When the Magisterium speaks and proposes something to be believed as revealed by Christ, baptized Catholics are committed to accepting the teaching as truly the Word of God.

Catholics believe the Magisterium is guided by the Holy Spirit. (Some people are scandalized at this thought. How can a mere man — e.g., the Pope — claim to be guided by the Holy Spirit? Of course, the people who ask such a question usually have no difficulty accepting the books of Scripture as inspired by the Holy Spirit. Since the human authors of the books of the Bible were mere men inspired by the Holy Spirit, why is it not possible for the same Holy Spirit to guide the Pope and the bishops when they interpret Revelation?)

The work of the Holy Spirit did not suddenly end with the completion of the last book of the New Testament. The Holy Spirit is at work today and always in the Church, and He guarantees that the Magisterium always authentically interprets Revelation for the faithful. Revelation, found in Tradition and Scripture, is authentically interpreted for the faithful by the Magisterium — by the Pope and the bishops teaching in union with him.

Revelation was completed by Christ. There is nothing further that God can tell us or show us about Himself after Christ. Therefore, Revelation ended with the death of the last person to have seen the Lord. Once there was no one on earth who had seen the Lord while He lived, there was no personal eyewitness to relate what Christ said and did. Since Revelation was completed by the beginning of the second century, c. A.D. 100, one might think that the Magisterium knew from the earliest days of the Church everything found in Revelation. Since the entire Word of God, Revelation, has been entrusted to the Church by Christ, the Magisterium did know everything in Revelation, at least implicitly. However, through study and experience, under the guidance of the Holy Spirit, the Church does come to a greater and greater explicit understanding of Revelation. "Thanks to the assistance of the Holy Spirit, the understanding of both the realities and the words of the heritage of faith is able to grow in the life of the Church: —'through the contemplation and study of believers who ponder these things in their hearts' (See DV, no. 8.) . . . —'from the intimate sense of spiritual realities which [believers] experience' (See DV, no. 8.) . . . —'from the preaching of those who have received, along with their right of succession in the episcopate, the sure charism of truth.' " (See CCC, no. 94.)

In other words, the Church throughout history gradually comes to an explicit understanding of what is implicit in Revelation. This process is called the development of doctrine. As we will see, false teachings contrary to the doctrine of the Church (heresies), sometimes elicited from the Church a development of doctrine — that is, the false teachings caused the Church to come to an explicit understanding of something that had up to that time been implicit in Revelation.

IV. What Is a Heresy?

When the Church proposes a particular truth as part of the content of Revelation, Catholics are committed by their Baptism to accepting it. "*Heresy* is the obstinate post-baptismal denial of some truth which must be believed with divine and catholic faith, or it is likewise an obstinate doubt concerning the same." (See CCC, no. 2089, and CIC, can. 751.) In other words, when a Catholic refuses obstinately to accept a teaching which the Magisterium officially proposes as revealed by God, that Catholic is guilty of heresy. Heresy is not merely a doubt; it is a stubborn refusal to assent to a teaching of the Church.

The aspect of stubbornness or obstinacy implies that the person refuses even to try to come to a belief in the particular teaching through study, prayer, and reflection.

Heresy is not simply a question of not understanding a particular teaching. Heresy involves a decision in the will to refuse even to consider the teaching. Further, only the baptized can be guilty of heresy because it is the "post-baptismal denial" of a truth proposed by the Church. Those who are baptized are committed by their baptismal promises to accept the Church's teaching. When they refuse to accept Church teaching, they break their baptismal promises.

Heresy, then, is fundamentally a breaking of the baptismal promises. However, those not baptized are obviously not obliged to accept the Church's teaching and therefore cannot be guilty of not accepting the Church's creed.

Most heresies (not all) began as an attempt to explain the teachings of the Church. Since most "heretics" began with the faith and were attempting to understand the faith more fully, they were not technically heretics according to the definition above. They did not obstinately refuse to accept Church teaching. Rather, they were trying to do the very opposite of refusing: they were trying to adhere to Church teaching while explaining it. However, in most cases, those who proposed teachings contrary to the doctrines of the Church came to a point of decision; they had to give up their ideas and accept the Church's creedal statements of belief or continue to promote their own ideas and reject the Church's beliefs. If they rejected the

Church's teaching, they became formal heretics in the sense of the definition given above.

Nevertheless, this definition of heresy focuses on the individual "heretic" and his or her motives. The more common understanding of heresy focuses on what is taught, not so much on the person teaching the heresy. In this second sense, heresy is any teaching publicly proclaimed which contradicts Church teaching. The public statement is included in this second sense of heresy because without a public statement, no one (but the individual who believes the false teaching) would know about it. It is in this second sense that heresy is used in this book. We will examine the major and some of the minor heresies proposed in the long history of the Church.

Since heresy is used in this study with an emphasis on what is taught, rather than on the individual, in a few cases even the question of Baptism is not relevant. In the third century, a certain Mani proposed beliefs which came to be known as Manicheism. Manicheism posed a threat to the Church, but Mani and many of his followers were never Christians: Mani and at least some of his followers had never been baptized.

Manicheism is usually included among the Christian heresies because it did attract Christians and because Manicheism accepted Christ, but not as the incarnate Second Person of the Trinity. One cannot normally speak of heresy except in the case of a baptized person rejecting the faith, but by focusing on the ideas proposed rather than on the individual heretic, even the question of Baptism becomes less important.

Heresy is the proposal of ideas that are contrary to Church teaching. Schism "is the refusal of submission to the Roman Pontiff or of communion with the members of the Church subject to him." (See CCC, no. 2089. In this paragraph, the *Catechism of the Catholic Church* quotes the *Code of Canon Law*, can. 751.) Perhaps the most famous schism was the so-called Great Schism between 1378 and 1415 when there was a rival Pope in Avignon (France) to the Pope in Rome and then two rival Popes (one in Pisa and one in Avignon).

Some peoples and nations refused to give their submission to the legitimate Pope and were therefore technically guilty of schism. (Of course, it was difficult to discern in the midst of the schism which of the two and then three Popes was the legitimate successor to Peter. The Church has decided that the legitimate successor to Peter was the Pope living in Rome.)

In this work on heresies, schisms will be excluded unless they are the result of heresies (some were).

V. The Layout of This Book

We will discuss the heresies in four broad chronological periods, 33-325, 325-843, 843-1789 and 1789 to the present. It is noteworthy that the chronological order of the heresies roughly follows the outline of the creed. In other words, in the first period of the Church's history (33-325), the heresies turned on the question of the Trinity, found in the first part of the creed. In the second period (325-843), the questions were about the Person of Christ, found in the second part of the creed. In the third (843-1789), the issue was the Holy Spirit, especially as the giver of life, i.e., of grace through the sacraments, found in the third part of the creed. In the final period (1789- 2000), the heresies centered around the concept of the Church, mentioned in the last part of the creed. The last chapter of the work suggests the trajectory of the Church in the new millennium and how that trajectory answers some of the objections raised in the period between 1789 and 2000.

PART I

God as One and Triune:
Heresies from A.D. 33 to 325

We believe in one God, the Father, the Almighty . . .
We believe in one Lord, Jesus Christ,
the only Son of God . . .
We believe in the Holy Spirit, the Lord, the giver of Life.

AS MENTIONED IN THE INTRODUCTION, FROM THE FIRST PENTECOST (C. A.D. 33) through the Council of Nicaea in A.D. 325, most of the ideas proposed contrary to Church doctrine — i.e., the heresies — concerned the Church's teaching on God as simultaneously one and triune. In discussing the Trinity, there are clearly two possible mistakes: one is to collapse the three Persons into one by making Father, Son, and Holy Spirit simply characteristics or attributes of one Person; the other is to emphasize the distinct reality of the three Persons to the point of excluding the oneness of God — i.e., of making three distinct gods of the three Persons. Both these mistakes were made.

In this first period of the Church's life, the theologians and scholars who went astray were attempting to explain and elucidate Revelation. In their attempts to reconcile apparent conflicts and to make clear the full impact of the teachings of Christ, the theologians of this first era in the Church's life sometimes erred. In many, many instances, they did not begin with bad will; even less did they intend to stray from the orthodox path. However, in many cases, they became more interested in defending their own theories than in following the teachings of the Church, and this attitude led to difficulties. But before we consider the heresies regarding the mystery of the one and triune God, we need to consider the heresies born from the Church's emergence from Jewish culture.

The Judaizers

Christians and Jews

THE FIRST ISSUE WHICH ROCKED THE EARLY CHURCH TO THE POINT THAT A council was convened to settle the issue, the Council of Jerusalem, is recorded in the Acts of the Apostles as well as in the letters of St. Paul. The issue was whether a convert to Christianity first had to become a Jew before he or she could become a Christian.

At the very beginning of the Church this issue did not arise because the first Christians were all Jews. But since Christ had commanded the Apostles to preach to all nations, soon the Gospel was preached to non-Jews. Thus, a question arose: could the Church welcome non-Jews into its ranks without their undergoing circumcision and embracing all the traditional practices in accordance with Jewish (Mosaic) law.

Philip

Philip, one of the deacons ordained with Stephen, was one of the first to preach the Gospel to non-Jews. He traveled to Samaria and invited the Samaritans to be baptized. After some Samaritans accepted the Gospel, Peter and John visited them. The Apostles approved of Philip's practices. This was an amazing step for the early Church!

After preaching in Samaria, Philip explained the Word of God to an Ethiopian traveling in the Holy Land. Philip baptized this Ethiopian. With these Baptisms, the answer to the question of whether to baptize non-Jews seemed to be: "Yes." However, the question was yet to be definitively settled.

While Philip was in Samaria, some of the other disciples went to Antioch and preached the Gospel there to the Jews. When some non-Jews asked to be baptized, the disciples there did not hesitate to baptize them.

Peter

Peter also had an important experience. A certain Cornelius, a Roman centurion and a Gentile, saw a vision. The angel in the vision told him to summon Peter to his home.

Meanwhile, Peter had a vision too. A net with different kinds of birds, reptiles and four-legged animals descended from heaven. A voice told Peter to kill and eat. Peter refused because the food was unclean (Jewish law designated certain foods as unclean and therefore unfit to eat.) A voice told Peter that "What God has cleansed, you must not call common." (See Acts 10:15.)

The meaning of the vision was that Jewish law had been superseded. Immediately after this vision, Cornelius's servants arrived to bring Peter to Cornelius's home. After visiting with Cornelius and proclaiming the Gospel, Peter baptized Cornelius and his whole household.

When Peter returned to Jerusalem, he explained his vision, and the Christians marveled that God had extended His mercy even to the Gentiles. After this, the Church did not hesitate to baptize Gentiles. The leader of the Apostles, St. Peter, had approved the work of Philip and the disciples at Antioch.

By A.D. 40, about seven years after the Ascension of the Lord, the Church included Jews as well as Gentiles. But did non-Jewish Christians have to adopt Jewish laws and customs in order to be Christians?

Paul

It was St. Paul's missionary journeys that definitively raised this second question. It was Paul's usual procedure in the towns he visited to preach in the local synagogue. The synagogue in most eastern Mediterranean towns was for the Greek-speaking Jews. Some of these were descendants of the Jews who did not return to Jerusalem after the fifty-year exile in Babylon.

Inevitably, some non-Jews, neighbors to the Jews in these towns, heard the message and wanted to become Christians. Paul received these non-Jews into the Church. More importantly, however, he exempted them from all the Jewish laws and rituals. Further, Paul gradually developed a theology which supported the position that Jewish rituals, laws, and customs did not bind Christians. In his writings, the constant references to the law which had been superseded by Christ express this theological position.

Paul's preaching as well as his exemption of the Gentiles from Jewish customs caused conflict between Paul and some of the Jewish Christians, who are known to history as Judaizers because they insisted that all Christians had to observe all the Jewish customs. The Judaizers viewed Christianity as an outgrowth of Judaism, almost as a higher form of Judaism. Paul, on the other hand, believed that the Lord had superseded Judaism and Jewish customs. It is hard for us to imagine the passions aroused by this controversy, but it was a major crisis for the early Church.

St. Paul had just made converts to Christianity. He had taught them the Gospel and instructed them. Then, "some who had come down from Judea [to Antioch] were instructing the brothers, 'Unless you are circumcised according to the Mosaic practice, you cannot be saved.' " (See Acts 15:1.) In other words, the ones who had come down from Jerusalem were publicly teaching Paul's own converts a doctrine contrary to what he had taught. One authority, Paul, was being contradicted by another authority in front of neophytes who were hardly in a position to judge what was right and what was not.

The Judaizers were convinced that the Church was founded on the solid rock of Jewish beliefs and practices because Christ was Jewish and had been sent as the last and greatest of the prophets to the Jewish people. They represented the most rigid view of the relationship between Judaism and Christianity. On the other hand, Paul was equally convinced that Christ had intended to give a completely new law, a new set of beliefs and practices, which transcended the old law. This dispute was absolutely central to the growth of the Church and would have to be settled. But it would have to be settled by an authority both St. Paul and the Judaizers recognized — i.e., by Peter and the leaders of the Church in Jerusalem.

Council of Jerusalem

Paul and Barnabas together with those who had come down from Jerusalem decided to go to Jerusalem and consult the leaders of the Church, the Apostles. In this dispute, clearly Paul was on one side and the Judaizers were on the other.

Paul and Barnabas went up to Jerusalem to meet with the leaders of the Church (the Apostles) there. This first council of the Church, often referred to as the Council of Jerusalem, was held in A.D. 49. The Apostles, after debating the issue, decided that Paul and Barnabas should continue their missionary work among the Gentiles. Further, Paul's policy of receiving non-Jews into the Church without first asking them to observe Jewish laws was adopted in its major outlines as the accepted practice of the Church.

In the Acts of the Apostles, Peter makes a definitive speech supporting Paul's position. (See Acts 15:7-12.) The opposite point of view was contrary to Revelation because it questioned the absolute transcendence of the New Covenant of Christ over the old. By insisting that Christians had to observe the laws of the Old Covenant, those opposed to Paul were denying that Christ had established a new dispensation which subsumed the old law into the new.

The intensity of this controversy is not only shown by the actions of the Judaizers; it is also demonstrated by the continuance of the difficulty even after the decision of the Council of Jerusalem. Even Peter seemed subsequently a bit unsure. Shortly after the council, he arrived in Antioch, and at first he ate with the Gentile Christians. However, after some Judaizers from Jerusalem arrived, Peter withdrew from the Gentiles.

Paul questioned Peter about his refusal to eat with the Gentiles: "But when Cephas came to Antioch, I opposed him to his face because he stood condemned." (See Gal. 2:11.) In the end, Peter followed the decision of the Council of Jerusalem. In other words, he followed his own advice because he made the essential decision at the council. (See Acts 15:7-12.) But even this opposition by Paul to Peter's face failed to resolve the issue. There were those who simply refused to accept the teaching of the Church.

Certainly, even before the Council of Jerusalem, the opinion that Christians had to follow Jewish practices in order to be Christians was wrong (heretical), but only after the decision of the council was it clear that the Church had taught that Christ intended for all men and women (Jews or not) to become Christians without having to embrace Jewish customs. Paul's teaching and practices became the explicit teaching of the Church, and those who opposed Paul were opposing the Church. In other words, in a formal sense, after the council they were heretics and could no longer claim that they were simply trying to fathom the will of God.

The Judaizer Heresy

This heresy held that to become a Christian, one first had to be a Jew and accept all the Jewish religious practices and customs. Opposed by St. Paul, the Judaizer heresy was rejected by the Church at the Council of Jerusalem in A.D. 49.

2

Kerinthian, Ebionite, Elchasaite, and Mandean Heresies

The Religious "Melting Pot" of the First-Century Near East

THE DISPUTE BETWEEN THE JUDAIZERS AND ST. PAUL WAS THE PREDICTABLE result of both the circumstances of the Church's birth — within a Jewish religious culture and society — and the conversion of both Jews and non-Jews to Christianity. Equally predictable, in light of the new discussions within Judaism that Christianity inevitably caused, was a mixing of the new with the old to produce religious beliefs and practices that had elements of both. This tendency was strengthened when Jerusalem fell because both Jews and Jewish Christians left the city.

Many fled eastward across the Jordan. Separated from the Temple and Jewish customs, lacking the institutions of Jewish society and government, such as the Sanhedrin, both Jews and Jewish Christians had to a certain extent lost their moorings. The presence of exiled Jews and Jewish Christians meant that there was a plethora of religious ideas to respond to the general desire in the culture for sound answers to the profound human questions.

A group of notions included under the general name of Gnosticism was also found in this "melting pot" of religious ideas. The name "Gnosticism" comes from a Greek word, *gnosis*, which means knowledge. Gnosticism is named for the most fundamental tenet of its members: they believed that they possessed a special knowledge which was superior to the faith of the Church. This knowledge was about human beings, God, and salvation.

Gnostics believed in God, but they thought God did not create the material world. A lesser being who created the material world and ruled through the aid of evil beings was the creator of the world. Human beings exist in the material world created by the lesser god. But without the knowledge of this lesser god, human beings have been given a "spark," a divine element, which belongs to the true God. *Gnosis* is knowledge of this hidden divine "spark" which is in each of us. *Gnosis* also means knowing the true God and knowing that true human happiness consists through a union with God.

Gnosticism embraces a dualism. There are two principles: good and evil. Evil is material and physical. Good is spiritual and divine. There is an anti-god, who is not equal to God but who governs through evil and who created the material world. There is God, Who is all good and Who created the spiritual world. The point of life is to come to the God Who is all good and to escape the god who is evil.

Taking ideas and practices from Christian, Jewish, and Gnostic sources, a series of religious movements developed about the turn of the second century in the lands east and north of Palestine. Among these movements was one begun by a certain Kerinthos.

Kerinthians

According to Irenaeus (bishop of Lyons, c. 200), Kerinthos lived in Asia Minor about the end of the first century (c. 100). He was probably influenced by Gnostic ideas and heterodox Jewish movements as well as by the Judaizers within Jewish Christian circles

Kerinthos emphasized the observance of the Sabbath and the Jewish laws. He also taught that Jesus was the natural son of Mary and Joseph, but not God the Son. According to Kerinthos, God recognized Jesus' justice and wisdom and so at the time of Jesus' baptism, Christ (God the Son) descended on Jesus. From that time on, Jesus taught about the Father and performed miracles. But Christ left Jesus before His passion and death. Further, Kerinthos distinguished between the highest God and the creator of the world, who did not know the highest God. This last idea has tinges of Gnosticism and might have attracted some who held Gnostic beliefs.

Kerinthos's teaching on Christ is clearly heterodox, but in denying the divinity of Christ and the virgin birth as well as the concept of God dying for our sins, his ideas would have been more acceptable in Jewish circles but not to faithful Christians. Of course, his emphasis on the Jewish law and the observance of the Sabbath attracted the Jews as well as the Judaizers in Christian circles, but again diverged from orthodox Christianity and Judaism. The notion of a highest God and the god-creator also is unacceptable in an orthodox Christian context or for that matter in an orthodox Jewish belief system.

Kerinthos does not seem to have gained a very large following. Nevertheless, even at this early date in the life of the Church, Christians were troubled by anyone questioning the divinity of Christ. Irenaeus tells us that St. John wrote his fourth Gospel in response to Kerinthos. This is an intriguing remark. It would explain the wonderful emphasis in St. John's Gospel on the divinity of Christ. The truth is probably that Kerinthos's teaching was one stimulus among many (not excluding the divine influence of the Holy Spirit) which prompted St. John to give us the fourth Gospel.

Ebionites

The Ebionites had ideas very similar to those taught by Kerinthos and flourished in the same religious environment as Kerinthos. The Ebionites may have originally been orthodox Jewish Christians who fled east of the Jordan after the fall of Jerusalem in A.D. 70.

Justin Martyr (d. 165) distinguishes between two groups of Jewish Christians: one group held to the divinity of Christ and the other group denied that Jesus was God. Scholars believe that this second group are the Ebionites. Since Justin made this remark about A.D.150, scholars date the appearance of the Ebionites around the middle of the second century (150 or so).

The Ebionites believed that God had established two principles: one that was good and one that was evil. The evil principle governed the world. The good principle, Christ, governed the world which was to come. For them, Jesus was the natural son of Joseph and Mary who was recognized by God on the day of his baptism and given divine power, becoming the Messiah, the Christ. It was their view that Christ had already appeared in the persons of Adam and of Moses. The Messiah did not die on the cross because Christ left Jesus before the crucifixion.

The similarities to the teaching of Kerinthos are notable. The Jewish and Christian elements are obvious. Gnostic influences are also clear: the two principles of good and evil with evil in charge of the world. The Ebionites had drawn from the entire religious culture of the early second century, as had Kerinthos. Both were influenced by Christian, Jewish, and Gnostic ideas and practices. The Ebionites differed from orthodox Christianity in accepting the Gnostic dualistic notions and in denying that Jesus was God the Son made man.

Elchasaites

Another sect demonstrating Christian, Jewish, and Gnostic elements was a group called the Elchasaites. A man named Elchasai who lived near Syria in the first decades of the second century (c. 110-130) founded them. This group actively conducted missionary work and extended their teaching as far as the Tigris and Euphrates rivers in the East and even to Rome in the West at the time of Hippolytus (c. 220).

The Elchasaites held rigidly to the traditional Jewish law, but rejected Old Testament sacrifices and certain parts of the Scriptures. They were deeply opposed to St. Paul. They believed in two gods: a female goddess called the holy spirit and a male god called Christ who had repeatedly been incarnate (in various people throughout history). To them, Jesus was a mere man — a prophet, but not divine.

The Elchasaites practiced ritual washings reminiscent of some Jewish movements, as well as baptism. The Elchasaites were probably more significant than the Ebionites or Kerinthians because they were more successful in their missionary works. They drew their beliefs and practices from the same triple influences as the Ebionites and Kerinthians did: Jewish, Christian, and Gnostic. From an orthodox Christian perspective, the Elchasaites present the same difficulties as the Kerinthians and the Ebionites.

Mandeans

The teachings of the Kerinthians, Ebionites, and Elchasaites have all disappeared, but a fourth sect, which developed about this same time in the same region, still exists. Today, the, Mandeans number about five thousand in the region of the Tigris and Euphrates rivers.

Strictly speaking, the Mandeans cannot be classified as a heretical sect because their origins are more Jewish than Jewish Christian. In this respect, the Mandeans differed from the Ebionites, Elchasaites, and

Kerinthians, who all had roots in Jewish Christian circles. The Mandeans are included here because they still exist and because they originated in the same religious culture as the Kerinthians, the Ebionites, and the Elchasaites.

The Mandeans regarded Jesus as a false prophet. (This point of view differs from almost every other heresy or religious movement of the time. Most acknowledged the Lord to have been at least a great teacher, if not divine.)

The Mandeans exalted John the Baptist and practiced baptism by immersing the candidate in flowing water three times. They also believed in the ascent of souls after death to a realm of light. For them, there was the Great Mana, their god, but there were also lesser gods, lesser manas. Opposing the Great Mana were demons inhabiting a world of black water. (Of course, the belief in a Great Mana, lesser manas, and opposing demons is confirmation of Gnostic influences.) The Mandean Gnostic dualism and the denial of the divinity of Christ made this sect totally unacceptable to Christians.

Kerinthian, Ebionite, Elchasaite, and Mandean Heresies

These heresies had the common Gnostic belief in multiple gods and took elements from Christian and Jewish sources as well. For their multiple gods of various ranks and the denial of the divinity of Christ, Christians rejected all these heresies.

3

Gnosticism

[handwritten margin note: around 150 A.D. Islam copied some of the followers of Gnosticism. e.g Belsides !]

The Gnostics

As we have seen, in addition to Jewish and Jewish Christian sources, Gnosticism was an important influence on Kerinthos, the Ebionites, the Elchasaites, and the Mandeans. In fact, the constellation of ideas called Gnosticism was probably the most important religious movement (other than Christianity) in the first two and a half centuries of the Christian era. Gnosticism offered answers to questions many people at that time were asking. There was a thirst for religious truth. Gnosticism offered an interpretation of the world and of humanity which made it a competitor with Christianity itself. Not the least attractive feature of Gnosticism was its liturgy, which it borrowed from the mystery cults and Christian sources. The Gnostics also organized themselves into communities and, seeing the Church as their true rival, organized Gnostic groups within Christian communities.

Gnostics claimed a special knowledge, a *gnosis*. Included in this special *gnosis* was an understanding that there was God Who created the spiritual world and a lesser anti-god who was responsible for the material (evil) world. Gnosticism represents a belief in dualism. There is a good and an evil. Evil is material and physical. Good is spiritual and divine. *[handwritten margin note: dualism good & evil]*

According to the Gnostics, a disaster at the beginning of the world had imprisoned a divine "spark" in human beings, i.e., in the evil world of material Creation. This divine element had lost the memory of heaven, its true home. Salvation consisted in knowing that this "spark" existed and liberating it from the human body. The liberation of the divine "spark" was only possible at the moment of death.

There were many different branches of Gnosticism. Further, there was not one defined Gnostic creed. Gnosticism represented a constellation of ideas taken from various sources, and it is next to impossible to identify one single individual as the founder of Gnosticism.

Gnosticism seems to have pre-dated Christianity, at least in regard to its belief in two principles: God Who is good and a lesser god who is evil. This dualism can be traced to ancient Iran. When these dualistic beliefs encountered the Genesis account of Creation in the Old Testament, the Creator God of Genesis became the evil and lesser god. And of course, as we have seen in some of the sects discussed above, the name Christ came to be associated with the god who was good. Gnosticism also had an element of astrology derived from ancient Babylon.

Valentinus

The loose association of Gnostic ideas allowed leaders in the various regions to emphasize one idea over others and even exclude certain ideas. As a result, Gnosticism is hard to identify, and it has a number of different manifestations. One of the more famous leaders, Valentinus, a philosopher in Rome (c. 150), drew heavily on the ideas of Plato, the Greek philosopher (c. 330 B.C.). Valentinus acknowledged Christ as the Redeemer. Christ was divine, i.e., He was the God Who is good, Who appeared to human beings in order to lead them back to the divine. However, the God of goodness could never have united Himself with the material world because the material world was evil. He could not have allowed Himself to be imprisoned by the principle of evil. Still, Valentinus needed to explain that the Gospels testify to the physical appearance of Christ. To solve this difficulty, Valentinus claimed that Christ's physical appearance was an optical illusion which those without special knowledge perceived to be real. Those with this special knowledge would have seen through the optical illusion. This teaching — that Christ's body was a mere apparition — is called Docetism.

Marcion

Marcion also drew many of his ideas from Gnostic sources. He was a native of Sinope in Asia Minor (modern-day Turkey) and owned a shipping business. Marcion rejected the notion that Christ truly had a body. To him, Christ's apparent body was merely a vision — a view almost identical to that of Valentinus. However, in rejecting the Old Testament, Marcion broke with Valentinus's ideas. For Marcion, the creator of the material world was the same as the god of the Old Testament. Since this god was the principle of evil, it was necessary to reject the entire Old Testament. Further, any passages in the New Testament that proposed a linkage between the god of the Old Testament and the good God of the New, had to be rejected.

Valentinus and Marcion founded the two most significant Gnostic sects, but Marcion represented a much greater threat. Excommunicated in Rome in 144 for his heretical ideas, he left the Church but retained fundamentally the same liturgy as the Church. Clearly, this meant that it was relatively easy for Catholics to become Marcionites. There was little or no difference in actual worship. Further, Marcion was a manager. (He had run a business.) He knew how to give his followers a systematic organization. In most places where there were Christians, Marcionite associations, including Marcionite bishops and priests, developed. Finally, since Marcionite theology was in some ways simpler than the theology of the Church, it attracted many Christians.

In addition to Marcion and Valentinus, there were a host of other lesser Gnostic leaders and sects.

Menander and Satornil

A group formed around Menander and Satornil was centered at Antioch in Syria. Menander proclaimed himself the Redeemer. Satornil taught that the Father created an upper world composed of angels and powers. The lesser god, the one he equated with the god of Genesis in the Old Testament, created the earthly world.

Basilides

Another Gnostic sect, also rooted in Syria, was called the Basilidians after their founder, Basilides. From the Church's point of view, Basilides was more important than Menander or Satornil because Basilides addressed Christians. He claimed that Christ had spoken secretly to the Apostle Matthias. Apparently, the secrets entrusted to Matthias were transmitted to Basilides and then revealed. One of those secrets was that Christ did not die on the cross. Rather, Simon of Cyrene died in the place of Christ. As with Valentinus and Marcion, Basilides taught that Christ only appeared to have a human body.

Barbelo-Gnostics, Ophites, Naassenes, and Sethians

Four other Gnostic sects identified in Christian literature are the Barbelo-Gnostics, the Ophites, the Naassenes, and the Sethians.

The Barbelo-Gnostics believed in a female goddess, named Barbelo. They believed that Barbelo came forth from the Father.

The Gnostic sect of the Ophites accepted Christ, but not as equal to the Father. To the Ophites, Christ was one of the highest of the lesser gods who came into the world through Jesus. The Ophites also emphasized the serpent. To some Ophites the serpent represented the evil principle, but for other Ophites the serpent was neither good nor evil.

The Naassenes were probably a sub-group of Ophites.

The Sethians believed in three gods who were each responsible for one aspect of the world: light, darkness, and *pneuma*. The Sethians also had a cult of the serpent. The Sethians had a veneer of Christianity and therefore, like Valentinus and Marcion, appealed to some in the Church.

Christian Difficulties With Gnosticism

What is crystal clear about Gnosticism is its eclectic nature. It took ideas and practices from mystery religions, from Jewish sources, from Christian sources, from pagan philosophy, and from the Syrian and Egyptian cultures. Each leader molded these ideas and related them one to another differently. The history of Gnostic thought and development shows clearly what can happen to the most profound religious ideas if left to the normal historical development of ideas. The story of Gnostic thought represents one of the strongest possible arguments for the necessity of an *authoritative* interpretation of Revelation.

From the point of view of orthodox Christianity, the difficulties with Gnostic teachings in themselves and with the particular teachings of Valentinus and Marcion are obvious. The dualism of the Gnostics denies the belief in one God. With the Gnostics, there are at least two principles: God Who is all good and Who created the spiritual world (Whom Christians call the Father); and another god, lesser in being than the Father, who is evil or at the very least is aided by evil beings, and who created the evil material world. But this is impossible, because there can only be one first principle, one origin of the universe. The Gnostic dualism flies in the face of the incredibly strong Jewish tradition of one God. The oneness of God, of course, is also a touchstone of Christian belief.

Gnostic dualism also denies the Creation account in Genesis because it regards the physical world as evil. Genesis repeatedly remarks that God saw that Creation was good. (See Genesis 1.) Following Genesis, Christianity has always taught that the one God created the world and that the world reflects the goodness of God. The Psalmist reflects this theme in a number of passages. "The heavens are telling the glory of God and the firmament proclaims his handiwork." (See Psalm 19.) "Praise him, sun and moon, praise him, all you shining stars! Praise him, you highest heavens, and you waters above the heavens! . . . Praise the Lord from the earth, you sea monsters and all deeps, fire and hail, snow and frost, stormy wind fulfilling his command! Mountains and all hills, fruit trees and all cedars! Beasts and all cattle, creeping things and flying birds." (See Psalm 148: 3-4, 7-10.) Of course, such passages are partly why Marcion, holding to the evil of the physical world, rejected the Old Testament.

But even if one were only to look to the New Testament, it is impossible to maintain that the world is evil and at the same time respect Christ. After all, He worked miracles using material Creation, e.g., the mud paste He used to cure the blind man: "As He said this, He spat on the ground and made clay of the spittle and anointed the man's eyes with the clay, saying to him, 'Go, wash in the pool of Siloam' (which means Sent). So he went and washed and came back seeing." (See John 9:6-7.)

Further, the Gnostic dualism, especially in regard to Christ, results in the denial of the double mission of the Lord: to reveal God — i.e. Revelation — and to save humanity — i.e. Redemption. If Jesus, the second Person of the Trinity, did not have a real body which was physically present and united with Him, then He could not have truly revealed the Father. In other words, the Lord's famous response to Philip when Philip said to Him, "Lord, show us the Father, and we shall be satisfied:" "Have I been with you so long, and yet you do not know Me, Philip? He who has seen Me has seen the Father; how can you say, 'Show us the Father'?" would have been a lie. (See John 14:8-9.) Without a true physical body, neither Philip nor anyone else was truly seeing Christ and they could not have seen the Father, which would mean that the Father was not being revealed. In fact, Philip and all the others who thought they were seeing Christ, would have been sadly deceived. They would have been duped, lacking the special *gnosis* given to the elect.

One cannot even argue that in the Gnostic view the Apostles and the others seeing Christ were experiencing a vision, because a vision is always given with the understanding that the one seeing the vision knows it is a vision. Philip and the others who saw Christ did not know it was a vision. They were, in the Gnostic sense, duped. Christ was playing a trick on them. With that, Christ's mission of revealing the Father falls. Without the Revelation of the Father by Christ, there is no Revelation and the entire basis of Christianity is lost.

In addition, human beings are the saddest of creatures because, not knowing the Father in whose image they are created, they cannot know themselves. As The Pastoral Constitution on the Church in the Modern World, *Gaudium et Spes*, teaches, Christ "reveals man to himself and brings to light his most high calling." (See GS, no. 22.) In other words, since human beings are images of God — i.e., they have minds and free wills — they cannot know themselves without knowing God. By revealing God, Christ reveals the identity and proper activity of images of God, that is, of human beings. But if Christ did not reveal the Father, then He does not reveal "man to himself."

Further, if the second Person of the Blessed Trinity did not truly become man and was not truly united to humanity, including a human body, then human nature was not assumed by Him. If human nature was not assumed by the second Person of the Trinity, then it could not have been "raised in us to a dignity beyond compare." (See GS, no. 22.) In other words, the Church teaches that, by assuming a human nature, Christ made humanity worthy of the divine. But if His body were merely a vision, not reality, then He did not assume human nature and our nature is not raised to the dignity of the divine.

Not only does Christ's mission of Revelation fail in the Gnostic vision, but also Redemption itself. If Christ's body was not real, then He did not die on the cross. If He did not die, then His passion and death were a sham. In other words, He did not really suffer and die because His body was not real. But if He did not suffer and die, then the entire concept of the Redemption fails because the Christian understanding of Redemption is founded on the principle that God the Son died in and through His (true) human nature — His human body united with His human soul, both forever united with the second Person of the Trinity.

In short, the Gnostic view of Creation and Christ destroys Christianity. In fact, any belief system purporting to be Christian that questions the union of the human and divine natures in the one Person of Christ cannot be called Christian because the very name Christian was given to those who believe that Christ is "God from God and light from light . . . Who became man." (See the Nicene Creed.)

Gnosticism also divided Christians into those who were spiritual and had the special knowledge of the interior "spark" of the divine within each human being and those without this knowledge. Those who were gifted with this special knowledge and the knowledge of how to reach this divine "spark" could properly interpret the world, God, and salvation. In effect, these special Christians were superior to other Christians who only had the Church.

Those lacking the special knowledge were in a lower class which the Gnostics called *psychic*. In effect, this set up an authority above and beyond the authority of the Magisterium. Obviously, unless the Pope and the bishops were all spiritual men, they would only speak on the level of the *psychic* Christians and obviously their teaching would be reviewed according to the *gnosis* of the "spiritual" men. Further, this division of Christians set up two levels of Church membership which, of course, the Church would not accept.

Christian Gnosticism

This heresy posited two gods: one who is good and created the spiritual world and one who is evil and created the material world. Christ was the good god, but He did not have a body because the human body belongs to the (evil) material world. Denying the Incarnation, Christian Gnosticism was obviously at variance with orthodox Christianity.

4

Subordinationism

Justin Martyr

WE HAVE SEEN THAT GNOSTICISM WAS ESSENTIALLY DUALISTIC, BUT AT FIRST glance there seems to be a dualism in Christianity as well. If there is only one God and He is in heaven and if Jesus is truly God, then there must be at least two divine beings: Jesus and the Father. But this interpretation of Christian belief in the divinity of both Father and Son might seem to conflict with the equally important Christian belief in the oneness of God.

Justin Martyr, the best-known among the Christian apologists of the second century, attempted to solve this problem by suggesting that the *Logos*, the Word of God, referenced in the prologue to St. John's Gospel, did not exist as distinct from the Father from all eternity. Rather the *Logos* came forth from the Father and was distinguished from the Father only at the time of the Creation. The Son, becoming a separate Person from the Father at the time of Creation, then became man and was born of Mary in Bethlehem. Therefore, the *Logos* was not equal to the Father and the oneness of God is preserved.

Of course, the difficulty with this position is that it makes Christ less than the Father. In this view, Christ, the second Person of the Trinity, is subordinated to the Father. This (false) viewpoint, called Subordinationism, was not challenged at the time it was suggested because it seemed to solve the problem of maintaining the oneness of God while admitting to the Sonship of Christ. It was only in light of subsequent teaching that it was understood that Justin Martyr and some of the other second-century apologists had erred in their understanding of the Trinity and the absolute equality of the three Persons in the Trinity.

The Church was gradually probing the mystery of the Trinity and the Incarnation, but these mysteries are beyond human understanding. It was difficult for the Church to express what was understandable in these mysteries in precise and accurate language because in the second century the language and tools for such statements did not yet exist. In fact, Justin Martyr and the other second-century apologists were helping the Church to develop adequate intellectual tools and an appropriate language for a more precise formulation of the Church's teaching on these mysteries.

Subordinationism

This heresy denied the existence of the Second Person of the Trinity for all eternity, claiming that the Second Person came forth from the Father and was divine, but only at the time of the Creation.

5

Montanists

Second Coming of Christ

SHORTLY AFTER JUSTIN MARTYR DIED, ANOTHER HETERODOX SET OF IDEAS developed. In Phrygia (present-day Turkey) about 170, a man named Montanus proclaimed to his fellow Christians in rather strange language that he was the spokesperson for the Holy Spirit. Two women named Priscilla and Maximilla were associated with him and his movement. The two women uttered prophecies while they seemed to be in trance-like states. At the heart of the Montanist movement was an emphasis on prophecy.

The Montanists believed that the second coming of the Lord was very near. Some even predicted the date of the second coming and went out to meet Christ in the desert where He was to appear. The belief in the imminent second coming of Christ led to a rigorous and unbending insistence on fasting as a means of purifying oneself for the meeting with Christ.

The Montanists forbade any of their followers to flee martyrdom. In contrast, the Church taught that one could avoid martyrdom if it could be done without denying any of the truths of the faith. However, the Montanists taught that any evasion of martyrdom would demonstrate an attachment to the world. Such a worldly attachment would be unfitting for Christians expecting to be taken momentarily with Christ to the glory of heaven. For the same reason, worldly possessions meant nothing because the world was about to end.

Arguing from the same rationale, the Montanists concluded that marriages should not be celebrated and those already married should leave their spouses. The Montanists argued that marriage and family life were among the strongest bonds fastening men and women to this world. The focus of all Christians had to be on the world to come because Christ was coming to introduce everyone to that new kingdom. The Montanists extolled virginity at the expense of marriage because they believed that virginity was the best way of freeing oneself from the cares of the world.

Reaction of the Church

The Montanists had broken with the Church, but this was not apparent at the beginning of the movement. At first, they appeared to emphasize certain aspects of the faith, but every Christian movement does that. In fact, Pope Zephyrinus (199-217) regarded the Montanists favorably. The Church initially saw the Montanists as a movement teaching many of the same things that were taught at the very beginning of the Church's life: prophecy, the emphasis on the Holy Spirit, the fasting requirements, the heroic virtue of facing martyrdom, as well as the value of virginity and celibacy. It was only on closer examination that the Montanist positions were seen to be a distortion of Christian truth.

The distortion of truth was not so much in the denial of Christian truths, but in their exaggeration. The Church taught that some fasting was good. The Montanists said that if a little fasting is good, more would be better, and they went far beyond the norms of the Church. If the Church taught that virginity and celibacy were good, but marriage was also good because it was established by God, the Montanists said that only virginity and celibacy should be embraced, not marriage. If called to martyrdom, the Church said that one should embrace the graces given to make such a heroic sacrifice possible. The Montanists said that martyrdom should never be evaded, even if it could be avoided without denying the faith. In fact, Montanism falsified Christian truths by exaggerating them. Montanism might be called a movement of enthusiasm. It enthusiastically exaggerated some Christian teachings.

Tertullian

The first great Latin theologian, Tertullian, came to embrace Montanism. Tertullian, born about 160, became a Christian about 195. His first works appeared between 200 and 207. He wrote against all the heresies of his time. He borrowed ideas and language from Irenaeus, Justin Martyr, and other Church Fathers. Most importantly, Tertullian wrote in Latin. He gave the western Latin-speaking peoples of the Roman Empire a theological language as well as access to the ideas that had developed in Greek over the course of the second century. Tertullian's achievement is even more remarkable when one remembers that there was no predecessor, no model to follow, in Latin.

Unfortunately, Tertullian gradually came to embrace the views of Montanus. Tertullian seems to have been attracted to the Montanists because of the rigor of their teachings. The Montanists' enthusiastic and unbending embrace of everything Christian attracted Tertullian.

Tertullian may also have been drawn to Montanism by its emphasis on the role of the Holy Spirit, because by claiming the inspiration of the Holy Spirit, a person places himself or herself above all human authority. Only the one who receives it knows the gift of inspiration. Such gifts are subjective and rest on the personal claim of the prophet. But claiming the authority of the Holy Spirit, the prophet cannot be judged by any human tribunal: martyrs, bishops, or even the Pope.

Tertullian did modify some of the Montanist teachings. He did not reject marriage as the Montanists had. Rather, he rejected second marriages, even after a previous spouse had died. (Clearly, though Tertullian's view represents a moderating of the Montanist position, it still conflicted with Church teaching.) Tertullian denied that women could have any speaking or priestly role in divine worship and taught that even if women had the gift of prophecy, they were not to speak publicly.

This position, of course, represented an implicit denial of the prophecies of Priscilla and Maximilla, the two women closely associated with Montanus at the beginning of the Montanist movement. While he denied the role of the feminine prophets, Tertullian did not embrace the priesthood as the Church presented it. Rather, he held that only Montanist (male) prophets retained the full priestly authority of Christ, e.g., the power to forgive sins.

Montanism spread rather successfully. The Christian communities of what is modern-day France in Lyons and Vienne had heard of it. It was known in Rome and, as mentioned above, Pope Zephyrinus had heard of it and actually wrote some letters to the Montanists. It was known in North Africa where Tertullian lived and worked.

Montanists and the Magisterium

One of the first difficulties to confront the bishops of the Church was the Montanist emphasis on prophecy and the private inspiration of the

Holy Spirit. Some bishops wanted to test the claim of the Montanist prophets. The bishops wanted to verify that it was indeed possible that the Holy Spirit and not some evil spirit was speaking through these people. (Such a test is made by an examination of the prophet and the prophet's teaching. If the prophet does not claim anything contrary to Church teaching, then it is certainly possible that the person is truly receiving inspiration from the Holy Spirit.)

The Montanists wanted no interference from the bishops. In other words, the Montanists wanted their subjective claims of inspiration by the Holy Spirit to be accepted by everyone and especially by the Church. The bishops in Asia Minor eventually rejected the claims of the Montanist prophets to speak with the inspiration of God. (Refusing to submit to an examination by the bishops is sufficient reason to doubt the claim that someone is inspired by God.) In effect, the bishops, speaking for the Church, were demanding that the claims of inspiration and prophecy be verified by objective (as opposed to subjective), criteria. Their own authority rested on Tradition, Scripture, and the promised guidance of the Holy Spirit, but these had to accord with one another and two were verifiable: Tradition and Scripture. This position of the bishops meant that the Church would rest on a solid, objective foundation.

Montanism

This heresy proposed that the end of the world was imminent. From this principle, exaggerated Christian practices regarding fasting, martyrdom, virginity, and celibacy were proposed. The heresy conflicted with the Church's Magisterium almost immediately.

6

Adoptionism and Modalism

The Holy Trinity

THE GNOSTICS HAD RAISED A VERY DIFFICULT QUESTION WHEN THEY SUG-
gested that there were two divine beings — a good God and an evil anti-
god. The response of the Christians was that there is only one God, the
Creator, Who is all good. But if there is only one God and He is in heaven,
how is it possible to claim that Jesus is God? If God is in heaven and Jesus
walked the earth (and there is only one God), then Jesus must not be God.
This was the conclusion that many Jews reached at the time of Christ. This
is precisely why the Lord was put to death.

Of course, the Christian answer to the dilemma is the doctrine of the
Trinity. In one God, there are three Persons: Father, Son, and Holy Spirit.
God the Son, the second Person of the Blessed Trinity, became man: Jesus.
However, this answer is founded on almost two thousand years of Chris-
tian reflection. In the early third century, there were many opinions on how
the Trinity might be explained. Two essential points should always be kept
in mind. One cannot emphasize the oneness of God to the exclusion of the
Trinity, and one cannot put so much weight on the Trinity of Persons that
the unity of the Godhead is destroyed. Every false attempt to explain the
Trinity makes one of these two mistakes.

The Christian response to the Gnostics emphasized the unity and
oneness of God in direct contrast to the dualistic approach of the Gnostics.
This viewpoint then called into question Subordinationism, the teaching
of Justin Martyr, who had said that the *Logos* was divine, but not equal to
the Father. Even this nuanced position still defended the divinity of Christ
and the divinity of the Father and therefore fell to the requirement of maintaining the oneness of God. It seemed that there was no way to maintain
the divinity of both the Father and the Son (because if God is one without
the trinity of Persons, then Jesus is not God the Son).

Adoptionism

Those who emphasized the unity of God (against the Gnostics) found it impossible to argue for the divinity of Christ. They argued that Jesus was especially blessed by God and that God's spirit dwelt in Him as in no other. But, they denied Jesus' divinity. This position is called Adoptionism or Dynamist Monarchianism — Monarchianism because there is only one God, a single Monarch, and Dynamist because they spoke of a *dynamis* or power which descended on Jesus when He was "adopted."

This belief seems to have been professed by Paul of Samosata (c. 260) as well as others. The adoptionist theory was difficult to maintain, especially since the Gospel of John proclaimed the divinity of Christ as did the Subordinationism proposed by Justin Martyr and some of the other second-century apologists. (Even though Subordinationism was not an accurate interpretation of Revelation, it was the best available at the time. The problem was to find a way to save the teaching of the prologue of St. John's Gospel without compromising the oneness of God.)

Modalism

Another proposal was made by Sabellius (c. 200) to resolve this dilemma: the name Jesus and the name Father were simply different names for the same Individual. In this view, the names simply named different aspects of the one God. We might apply this point of view in our own lives. Most of us do more than one thing. If a man is an employee of IBM, some might identify him as someone who works for IBM. But his wife would call him husband. Both names, employee and husband, name the same individual, but they indicate different roles the one person has. Similarly, it was proposed that the name Jesus and the name Father simply named different aspects of the one God.

Sometimes this theory is called Modalism because the proponents of this theory claimed that the names of Jesus and God simply identify different modes of the same Individual. Another name for those who held this belief was Patripassionists (which means, literally, Father-sufferers). They were called this because their theory would require that when Jesus died on the cross, the Father (not separate and distinct from the Lord in any way) suffered and died. It is also called Sabellianism after one of its chief proponents, Sabellius. It even has a fourth name — Modalist Monarchianism

(Monarchianism because it holds to the oneness of God, the single Monarch, and Modalist because the names of the Trinity were simply different modes or functions of the same one Individual.)

Difficulties With Adoptionism and Modalism

Of course, the difficulty with Adoptionism is that, in maintaining the oneness of God, it denies the essential Christian belief that Jesus is "God from God and light from light." If this teaching is denied, the mission of Christ to redeem us fails, because God the Son would not have become incarnate and God the Son would not have died on the cross. If Jesus were not God, His sufferings and death would not possess infinite value and thus would not atone for all the sins of men and women. Further, the mission of Christ to reveal the Father also fails because if Christ were not God, He cannot fully know and thus cannot show us the Father. For both these missions of Christ to have been accomplished, it is not sufficient for Him to be adopted by the Father. He had to be divine. Further, it is not sufficient to say that Jesus (or the *Logos*) was another name or a different mode of the Father. In this case, all three divine Persons would have been incarnate and there would have been no distinction between the incarnate Son and the Father. Yet, Jesus offered prayers to the Father, e.g., in the agony before His death. Was He praying to Himself? Scripture clearly reveals that Jesus and the Father are distinct and therefore Modalism fails.

Nevertheless, these ideas did not develop in a vacuum. They were a response to a serious threat to Christianity: Gnosticism. They *did* successfully defend the oneness of God. If in so doing they *did not* maintain the divinity of Christ as they should have, this failure can be as much attributed to the lack of a precise language and theological tools at this time in the Church's history as to anything else.

There is no question that erroneous theories such as Adoptionism and Modalism stimulated the Church to develop, in reaction, a clearer understanding of Revelation. Had certain theories and ideas not been proposed for discussion, how could the Church have developed better insights into the content of Revelation? Of course, there were those who maintained their ideas even after the Church had rejected them and in the process became formal heretics. But such were relatively few.

Adoptionism and Modalism

These heresies denied the divinity of Christ in order to maintain the oneness of God.

7

Manicheism

Mani

AN EVEN GREATER THREAT TO THE CHURCH THAN GNOSTICISM WAS MANIcheism. Most people are familiar with Manicheism through St. Augustine. Augustine was a member of this religion for ten years and later wrote extensively against Manicheism.

Born in 216, Mani, the founder from whom Manicheism receives its name, was brought up in a religious sect (which may have been the Mandeans, but we are not sure) that rejected meat and wine. Mani claimed to have received private revelations inspiring him to found a new universal religion and to engage in missionary activities. He went to India and afterwards managed to obtain permission to preach in his native Persia. Some of his missionaries are known to have been in Egypt.

Mani's preaching was founded on a radical dualism which went beyond anything the Gnostics had taught. For Mani, there were two absolutely equal, eternal, and unbegotten gods: one the god of light, the other the god of darkness. (For the Gnostics, the god of darkness was always of lesser rank than the god who created the spiritual realm and was good.) The god of light creates the spiritual world and the god of darkness creates the material world. But there is a constant battle between these two gods and their respective worlds. The evil material world seeks to swallow up the spiritual world.

To defend his realm, the god of light creates the first man, who engages in the battle but loses to the material world. The first man calls out to the god of light for help, and in response, the god of light sends forth from himself a spirit who frees the first man from the evil material world. The process of liberation from the evil material world continues for all human beings because the god of light sends his messengers to let all people know that their true destiny lies with the god of light.

The messengers were Buddha, Zoroaster, Jesus, and, of course, Mani, who is the final messenger and the last hope for all people everywhere. One can easily perceive the Gnostic elements in this system of thought. However, the Manicheans went beyond the Gnostics, first in maintaining that the evil principle, the god of darkness, was equal to the god of light, but also in their requirements that all followers of their religion avoid evil, including avoiding the evil of the material world.

For human beings, as physical beings, it is very difficult to avoid the physical and material world! Consequently, the Manicheans demanded heroic sacrifices. For example, sexual activity, because it was a union of material bodies, was evil. The Manicheans encouraged their members to abstain from all sexual activity. They also rejected menial work because it involved working with matter in the evil material world. Further, all physical pleasures were to be avoided because they brought one into contact with the evil material world. So, for example, one was not to enjoy the pleasures of eating and drinking. For this reason, there were elaborate fasting and abstinence requirements. Of course, such demands were almost impossible to fulfill, and so the Manicheans divided their membership into the elect, who fulfilled the Manichean requirements as far as possible, and the hearers, who served the elect and aspired to become members of the elect.

The radical view of the Manicheans towards the material world differs even from the Gnostics. While the Gnostics did hold that there was a "spark" of the divine, present in all human beings, which needed to be liberated, this liberation happened at the moment of death. For the Manicheans, the goal was to liberate oneself from the material world while still living in the world — a practical impossibility!

Although Mani regarded himself as the greatest of the four messengers from the god of light, Jesus had the most important mission of the other three. In fact, Mani even refers to himself as the "apostle of Jesus Christ." Mani claimed that the Holy Spirit, sent by Christ, had descended on him and that he and the Holy Spirit were one. However, Mani did not believe that Jesus had a true body because, if he had, he would have imprisoned himself in an evil, material world. (There is an inconsistency here. If all the material world is evil and Christ could not have had a true body — because he would have imprisoned himself in the evil world of matter — it is difficult to see how the Holy Spirit could have united himself with Mani, who obviously did have a human body and was imprisoned in the material world.) Further, Mani rejected most of the Old Testament Scriptures because he believed the God of Genesis and the Old Testament to be the god of darkness.

Mani cannot be called a formal heretic because he never embraced Christianity. Still, his ideas brought many Christians into his new religion. As a serious threat to the teachings of the Church, even though this threat came from the outside, as it were, his movement needs to be considered among the divergent religious teachings proposed to third- and fourth-century Christians.

Christian Elements in Manicheism

The Christian elements included by Mani were intended from the very beginning to attract Christians to his new universal religion. He had incorporated similar elements from Buddhism and Zoroastrianism for his missionary work in the East. But there was more to it than that. Mani believed that his new religion was the fulfillment of all the others. The previous religions all had elements of the truth, but they also had falsehoods. The true elements needed to be accepted, united with the full truth, and incorporated into a complete, coherent, universal religion. The false elements of the previous religions needed to be discarded. Mani was successful in converting Christians. Within the Empire, the acknowledged sphere of Christian influence, the Manicheans were strongest in the East and in North Africa.

The incorporation of Christian elements accounts for some of Mani's success in Christian circles. In addition to the emphasis on Jesus, Christians were attracted by some of the Manichean prayers, for example, "Come to me, living Christ! Come to me, O light of the day! O merciful one, O comforter, I cry to you so that you may turn to me in the hour of tribulation. Your sweet yoke I have taken upon me in purity. Honor and victory be to our Lord, the comforter and to his holy elect and to the soul of the blessed Mary."

Further, Mani offered his followers a coherent system of thought. Mani proposed explanations for many questions. For instance, the problem of evil was given a solution. Evil existed because of the god of darkness. Mani also attracted Christians with the structure of his new universal religion.

Manicheism had a well-organized hierarchy, with apostles, bishops, priests, and deacons.

Finally, the Manicheans, taking their cue from their founder's own life, had an active and zealous missionary program. Manichean missionaries sought converts among Christians, among pagans, among any who would listen. The Manichean missionaries believed that they possessed the full religious truth and wanted to give this to all Christians, who unfortunately were duped into believing falsehoods. Since Mani did not allow his followers to be members of another religion, when a Christian was converted, he or she left the Church. Further, the Manichean missionaries were in competition with the Christian missionaries for the hearts and souls of the pagans. Manicheism was definitely a serious threat to the Church.

Reaction of the Church

The Church responded by preaching against the Manichean teachings. Christian writers argued forcefully against the Manichean beliefs. St. Augustine wrote extensively against the beliefs of his former religion. In addition, the Church was cautious about accepting converts from Manicheism. When a former Manichean joined the Christian Church, he or she had to agree to renounce the Manichean beliefs in special and specific formulas. These requirements were put in place because the Manicheans employed Christian formulas to express their beliefs (while intending something different than the Christians did in using those formulas) and employed Christian language in some of their prayers and devotions.

Manicheans and the Roman Empire

It was not only the Church that had problems with the Manicheans. Even before Christianity was tolerated, Diocletian (284-305) began a persecution against the Manicheans in 297. In the fourth century, during Constantine's reign (306-337) and after, the Empire continued to persecute the Manicheans. Although the persecutions probably had little effect on the growth or, for that matter, on the decline of the Manicheans, they were beginning to decline by the end of the fourth century. St. Augustine hardly mentions them after 400 — an indication that their influence had declined.

Difficulties of Manicheism

The Manichean religion had all the flaws of Gnosticism. Clearly, the dualistic concept of two equal and eternal gods was untenable in a Christian or Jewish context. There is only one God, not two. Second, Christ is not merely one of the great messengers of God, but is God. Third, the claim that the Holy Spirit descended on Mani is a claim on Mani's part to speak with the authority of God Himself. Obviously, from the point of view of the Church, this puts Mani above the Pope and the bishops and cannot be maintained. Fourth, the concept that the material world is evil does not accord with the Church's confession that the world reflects the goodness of God. Fifth, the division of members of the Manichean Church into elect and hearers runs contrary to the spiritual equality of all men and women before God.

It should be noted here that the division in the Manichean system was not a hierarchical division — not like the division in the Church which exists between the ordained and the non-ordained. The division between the ordained and the non-ordained is a division in roles of service. The ordained exist for the service of the faithful, but the ordained and the non-ordained are asked to observe the same discipline, following the commandments and leading virtuous lives. All are asked to observe the same commandments, the same virtues. Whether deacon, priest, bishop, pope, monk or nun, brother or sister, married or single, all Catholics are called to holiness, to sainthood, and can achieve it in their individual vocations. Of course, there are differences among the individual vocations. A monk or priest makes promises that a married man does not. But the fundamental point is that holiness and true sainthood are possible in any vocation if it is lived properly.

The Manichean division was based on a radically different discipline for the elect as opposed to the hearers. Further, the hearers could not come to holiness or sainthood without joining the elect. A comparable system in the Church would require everyone to be a monk or nun in order to be saved. In Manicheism, there was clearly a two-tiered membership system with different rules of conduct. Such a system is alien to Christianity. With all these differences, it may surprise some that the Manicheans were successful in converting Christians.

However, the dualism offered by Mani and to a lesser extent by the

Gnostics seemed to answer some fundamental questions common to all people everywhere. This dualism will resurface in the Church repeatedly throughout the ages. The dualistic approach seems to be one way the human mind grapples with the problem of good and evil. Dualism appeals probably because it is straightforward and relatively simple. Unfortunately, it is false.

Manicheism

This heresy was radically dualist with two gods: a good god who created the spiritual world and an evil god who created the material world. For the Manicheans, these two gods were absolutely equal and there was a struggle between them.

8

Controversies on Baptism, Penance, and Papal Primacy

St. Cyprian

THE MANICHEANS HAD BEEN VERY SUCCESSFUL IN MAKING CONVERTS FROM Christianity in North Africa. Of course, this very fact testifies to the strength of the Church in North Africa. (If there had not been flourishing Christian communities, the Manicheans could not have made many converts from those communities for the simple reason that either they would not have existed or they would have been very small!) We also know the strength of the Church in North Africa through the work of Tertullian.

In the middle of the third century, there were synods (meetings) of bishops in North Africa with over seventy bishops present. Each bishop represented a diocese. (By comparison, the United States in the year 2000 has about 175 dioceses. One also must remember that the total population of the world in Roman times was far less than today.) For North Africa to have had seventy dioceses testifies to the extraordinary strength of the Church in this region in the third century.

St. Cyprian (d. 258) lived and worked in North Africa. He was the bishop of Carthage. While Cyprian was bishop, the Emperor Decius (249-251) issued an edict (in 249) requiring all inhabitants of the Empire to offer worship to the Roman gods. Although such a requirement had long been Roman law, Decius' decree was different in that it set up commissions throughout the Roman Empire which would issue certificates to all those who had worshiped the Roman gods. By a given date, everyone had to present a certificate to the authorities. If someone subject to Roman authority did not have a certificate, he was subject to arrest, imprisonment, torture, confiscation, and even death if he did not consent to offer sacrifice to the Roman gods.

Under this kind of pressure, many Christians did not find the courage to resist, and they submitted to the Roman demands. Some worshiped the gods immediately, some after some days in prison, others only after torture, but many bowed to Decius' decree. All these were guilty of apostasy, of denying the faith. There were others who managed to bribe the authorities and obtain certificates without offering sacrifice to the gods. Obviously, these were less guilty than the others.

Fortunately, while vicious, the Decian persecution ended in 251. Many Christians who had apostatized or who had obtained certificates wanted to return to the Church. The Church had to face the very practical question of what to do about those who had not found the courage to suffer martyrdom for their faith.

Penance and Forgiveness

It brought the question of penance and forgiveness into play in a very practical way. This question was not new to North Africa. Tertullian, in his Montanist days, had taken a very stern stand against the Church's offering forgiveness to anyone. In his later (Montanist) writings, Tertullian had held that only the Montanist prophets could forgive sins.

Since there were many Christians in North Africa during the Decian persecution, there were many who had fallen away. (There were also a good number of martyrs.) St. Cyprian had to decide what to do about those who wanted forgiveness for their sin against the faith. Following the tradition of Tertullian, there were some who said that those who had sinned against the faith could not be forgiven. There were also some priests who were accepting the lapsed back without any work of penance whatsoever. Further complicating the issue were many of the fallen away who had managed to persuade the martyrs before they died to write letters recommending forgiveness.

Often the martyrs granted letters to those who asked. We do not really know what motivated the martyrs to grant these letters. It is possible that friends and relatives approached the martyrs requesting the favor of a letter. There were many martyrs, and the Christian community was relatively close-knit. It is probable that almost everyone knew at least one of the martyrs, either as a friend or family member. Some of the martyrs might have wanted to spare their family and friends any further losses — to ease their pain, but also to preserve some semblance of the family. If most family members were martyred, especially the male members, who would earn a living and care for the others? Further, the martyrs knew the courage it took to do what they were doing and realized that others might not have that same virtue. There were two questions: Should some penance be imposed for those who wanted forgiveness for denying the faith? And did the letters from the martyrs constitute absolution of the sin of apostasy?

St. Cyprian refused to allow his priests to forgive the sins of those who had fallen away without any penance. Priests who violated this policy could lose their position. St. Cyprian also made it clear that the letters from the martyrs were only recommendations to the Church authorities. He clearly held that the letters did not constitute forgiveness of any sins. Cyprian made some special provisions for those who were dying: he allowed his priests to reinstate those who had worshiped the Roman gods provided they had letters from the martyrs or had previously done some sort of penance for their sins.

Many accepted St. Cyprian's policies, but there were a number of those with letters from the martyrs who maintained that they had already been forgiven and did not need to do any further acts of penance. Those who insisted that the letters of the martyrs were sufficient for forgiveness set up a rival community in Carthage. The leaders of this community included the priest Novatus. This rival community grew in numbers and they regarded themselves as the legitimate Catholic community of Carthage. When those who disagreed with Cyprian approached Pope Cornelius (251-253), the Pope did not condone their position. Pope Cornelius supported Cyprian.

Novatian

All this would only be of interest to those following the development of the Church's understanding of forgiveness and the sacrament of Penance, except that a priest of the diocese of Rome, Novatian, came to believe that those who had left the faith could not be forgiven. Novatian was secretary of the college of priests in Rome between the death of Pope Fabian in the Decian persecution (January 250) and the election of Pope Cornelius in 251. As secretary for the priests and in the absence of a Pope (after January 250 and before 251), Novatian handled the correspondence between the diocese of Rome and other sees. He corresponded with Cyprian and agreed with the bishop's policies. However, it seems that he expected to be elected bishop of Rome — that is, Pope. Instead, Cornelius was chosen. With the help of Novatus, the priest in Carthage who had been one of the leaders of the anti-Cyprian Catholic community there, Novatian managed to make himself a rival to Pope Cornelius.

Of course, this was a schism, a break in jurisdiction. This schism quickly became heretical when Novatian began to retract his previous statements on the forgiveness of those who had abandoned the faith. As a claimant to the see of Peter and a rival to Pope Cornelius, Novatian taught that the Church could not forgive the sins of those who had worshiped the Roman gods. According to Novatian's new viewpoint, if the Church forgave those who had abandoned the faith, the Church would tarnish its holiness.

Novatian set up a Church structure and even persuaded some bishops to join him. He wrote the African bishops, and one wavered for a time, but then was convinced of Novatian's error by a letter from Cyprian. Bishop Marcian in Arles joined the Novatianists and held to the principle that the lapsed could not be forgiven by the Church. Novatian found some support in Spain, Syria, Palestine, Asia Minor, Armenia, and Mesopotamia. However, with the death of Novatian in the persecution of Valerian (257-259), the schism ended and the unity of the Roman See was restored. However, the rigorist idea that the Church's sanctity precluded the forgiveness of serious sins continued to persist in small communities, especially in the East.

Baptism

The Novatian schism and heresy resulted in a dispute about Baptism between Cyprian and Pope Stephen (254-257). (Pope Stephen was not the immediate successor of Pope Cornelius. Pope Lucius I succeeded Cornelius, but Lucius died in 254.) A bishop in North Africa wrote Cyprian asking if someone who was baptized by the Novatianists should be rebaptized when admitted to the Catholic Church. In other words, was the Baptism done by a heretical or schismatic sect valid?

Cyprian and several African synods unequivocally held that heretical Baptism was invalid because Baptism is one of the sacraments and the sacraments have been given to the Church. Anyone not in full communion with the Church cannot confer any sacrament because the sacraments are always celebrated by the Church. Further, anyone not in full communion with the Church does not possess the Holy Spirit, and since the sacraments confer the Holy Spirit, no one outside the Church may validly celebrate the sacraments. This position was also the one held in Asia Minor and the one that Tertullian defended. However, the practice at Rome was not to rebaptize those who had been baptized in heretical sects.

A synod meeting at Carthage in North Africa in 256, considering this matter of re-Baptism, wanted to consult Rome. Cyprian was directed to write Pope Stephen and ask about the re-Baptism of those baptized in heretical sects. St. Stephen responded, conscious of his position as the successor of Peter, that the Church should accept heretical Baptism as valid, that people baptized in heretical sects should not be rebaptized as long as the Baptism had been done in the name of the Trinity. He defended his teaching as traditional and the practice of re-Baptism as an innovation. Not only did Pope Stephen write St. Cyprian, he also wrote the bishops of Asia Minor who were also rebaptizing those baptized in heretical sects.

Cyprian was offended by the tone of St. Stephen's letter, by what he regarded as Stephen's presumptuous interference in other bishoprics, and, of course, by Pope Stephen's acceptance of heretical Baptism. St. Cyprian called another African synod, and this synod also supported his position. When the decisions of this council were taken to Rome to be presented to the Pope, Stephen would not receive the decisions or the messengers carrying them. However, the controversy ended with the death of Pope Stephen in 257 and the death of Cyprian (258) in the Valerian persecution.

Cyprian and Pope Cornelius had agreed against the schismatic Novatian that the Church could forgive sins, even serious sins. They also agreed that penitents should perform an appropriate penance. On the question of accepting the validity of Baptism by heretics, Cyprian forcefully disagreed with Pope Stephen I and actively resisted the Pope's position. Cyprian even called a synod to support his own position after he had received Pope Stephen's letter. Obviously, Cyprian was his own man.

Differences in Understanding the Church

However, the difference in his attitude towards Rome regarding these two issues clearly reflects Cyprian's view concerning the structure of the Church. Cyprian believed that the bishop was the sign of unity in each diocesan Church. The bishop was answerable to God alone for the administration of his diocese. The whole Church formed a unity because each bishop was in communion with all the other bishops. During the papacy of Pope Cornelius, a work of Cyprian on the unity of the Church gave glowing praise to the importance of the Church of Rome as the ultimate source of unity among the bishops of the world. After Cyprian's quarrel with Pope Stephen, Cyprian revised his text and toned down his appraisal of the role of the papacy, reserving to it simply a pride of place.

For his part, Pope Stephen claimed a primacy because he was the successor of St. Peter. Stephen consciously interpreted Matthew 16:18-19 — "You are Peter, and on this rock I will build my Church, and the powers of death shall not prevail against it. I will give you the keys of the kingdom of heaven, and whatever you bind on earth shall be bound in heaven, and whatever you loose on earth shall be loosed in heaven" — as conferring on the see of Rome, the see of Peter, a particular primacy. For this reason, Pope Stephen believed it proper to write to other bishops regarding their beliefs and practices. Pope Stephen's decision on heretical Baptism and his letters to Cyprian and the bishops of Asia Minor show a development in the Church's understanding of its own structure.

Difficulties With Novatianism

The difficulties with Novatianism — i.e., with the non-acceptance of heretical Baptism — are clear from a Catholic perspective. In denying the Church's power of forgiveness, Novatian was denying that the Church had been given the power to bind and loose by the Lord. Novatian denied the obvious meaning of Matthew 16:19: "Whatever you bind on earth shall be bound in heaven, and whatever you loose on earth shall be loosed in heaven." If the Church cannot forgive all sins, then the Church does not have the power of Christ. Obviously, this is an untenable position from the Catholic point of view.

The problem with the non-acceptance of heretical Baptism was that such a stance calls the sacraments into question. If a priest did not believe everything that the Church taught, then would the sacraments he celebrates be invalid? Such a stance would call into question every sacrament of the Church. The sacraments cannot depend on the faith of the one conferring them. For the sake of all members of the Church, sacraments must depend on the observance of their essential elements (e.g., water and the proper words in Baptism; bread and wine and the words of consecration in the Eucharist). One can objectively perceive the essential elements of the sacraments. Even the question of intention is verifiable because if a particular priest is using the words and the elements of the Eucharist, it can be inferred that he is intending to do what the words say.

Cyprian's argument about the Holy Spirit would mean that a priest in the state of serious sin could not validly confer the sacraments because in that state he would not possess the Holy Spirit. Pope Stephen's insistence on not making Baptism dependent on the beliefs or holiness of the individual conferring the sacrament is the only way to guarantee the sacraments for the whole Church. Ever since the reign of Pope Stephen I, as indeed before his reign, the Church has taught what he taught.

Difficulties With Cyprian's View of the Church

We have already seen the conflict between Cyprian's view of the autonomy of each bishop answering only to God and the doctrine of Roman primacy maintained by Pope Stephen: Cyprian's view conflicts with Matthew 16:18. Pope Stephen's traditionalist understanding of his own position and role in the Church was the understanding the Church held in the past and would continue to maintain forever after.

Issues Arose From Genuine Pastoral Problems

The controversy over offering forgiveness to the lapsed arose because of a need. There were those who had abandoned their faith and wanted to return. What was the Church going to do with these people? Thus, the whole question arose not out of theoretical discussions on the nature of God, but rather out of a specific pastoral problem. The discussion of the question by the North African bishops and among the clergy of Rome led to a development in the Church's understanding of its own powers of forgiveness. Officially, it repudiated forever the rigorist position which held that there were sins the Church could not forgive.

The question of the re-Baptism of those baptized in heretical sects also arose out of a specific pastoral problem and led to a development in the Church's understanding of the sacraments. In affirming that the sacraments did not depend on what the celebrant of the sacraments believed or how holy he was, the Church clearly came to a better understanding of what Christ intended when He entrusted the sacraments to the Church.

In addition, Pope Stephen's exercise of the privileges he possessed as the successor of Peter was not a theoretical test of the acceptance of papal authority. This authority was used because there was a need to use it: the question on heretical Baptism needed to be settled.

Each of these questions was a practical problem that had theoretical implications. On the practical questions, people disagreed. Without these disagreements, there would never have been a full discussion of the issues and the important development of doctrine would not have occurred.

Certainly in beginning the schism, Novatian went beyond the point that faithful Catholics should go. On the other hand, Cyprian can only be charged with forcefully defending what he considered to be not only viable decisions, but ones necessary for his own diocese. St. Cyprian was not guilty of formal heresy, even though he defended positions on re-Baptism and on the primacy of the Pope that were in error. Except for Pope Stephen's position, the question of re-Baptism was an open one. Many dioceses rebaptized and others did not.

The acceptance of Pope Stephen's position depended on the acceptance of papal primacy. Cyprian retreated from his earlier understanding of the papacy's role in the structure of the Church. But he cannot be accused of formal heresy on this point either. The Church had not yet made a formal statement on the position of the Pope in the Church even though Pope Stephen exercised his rights to intervene in other sees as earlier Popes had done, e.g., Victor I (189-198). There was no universal understanding (as there would be later) that the successor of Peter exercised a certain authority over all the other sees.

In other words, there was no universally held belief in the primacy of the Pope, just as there was no universally held position on the question of re-Baptism. In this sense, Cyprian believed he had the right to disagree. Cyprian's views on these two matters did not represent the future. Nevertheless, without him and even without Novatian, the Church might not have had the stimulus to develop its understanding of Revelation on the subjects of forgiveness of sins, the sacraments, and the primacy of the Pope.

Novatianism

This heresy held that the Church could not forgive certain sins because they were too serious.

St. Cyprian believed that those baptized by heretics or schismatics should be re-baptized and in the wake of a quarrel with Pope Stephen, he retreated from his earlier policy of endorsing a more active role of the papacy outside Italy.

Conclusion to Part I

WE BEGAN THIS SECTION WITH A QUOTATION FROM THE NICENE CREED: "We believe in one God, the Father, the Almighty. . . .We believe in one Lord, Jesus Christ, the only Son of God. . . .We believe in the Holy Spirit, the Lord, the giver of Life." This quotation points to the major doctrinal issue of the first three centuries of the Christian era: the mystery of the one and triune God. Of the eight topics discussed in this part, five concern God in His oneness or as a Trinity of Persons: Kerinthians, Ebionites, Elchasaites, and Mandeans; Gnostics; Subordinationism; Adoptionism and Modalism; and Manicheism. The other three heresies of this period — the Judaizers, who wanted to insist that Christians become Jews before they became Christians; the Montanists; and the Novatianists (together with those ideas of St. Cyprian which the Church came to reject definitively) — did not directly concern the mystery of God. However, none of these, not even the Montanists, can compare with the appeal, the organization, or the missionary work of the Gnostics or the Manichees. The Gnostics and Manichees made a far greater impact on the religious world of the second and third centuries than the Judaizers, the Montanists, or the Novatianists all combined.

It is clear from an analysis of the heresies proposed in these centuries that the major difficulty was the nature of the one and triune God. Some were definitely not trying to advance the Catholic understanding of God. Certainly, the Gnostics and the Manichees cannot be accused of attempting to understand God in the Christian sense. The Kerinthians, the Ebionites, the Elchasaites, and the Mandeans also did not contribute much to the Christian understanding of God. But the Subordinationists, the Adoptionists, and the Modalists were certainly making an attempt to fathom the mystery of God as one and triune. Therefore, either in proposing dualistic theories or in trying to understand the mystery of God Himself, the most significant heresies of the first three centuries of the Church revolved around the statement: "We believe in One God, the Father, the Son, and the Holy Spirit."

PART II

Was Christ God the Son?
Heresies from 325 to 843

We believe in one Lord, Jesus Christ,
the only Son of God
eternally begotten of the Father,
God from God, Light from Light,
true God from true God,
begotten, not made, one in
Being with the Father.
Through him all things were made.
For us men and for our salvation
he came down from heaven:
by the power of the Holy Spirit
he was born of the Virgin Mary,
and became man.

WHILE THE THEOLOGICAL ISSUES OF THE FIRST THREE CENTURIES OF THE Church's life (33-325) were primarily concerned with the mystery of God as one and at the same time triune, the theological issues in the next period (between the Council of Nicaea in 325 and the end of Iconoclasm in 843) concerned the divinity of Christ and the relation of His divinity to His humanity.

Christian belief in the Trinity had direct implications for the teaching on the divinity of Christ. If there are not three distinct Persons in the Trinity, then the divinity of Christ is hardly plausible. Further, if there are really two principles or two first causes, one who created the (good) spiritual world and one who created the (evil) physical world, then the humanity of

Christ (as united with His divinity) is called into question. How would it have been possible for God (the good one) to unite himself with the (evil) physical world? Thus, the various false teachings on the Trinity discussed in the last part resulted in certain false conclusions about Christ. However, the starting point of these ideas was the nature of God as one and triune.

In the first period, 33-325, the question asked was: What and Who is God? The false doctrines proposed in the time period discussed in this part often result in teachings about Christ which resemble the (false) ideas about Christ discussed in the last part. However, the starting point for the (false) teachings about Christ discussed in this part is Christ Himself, not God in the mystery of the Godhead.

The question asked by those proposing (false) teachings about Christ in the second period, 325-843, was: What and Who is Christ? Even though some of the (false) teachings discussed in this part about Christ are similar to some of the ideas proposed by men of the previous era, there are differences in detail because the starting point of a discussion usually determines, at least partially, the result.

The most significant heresies about Christ in the period between 325 and 843 were in chronological order: Arianism, Nestorianism, and Monophysitism. But there were other heresies following the Monophysite heresy which raised questions about Christ. The heresy of the Three Chapters (which will be explained) was an attempt to heal the divisions in the Empire which resulted from the Monophysite heresy. The Monothelete heresy was also a proposal to reconcile the Monophysites to the Empire. It failed because it was found to be inconsistent with the teaching of the Church. Iconoclasm rocked the Church in the East in the eighth century and was fundamentally a questioning of the propriety of depicting Christ and the saints in images. In effect, this was a question of whether the humanity of Christ, depicted in art, truly represented *Him*, both in His divinity and humanity, and whether artistic portrayals of human persons (which portrayed only the bodies of the subjects) could truly reflect the holiness of human persons.

9

❦

Arianism

Origin of Arianism

ARIANISM WAS ONE OF THE MOST IMPORTANT HERESIES IN THE HISTORY OF the Church. It had effects well into the seventh century. The Church was dealing with Arianism almost throughout the entire period between 325 and 843. Arianism was the reason the Council of Nicaea was convened in 325, the chronological starting point of this part.

Arianism is named after its originator, the priest Arius. He grew up in Libya and was trained at the theological school at Antioch. (By the beginning of the fourth century, there was a theological school at Antioch in Syria and one in Egypt at Alexandria. These two schools were rivals, and each fought against the other for influence in the Church. The story of the heresies in this period is in large part the story of the rivalry between these two schools.)

In 318, Arius was a pastor at one of the parishes in Alexandria, even though he had attended the school at Antioch. (His association with Libya, Antioch, and Alexandria is one demonstration of the ease of travel and movement in the Roman Empire and also evidence of the cosmopolitan nature of the Church in the early fourth century.) In a series of sermons in 318 and 319, Arius gave his interpretation of the *Logos* (the Greek word for the Word of God used in St. John's Gospel: "In the beginning was the Word. . . ." See John 1:1.), and the relationship between the *Logos* and the Father. Hearing of the sermons, Bishop Alexander of Alexandria was not concerned but thought there should be a theological discussion of the points made by Arius.

The bishop convened a meeting. On this occasion, Arius presented his views and others presented opposing theories. The fact that Bishop Alexander was not at all concerned about Arius's teaching but wanted a theological discussion shows that important questions about the Incarnation had not yet been settled and remained open for discussion. Arius was suggesting a solution to a difficulty. In presenting his ideas, he was not defying the Church or teaching ideas contrary to what the Church had defined as part of the content of Revelation. Further, such ideas stimulated the Church to develop a better understanding of Revelation.

In his presentation at the meeting, Arius suggested that the Son of God was created and that therefore there was a time when He did not exist. In Arius's view, the *Logos* was a creature made by God who was capable of virtue but also of vice. Those opposed to Arius insisted that the Son of God was somehow really God. (Please note that the Nicene Creed had not yet been formulated and so the phrase "one in being with the Father" was not in place.) It is noteworthy that, with Arius's suggestion that the Son was created, those opposed to Arius immediately asserted that the Son is one in being with the Father. With this statement, although the starting point had been the Son, the entire controversy became an argument about the relationships in the Trinity. At the conclusion of the discussion, Bishop Alexander accepted the arguments of those opposed to Arius.

The bishop also told Arius never to propose his ideas again. However, Arius refused to comply with the bishop's mandate. With this refusal, Bishop Alexander excommunicated Arius. At this point, in refusing the clear and direct order of his bishop, Arius can certainly be faulted.

Knowing that many bishops and theologians outside of Egypt agreed with his ideas, Arius contacted Bishop Eusebius of Nicomedia, a former fellow student of his at Antioch. (Nicomedia is in modern-day Turkey, across the Bosporus from Constantinople, modern-day Istanbul. The Emperor Diocletian, 284-305, had built a palace there.) This step forced Bishop Alexander to seek support.

The Bishop called a synod of all the bishops of Egypt in 319. This synod affirmed the excommunication of Arius and extended it to all those who followed him. Bishop Alexander communicated the decisions of the Egyptian synod to all the bishops of the Church, but was under considerable pressure from other bishops to rescind the excommunication of Arius and those who agreed with him. Alexander defended himself, writing to all the bishops of the East and even to Pope Sylvester I (314-335).

Clearly, the disagreement had overtones of a struggle between those of the Antioch school (Arius and fellow students like Bishop Eusebius of Nicomedia) on the one hand and those from the Alexandrian school (mostly in Egypt) on the other. Further, the dispute had spread to the entire Church of the East. Bishops and theologians, priests and deacons immediately took sides, either with Arius or with Bishop Alexander. Those taking sides sometimes did not know the particulars of the problem. As is often the case in such situations, positions hardened rapidly and it became more and more difficult to mediate the dispute. Had the issue not spread beyond the Alexandrian diocese, it might have been possible to find a way out of the impasse. Once spread beyond the diocese, the problem became more and more difficult to resolve.

Even Emperor Constantine (305-337) heard of the problem and, apparently without understanding the issue at stake, wrote a letter to Bishop Alexander suggesting that Arius and the bishop should reconcile because their differences were not about anything essential! Further, the Emperor believed that on such an unimportant point, people could reasonably differ.

The Emperor's letter clearly demonstrates that either he did not grasp the nature of the discussion or had a very poor understanding of the nature of Christ and the importance of Christ in the faith of the Church. Actually, the Emperor's letter was probably the result of both these factors: he did not grasp the issue at hand and also did not have a good understanding of the faith. He had not yet been baptized, although he did regard himself as a Christian. (Many urged him to delay Baptism — partly the result of the notion that Baptism forgives all sins and one should wait until it was unlikely for one to commit any more sins before receiving Baptism — until death. The Church never officially endorsed such ideas, but Constantine seems to have followed this advice and did not receive Baptism until he was dying.)

Council of Nicaea

Constantine and his advisors decided that the issue needed to be settled when his plan for reconciliation failed. So he decided to call a general council of the Church to settle the dispute along with some others (including the date of Easter).

In calling a council, the Emperor was acting as a religious leader. This was a traditional task of the Roman Emperors. Since Octavian (27 B.C. – A.D. 14), the Roman Emperors had held the title *pontifex maximus,* or chief priest (literally, bridge-builder). In virtue of this office and title, the Emperor was the chief representative of the official Roman religion.

The Emperor Constantine naturally continued to exercise a leadership role in the Church, just as his predecessors had exercised a leadership role in the pagan religion. Further, since Constantine had placed himself and his army under the protection of the Christian God before his final victorious battle over his rival Maxentius, he believed that he was designated by God to rule the Roman Empire. In return for this favor, Constantine believed that he had a grave obligation to promote Christianity.

This belief, in addition to the imperial traditions associated with the *pontifex maximus* title, led to Constantine's assumption of a religious role within Christianity. By associating a leadership role with the imperial powers, Constantine set the stage for numerous difficulties both in the East and the West. What would happen if there were conflicts between the Emperor and the bishops? Was the Emperor to decide Church policy and doctrine? What if the Emperor used his influence to promote heretical teachings? Many of the problems of the Arian crisis are attributable to Constantine's continuance of imperial prerogatives in religious matters even after Christianity became the dominant religion of the Empire.

Constantine called the Council of Nicaea. It was the first general council of the Church since the Council of Jerusalem. It had been impossible for the Church to function on such a scale before Constantine because of the persecutions and the laws against Christianity.

The council was called to meet in Nicaea, a town in Asia Minor (modern-day Turkey), a bit south of Nicomedia, where Eusebius, one of the defenders of Arius, was bishop. While the Pope did not attend Nicaea personally, he sent representatives. By sending representatives, the Pope ratified the decision of the Emperor to convene the council. Many bishops from the East were present, but few from the West because of the distance they would have had to travel.

The council opened at Constantine's own palace in the city on May 20, 325. The council, after some heated discussion, adopted the creed which is now known as the Nicene Creed. Further, the council specifically condemned any teaching that Christ was created or that there was a time when He did not exist.

"One in Being with the Father"

The major dispute at the Council surrounded the phrase "one in being with the Father." This is an exact translation of the Greek phrase *homoousios* — important both because of its earlier and later history. *Ousios* means being and *homo* means one or the same. This phrase, *homoousios*, made some of the eastern bishops very uneasy because Paul of Samosata had used it in an Adoptionist sense, i.e., that Jesus was only a human being but one who was blessed, or adopted, by God.

According to the Adoptionists, God's spirit descended on Jesus. (See above, chapter 6, on Adoptionism.) Paul of Samosata apparently used *homoousios* to mean that God was one in being without a distinction of Persons. Therefore, the divine spirit or the divine wisdom that descended on Jesus was not a separate Person in the Godhead, but rather a power of the one (Person of) God.

Paul of Samosata's understanding was not accepted, and it is clear that Nicaea used *homoousious* in a completely different way than Paul of Samosata had used it. Nicaea uses this same word to mean that all three Persons of the Trinity are one in being with the others. In other words, there is only one Godhead. Another way of putting the same concept is the phrase "God is one." (Of course, today we have well-defined terms thanks to later theological development. The one-in-being phrase to us is the same as saying that God has one divine nature.)

The Latin bishops from the West, although few in number, did not have the same difficulties with *homoousios* as some bishops from the East because they saw in *homoousios* the same meaning as *consubstantialem* which Tertullian had used to describe Christ. But in defining *homoousios* as *consubstantialem*, the western bishops raised a difficulty of language, because the council also decreed that Christ and the Father are of the same substance and used the Greek word *hypostasis*.

Obviously, the western bishops are equating *consubstantialem* (i.e., "with the same substance") and the Greek *homoousios*. But the Greeks are using *hypostasis* to mean substance. The Greeks are making a distinction between *homoousios* (being) and *hypostasis* (substance), while the Latins do not seem to have a different word for these two Greek terms. Even though *homoousios* and *hypostasis* were used interchangeably by the Greeks until the 370s, the very fact that there were two words shows that there were at least different shades of meaning and emphases between them. The Latins did not understand these subtleties. This language problem is typical of the difficulties in defining the mysteries of Revelation.

The bishops and theologians were struggling for terms to at least describe, if not to explain as far as possible, some of the deepest mysteries of the Christian faith. The language problem surrounding *homoousios* and *hypostasis* is also typical of the possibility for misunderstandings between the East and West. The East was using Greek and the West was using Latin. The two languages, especially on these very fine points, were different enough that there were not always exact translations. This led to difficulties for each group in understanding the other.

Nevertheless, we can see the fruit of Nicaea's technical discussions of words in the Nicene Creed: "We believe in one Lord, Jesus Christ, . . . the only Son of God eternally begotten of the Father . . . one in Being [*homoousios* or *consubstanialem*] with the Father. Through him all things were made." With the acceptance of the Nicene Creed by the council and the issuance of the decrees specifically directed to the Arian position, it was difficult to interpret Nicaea in an Arian sense. In fact, the Arians had lost.

Even though they were a very strong party at the council, they were unable to prevail because the other side not only had the stronger argument but also had the greater numbers. Further, those sympathetic to the Arian position did not want to risk offending Constantine, who also accepted the Nicene Creed and the decrees of the council.

Nicaea: The Pattern for Future Councils

The importance of Nicaea cannot be underestimated in the life of the Church. It was the first truly ecumenical council. (The Council of Jerusalem in 49 is not generally counted among the councils of the Church because it was more a meeting of the leaders of the Church in Jerusalem, including, of course, Peter. Further, with Peter and some of the others who had seen Christ, the decision was made on the basis of what they had seen and heard Christ say and do. This scenario is far different from

POOR CHOICE OF WORDS BY AUTHOR: IT SEEMS TO IMPLY Concl for decisions are the work of Men and not of the Holy SPIRIT. PTY.

a deliberation by the bishops of the Church after the death of the last Apostle.

Nicaea made very important doctrinal decisions through sometimes heated discussions among the bishops. In other words, they promulgated dogmas that were to be accepted and believed by all faithful Christians. They consciously exercised a teaching authority, a very important development in the structure of the Church.

Further, this first council followed a process which is still, even today, in place. Even though styles and procedures vary somewhat from age to age, the Nicene pattern of discussion of all the issues — followed by acceptance of specific formulae by most, if not all, of the bishops present — is still in place today for councils of the Church. Nicaea established the pattern for conciliar activity in the Church, and this was almost as important as the dogmatic decisions themselves.

Unfortunately, Nicaea did not end the controversy. The Arian sympathizers, even though they had signed the creed and decrees of Nicaea, continued the struggle to have Arius's views accepted. Of course, after Bishop Alexander excommunicated Arius and his followers, and certainly after Nicaea, Arius and those agreeing with him were guilty of formal heresy. In fact, after the close of Nicaea, but in the same year, 325, two bishops supporting Arius, including Eusebius of Nicomedia — Arius's original supporter among the bishops — informed Constantine that they were withdrawing their consent to the decrees of Nicaea. There is no question that this represented a formal break with the Church. Constantine sent the two bishops to Gaul (modern-day France), exiling them from their bishoprics. He also appointed new bishops to their two sees.

In 328, Constantine seems to have changed his mind, possibly under the influence his half-sister Constantia, who lived in Nicomedia and may have interceded with Constantine in favor of her exiled bishop, Eusebius. Along with Eusebius, Arius and the other members of the anti-Nicene party were recalled from exile and restored to their positions. Of course, they did sign a confession of faith, but it was vague and open to many interpretations. Further, the sincerity of those who signed this confession can be questioned.

Still, the anti-Nicene party had recovered, and with the support of the Emperor, they launched a full-scale attack against those in favor of the

Nicene formulations. The Arians accused Nicene bishops of all sorts of crimes, including adultery and spreading rumors about the Emperor's family.

Athanasius

St. Athanasius, who had succeeded Bishop Alexander in Alexandria, was accused of undue severity toward certain members of his flock and even of threatening to prevent the sending of grain shipments from Alexandria to Constantinople. The anti-Nicene party used every possible political, personal, and moral weapon against the supporters of the Nicene formulas.

What is astounding is that rarely did the anti-Nicene party engage in theological debates. Presumably, they could not because, in the face of the decrees of Nicaea, they were clearly in the wrong. Including Athanasius, there were twelve bishops deposed in synods between 326 and 335. Without the authority and power of the Emperor behind them, the Arian synods could never have enforced their decrees. However, with the cooperation of the Emperor and the full authority of the state, the Arians were able to impose their decisions. Athanasius, the great warrior against Arianism, appealed to the Emperor, but to no avail. He spent the next two years in Trier, a town in modern-day Germany on the border of Luxembourg.

It is hard for most of us to understand why people became so intense on what often seems to the modern mind to be a rather abstruse theological discussion. Our attitude is usually "So what?" What difference did either position really make in everyday life? If Jesus is created, but still blessed by God (the Arian position), is there truly any earth-shattering difference between that idea and Jesus as one in being with the Father (the Nicene formula)? What difference in everyday life can it make if Jesus is just a manifestation of one of the characteristics of God (the Modalist position) as some misinterpreted the Nicene formula?

But these were fighting words for Emperors, Popes, bishops, priests, deacons, and even lay people. Gregory of Nyssa mentions that if one goes to the public baths and asks if the bath is ready, the reply is that the Son came from nothingness (the Arian position). If one goes to buy bread, the baker remarks that the Father is greater than the Son! In other words, everyone was discussing these issues. Obviously, to many people of the fourth century, these ideas made a huge difference.

The various ideas proposed were an attempt to answer the question: Who and What is Christ? These answers were absolutely central to Christianity. If the Arian formula were accepted and Jesus is not "God from God and light from light," then how could one accept the basic tenets of Christianity about Revelation and Redemption? How could the Gospels be accepted at face value, especially the Gospel of John? If the formula of Nicaea were accepted in a modalist interpretation, then Jesus is also not God. He would have been blessed with a characteristic of the Father, e.g., with the Father's wisdom, but he would not be God made man and if he were not God made man, then the result is the same as if the Arian position were accepted.

But if Nicaea is accepted, how can it possibly be true that God is one and yet Jesus is also God distinct from the Father. In the Nicene formula, if emphasis is put on Christ as God the Son (rather than on the oneness of God), is there not in effect a confession of three gods? And if there are three gods, then neither the Gospels nor the Jewish rock-solid faith in the oneness of God can be accepted. In other words, these ideas did have impact on how people lived their daily lives.

Further, in the fourth century, Christianity had a new freshness about it. It had just been accepted as a lawful expression of religious belief and as the religion of the Emperor. (Even though not baptized, Constantine regarded himself as a Christian after 312.) With its new status and the imperial protection, the Church was able to grow both within the Empire and outside of it. Within the Empire, more and more pagan shrines were destroyed and converts were made from paganism. Bishoprics were established. In North Italy in 300, there were five or six bishoprics. In 400, there were fifty. Similar growth occurred throughout the Empire.

Outside the Empire, the Church sent out missionaries who brought many into the Church. Christianity had become the trend in society! In addition, it made good political sense to be Christian if one wanted to "get ahead," because the Emperor favored Christianity. The excitement this growth and new freedom generated in Christian and even non-Christian circles led people to discuss doctrinal issues often in the same sense that passionate sports fans today discuss the latest trades or game scores.

Not only did the issues matter to Christians, but these issues were interesting and new. Further, they had political overtones and were among the most exciting movements within the Roman Empire in the fourth century.

Other factors also motivated people to discuss these theological issues. In the twenty-first century, most of us are inundated, almost surfeited, with entertainment possibilities. In fact, for many of us, there are simply too many possible choices. This was not true in the ancient world. The discussions about Christian doctrines offered true entertainment. The points of view were interesting because the doctrinal issues involved the application of old ideas in new ways and the introduction of new concepts. There was emotional involvement; heroes were to be defended. Today we have a saying that "We don't discuss religion or politics." Of course, the reason for this "ban" is that both these areas can result in heated discussions and make enemies of former friends. If we can become so passionate about religion with all the other possible diversions we have, how much more was that true for the people of the fourth century? The discussions were intellectually stimulating.

Nevertheless, the intensity of the Arian controversy among some — for instance, the bishops — seems out of proportion to the discussions of the previous centuries. The Adoptionist and Modalist positions had similar implications for the Christian understanding of Christ, but they never reached the level of discussion which the Arian controversy did. The question that comes to mind is: How is it possible to account for the genuine viciousness of some bishops toward other bishops on the Arian question in the fourth century when in the previous century, on similar issues, the bishops did not react in the same way? Presumably, the bishops of both centuries would have been equally interested in the doctrinal questions. Thus, the new freshness or excitement surrounding Christianity in the fourth century cannot completely account for the differing attitudes of the bishops in the two centuries.

New Freedom for the Church

The differing reactions of the bishops of the two centuries has to do with the new freedom granted the Church in the fourth century. Before Constantine, the Church was persecuted. There was an external threat.

While there were differences among Christians, these differences could never rise to the level of the Arian controversy because the external threat forced Christians into a united front against the State which was persecuting them.

Once the persecution was eliminated, the internal differences among Christians had nothing to hold them in check. No longer did Christians have to form a united front to face an external threat. Similar reactions have occurred in other periods in other lands.

In our own day, the Polish Solidarity movement, while it had differences within itself before the fall of the Polish communist government, presented a united front against the Polish communist government. The internal differences, while known and discussed, were never allowed to obscure the essential factor forcing a unity: the opposition to the government. Once Solidarity came to power, almost immediately various factions arose which were allowed to function freely.

The same occurred in the United States at the time of the Civil War. The Republicans put up a united front against the Democrats in the 1860 election even though there were differences among them. As soon as the southern states seceded and the southern Senators and Congressmen withdrew from the two Houses of Congress, there was little or no effective Democratic opposition to the overwhelming majority of Republicans in Congress. Immediately, the internal differences within the Republican party increased in intensity.

For all these reasons, the Arian dispute was very heated at all levels. The intensity of the discussion helps to explain why the anti-Nicene party led by Eusebius of Nicomedia used whatever tactics necessary to put party members in as many bishoprics as possible.

After the death of Constantine in 337, the Arian (anti-Nicene) party lost an important ally. Constantine's two sons, Constans and Constantius II, differed on the Arian question. Constans ruled the West and accepted the Nicene formulas. (Actually, Constantine was survived by three sons who divided the Empire, but Constantine II was ambushed and killed in 340 while preparing to do battle with Constans over the issue of Constans' equality in imperial authority with his brothers. After Constantine II's death, Constans and Constantius II divided the Empire between them.) Constantius II ruled the East and, while at times conciliatory toward the supporters of the Nicene formulas, generally allied himself with the anti-Nicene, Arian position.

At the beginning of his reign, Constantius II was relatively friendly towards the Nicene party. He allowed Athanasius and others of the Nicene party who had been exiled to return to their sees. Of course, Arian bishops had been appointed to the sees of these bishops. As a result, there were struggles in many of these sees between the Nicene bishop and the anti-Nicene, Arian bishop. The anti-Nicene party was dismayed at the return of their enemies and moved strongly to prevent them from formally assuming their episcopal offices. Athanasius can be used as an example.

Returning to Alexandria in late 337, Athanasius called an Egyptian synod which confirmed that he was the lawful bishop, but he was forced into exile again in 339 when the Arian party managed to install a new bishop in Alexandria, Gregory of Cappadocia, who was conducted into his cathedral city by a military escort. Athanasius appealed to Pope Julius (337-352),who convened a Roman synod which recognized Athanasius as the legitimate bishop of Alexandria. But without imperial support, Athanasius could do nothing. For the second time, he was exiled from his see and remained in Rome until 346.

The Emperors wanted unity in their realm. It was important to them that the Empire be united in religious beliefs and practices. Between 341 and 351, no less than seven different formulas were proposed to resolve the issue raised by Arius more than twenty years previously. Most of these formulas were attempts to replace the Nicene formula with something more acceptable to the Arians. However, most of these formulas were also not militantly Arian. The West rejected all these attempts, while in the East they continued to be proposed in an effort to bring religious unity to the Empire. In 346, when the Arian bishop of Alexandria, appointed in 339, died, Constantius invited Athanasius to return to his see. Of course, this move was a further attempt to bring the two parties together. Athanasius had become the leading figure in the East defending the Nicene formula, and so an invitation to him by Constantius was a gesture towards reconciliation. Athanasius returned to Alexandria and remained there for ten years, until 356.

However, the entire political situation changed again in 350 when Constans was killed by a usurper. Constantius II avenged his brother by defeating and killing the usurper. Constantius II was now the sole Emperor of both East and West. Even though generally sympathetic to the Arian party, Constantius II, out of a sense of loyalty to his deceased brother Constans, continued to support Athanasius even after becoming sole Emperor. But with Constantius II as the sole Emperor, the Arian party saw that it had an opportunity for a complete victory.

The Arians tried to impose their views on the entire Church and on the whole Empire. The first order of business was to silence and disgrace Athanasius. With the death of Pope Julius in 352, the new Pope, rejecting the claims of the Arian party against Athanasius, asked the Emperor to convene a synod.

When the synod met at Arles (in France) in 353, under the imperial influence, the only issue discussed was the deposition of Athanasius. Most of the bishops, not knowing the previous history of the whole question (it had been eighteen years since Athanasius was first forced from his see), succumbed to imperial pressure and agreed to the deposition of Athanasius. The Pope then asked the Emperor to call a general council of the Church. The Emperor called a meeting of the bishops. This meeting took place at Milan in 355 and again, under imperial pressure, the bishops agreed to the deposition of Athanasius. Of course, this was not the outcome Pope Liberius (352-356) had in mind when he asked the Emperor to convene a council.

The Pope resisted the decisions of the Milan meeting, as did a few other bishops including Bishop Hilary of Poitiers and Hosius of Córdoba (the papal delegate at Nicaea, who was almost one hundred years old). These and others who resisted the imperial will were exiled. (Of course, with the Pope's rejection of the meeting at Milan, it has never been recognized as a general council of the Church.)

After Arles and Milan, Athanasius' position in his see became impossible, and in 356 he began his third exile from his bishopric. This time he went to live with the desert Fathers. (These were the founders of monasticism — those who had joined St. Antony [c. 252-356] to live an ascetic life in the Egyptian desert.) With Athanasius in exile, Constantius II now made a supreme effort to unite the Empire in one confession of faith on the question of the divinity of Christ. A double synod of East and West was convened. The western bishops met at Rimini (on the east coast of Italy), and the eastern bishops met at Seleucia in Isauria (modern-day Silifke on the southeastern coast of Turkey).

Rimini-Seleucia

This double synod of East and West at Rimini-Seleucia in 359 was one of the strangest occurrences in Church history. It was suggested not only because it was difficult for the eastern bishops to travel to the West, and vice-versa, but also because the western bishops remained generally loyal to the Nicene formulas. (Although under pressure from the Emperor, most of the western bishops had agreed to the depositions of Athanasius in the 350s, most of them remained faithful to the Nicene formulas of the faith. In other words, by this time the linkage between the doctrinal formulas of Nicaea and the case of Athanasius was broken, at least in the minds of most of the western bishops.) By arranging for two meetings, the Emperor and the anti-Nicene party could apply pressure on the western bishops more effectively. Further, the meeting of the eastern bishops would not be disturbed by pressure from the western bishops against the anti-Nicene formulas.

As is clear from this brief historical sketch of a complicated controversy, after Nicaea the original theological controversy became mostly political. In all the struggles for influence and position, the primary issue seemed to have been overshadowed by secondary ones. Part of the reason for this development was the death of the chief figures in the original controversy.

Arius and Eusebius of Nicomedia were both dead by 342. But another reason why the primary theological issues all but disappeared was that no one on the Arian side wanted to discuss the Nicene formulas. The seven formulas suggested between 341 and 351 were attempts, not to oppose Nicaea, but to go around it. Those who proposed these formulas made almost heroic attempts not to define the relationship between God the Father and God the Son. By avoiding this central question, the proponents of these formulas avoided comment on the key problem: the Nicene one-in-being-with-the-Father phrase (*homoousios*). The difficulty in trying to find a solution while avoiding the central problem is obvious! Thus, there were absolutely no effective proposals on the central theological question for almost two decades, and the entire dispute became mostly a political one.

Before the double synod of Rimini-Seleucia, three possible theological proposals were made concerning the central question of the relationship between Father and Son. All of these were suggested as alternatives to the Nicene formula. None of those supporting these three proposals wanted to retain the Nicene wording.

In 356, a deacon named Aetius proposed that the Son was unlike (*anomoios*) the Father. However, Aetius's position went far beyond the original thought of Arius himself. Although many in the East were unwilling to accept the Nicene formula, "one-in-being," they were not prepared to admit to the unlike-the-Father idea.

A counter-proposal from Basil of Ancyra (modern-day Ankara in Turkey) came extremely close to the Nicene formula. He suggested that the relationship between the Father and the Son was best described as like-in-being-with-the-Father (*homoiousios*). Clearly, this was almost the Nicene formula, one-in-being-with-the-Father, as is clear from the indication from Athanasius, Hilary of Poitiers, and Pope Liberius that this formula might be acceptable as a genuine statement of faith if Liberius's words, like the Father in all things, were added to it. In other words, Basil's slightly modified like-in-being formula might be reconcilable with the Nicene statement of faith.

These two proposals were "on the table" as the preparatory meeting for the Rimini-Seleucia synod began. At the preparatory meeting, the representatives of the Arian party, unwilling to accept Aetius' formulation, unlike-the-Father, but also rejecting Basil's like-in-being because it was too close to Nicaea, proposed a third formula: like-the-Father (*homoios*). The man who came to be associated with this point of view is Acacius. The Emperor came to favor this third position, perhaps because those offering this idea were able to convince him that it was better to avoid the question of being (*ousios*), and this formula did so. (Of course, this idea was similar to the tactics used by the Arians since Nicaea, i.e., avoid the question as much as possible!)

In addition to the Nicene formula, "one in being with the Father," there were now three others: (1) Unlike-the-Father of Aetius; (2) Like-in-being with the Father of Basil (in the past, this like-in-being formula has sometimes been called semi-Arianism; and (3) Like-the-Father of Acacius. This like-the-Father or *homoean* formula is what is traditionally meant by Arianism, even though Arius never once used this precise wording. The bishops of the double synod of Rimini-Seleucia were to affirm Nicaea or pick one of the other three possible formulas.

At Rimini, the majority of the western bishops initially affirmed the Nicene formula. But there was a minority of bishops at Rimini, about eighty of the four hundred bishops present, who refused to accede to the majority decision. Both parties sent representatives to the Emperor.

Since Consantius II favored the formula like-the-Father, he refused to meet the representatives of the Nicene party of Rimini, but the representatives of Rimini representing the minority position (the Arian one) were able to meet the Emperor as soon as they arrived. They won the Emperor's endorsement and were able to infiltrate the representatives of the Nicene majority. After they "explained" their formula (actually blurring the distinctions between their formula and the Nicene statement of faith), the representatives of the majority at Rimini, under imperial pressure, agreed to the like-the-Father formula.

While there were these intrigues at the imperial court, the bishops at Rimini waited. The imperial guard refused to let them return to their dioceses, and after their representatives agreed to the Arian formula, the imperial guard at Rimini made it clear that the bishops would not be allowed to return home until they signed the decree stating that God the Son was like-the-Father.

This doctrinal decision was made by the Emperor. The Pope was not even invited to attend the Rimini synod. In the East at Seleucia, there were intense discussions among the one hundred fifty bishops present. They were divided among the three non-Nicene Arian formulas. The most radical position, unlike-the-Father, was rejected first. However, those who held for the like-in-being-with-the-Father formula were bitterly opposed to the like-the-Father wording. In the end, under imperial pressure, those supporting the like-in-being-with-the-Father position agreed to the like-the-Father phrase. Theoretically, the Empire was now united and the Arian controversy put to rest. It was about this time that St. Jerome made his famous remark that the whole world had become Arian.

In consequence of the Rimini-Seleucia decision, ratified by a "council" which met at Constantinople at the beginning of 360, the party of Acacius, the homoeans or the like-the-Father party, had imperial support

Those not agreeing to the like-the-Father phrasing suffered imperial displeasure. Many were exiled. The same process followed in the 330s was repeated in the 360s. Still, Athanasius proved troublesome to the ascendant party. He sent a letter to all the bishops of Egypt urging them to refuse their assent to the like-the-Father formula. As a result, Egypt remained faithful to the Nicene wording.

In 361, Constantius II died. He was succeeded by his cousin, Julian, who is called Julian the Apostate because he made an attempt to restore paganism as the religion of the Empire. As part of this attempt, he tried to foster divisions within Christianity and so permitted the return of the exiled bishops to their sees. Again there were rival claimants to various sees.

Antioch was especially troubled because in 362 there were no less than five different Christian communities there, all loyal to a different claimant to the see! Under Julian's policy, in 362, Athanasius was able to return to Alexandria, his diocese, for a few months but was forced again into exile later that same year. Instead of creating problems in Alexandria (which Julian expected and wanted), Athanasius' return had begun a reconciliation. Julian was more than disappointed and forced Athanasius to return to the Egyptian desert.

Julian died in 363, while fighting the Persians, and was succeeded by the Emperor Jovian, who died eight months later. The military and civil officials then selected Valentinian as the next Emperor. The military insisted that Valentinian choose someone as a second Emperor, following the pattern Diocletian had envisioned. Valentinian chose his brother Valens and gave Valens the East while Valentinian himself took the West.

Valens and Valentinian

There was not only a division politically between the two brothers; they also differed on the religious question. Valentinian in the West adhered to the Nicene formula, but Valens in the East was an Arian of the like-the-Father party. The situation was very similar to that of Constantius II and Constans in the 340s, especially since in 360 the western bishops, led by Hilary of Poitiers, met at a synod at Paris and repudiated the Seleucia-Rimini decrees. (In less than a year, the Arian victory and the supposed religious unity of the Empire had collapsed.)

The Arians had made a profound political mistake (if not a theological one) in dividing their loyalties among the three non-Nicene points of view: (1) the like-in-being (*homoiousios*) party; (2) the like-the-Father (*homios*) party; and (3) the unlike-the- Father (*anomoios*) party. Valens supported the homeans, the like-the-Father party, and the Nicenes, as well as the other two Arian groups, suffered under Valens. (Athanasius was exiled for a fifth time in 365 under Valens, but when disturbances broke out in Alexandria as a result of his exile, Valens allowed him to return in early 366 and he remained until his death in 373.) But the persecution of the three parties, instead of one, gave the persecuted parties reason to unite against the one persecuting them.

While it was impossible for the Anomoeans, the unlike-the-Father party, to unite with the Nicenes or with the like-in-being party, the latter two were very close. In fact, in 364 the homoiousians, the like-in-being party, did agree to the Nicene formula, but the agreement remained unfulfilled because Valens and the homoeans, the like-the-Father party, blocked a meeting of the homoiousians where the decision would have been implemented.

Between 365 and 370, while Valens was occupied with other serious problems and more or less ignored the religious question, the Nicenes were able to strengthen their position by filling important sees with their men. Presumably, this situation might have given the merger of the Nicenes with the homoiousians a chance to succeed. Unfortunately, the compromise of 364 collapsed in 365 when the homoiousians moved away from their acceptance of the Nicene "one-in-being" language.

But the failure of the compromise was more the result of a split on the question of the Holy Spirit. Inevitably, the question of the relationship of the Son to the Father raised the question of the relationship of the Holy Spirit to the Son and Father. Nicaea had affirmed the Church's belief in the divinity of the Holy Spirit, but some of the homoiousians had difficulties with this teaching. This hesitancy about accepting the Nicaean belief in the divinity of the Holy Spirit was the chief cause of the failure of the compromise of 364.

Turning again to religious issues, in 370 Valens began a persecution of all those who refused to accept Rimini-Seleucia. However, the Nicene bishop, Basil of Caesarea (not to be confused with Basil of Ancyra, who had proposed the like-in-being formula), impressed Valens when the Emperor attended Basil's Mass on Epiphany in 372. Valens gave up all attempts to force Basil to accept the homoean formula.

The Young Nicenes

The imperial leniency gave Basil the opportunity to become the protector of persecuted Catholics and, even more importantly, to work to strengthen the Nicene party. He filled vacant sees with Nicenes. He created bishoprics to increase the numbers who were in a position to support him. Basil and those close to him, including Gregory of Nyssa, Gregory Nazianzen, and Amphilochius, were all faithful to Nicaea and are often called the young Nicenes.

The young Nicenes realized that there could be no solution to the continuing theological difficulties unless the West and East could talk with each other and understand what the other was trying to say. Further, they understood that some solution to the question of the Holy Spirit had to be found. Basil distinguished the terms *hypostasis* and *ousia*. At Nicaea, the Greeks had understood *ousia* to mean being and *hypostasis* to mean substance. The Latins had used them interchangeably. Although defining them differently, the Greeks had also used the terms interchangeably during the entire controversy.

Basil suggested that God was one *ousia* (meaning nature) and three *hypostaseis* (what came to mean persons). This clarification was incredibly important. Words convey ideas, but if words are not precisely defined, then ideas are not clear. The lack of clarity, in addition to the problems of Latins and Greeks talking different languages, was a major contributing factor to the entire Arian controversy.

On the question of the Holy Spirit, Gregory Nazianzen taught that the Holy Spirit was one nature (*ousia*) with the Father, but he, Basil, Gregory of Nyssa, and Amphilochius preferred the formulation that the Holy Spirit was from-the-Father-through-the-Son. Nevertheless, the young Nicenes held to the *homoousios*, one-in-being, or as they defined it, one-in-nature formula for both the Son and the Holy Spirit. But unless imperial cooperation could be obtained, this work would no more offer a solution to this now almost sixty-year-old problem than all the other proposals that had been made.

However, the political situation changed rapidly. Valentinian died in 375. He was succeeded by his son Gratian, who was loyal to the Nicene position. When Valens died in 378, Gratian appointed Theodosius (379-395), a western military figure, as Emperor in the East. As a westerner, Theodosius also accepted the Nicene position. For the first time since 325, both East and West were ruled by Emperors loyal to the Nicene formula. The Emperors, like all their predecessors of every possible religious persuasion, wished for religious unity.

Gratian and Theodosius, together with Gratian's brother Valentinian (who was associated with Gratian in the West), jointly issued a decree in 379 that enjoined all heresies and officially sanctioned only the Catholic religion. This decree simply begged the question; what was the Catholic faith?

The next year, 380, the eastern Emperor, Theodosius, issued an edict to the people of Constantinople which had important implications for all his subjects. In this edict, Theodosius asked that all people live in the religion handed down from Christ through Peter to the Romans, which was professed by the Pope and the bishop of Alexandria (Athanasius' see): namely, that everyone should believe "in the one divinity of the Father and the Son and the Holy Spirit in equal majesty and holy Trinity."

First Council of Constantinople

In 381, Theodosius identified his profession of 380 specifically with the Nicene formula, and early in the same year Theodosius called a council of the Church to meet in Constantinople in May 381.

This council, the First Council of Constantinople, the second ecumenical council of the Church, was attended by one hundred fifty bishops, mostly from the East. It finally resolved the Arian issue. With such a relatively small number of bishops present, especially in light of the five hundred fifty present at the double synod of Rimini-Seleucia, the First Council of Constantinople did not look much different from many of the other meetings of bishops that had occurred throughout the Arian controversy. In fact, it was not until seventy years later at the fourth ecumenical council of the Church — Chalcedon in 451 — that the 381 meeting of bishops at Constantinople was definitely recognized as an ecumenical council of the whole Church. Chalcedon recognized the first council of Constantinople because of its contributions to the Church's understanding of the faith.

The bishops at the First Council of Constantinople reaffirmed the Nicene formula, accepting that the Son was "one-in-being-with-the-Father" (nature or substance could also be used here), *homoousios*. As a compromise to the like-in-being-with-the-Father party, which had difficulty with applying the same oneness in being with the Father to the Holy Spirit, the bishops did not insist on applying *homoousios* to the Holy Spirit. However, they did add to the simple statement of Nicaea, "We believe in the Holy Spirit," the phrases, "the Lord, the giver of life, Who proceeds from the Father. With the Father and Son He is worshiped and glorified. He has spoken through the prophets."

By giving the Holy Spirit the title Lord, the bishops of the council were clearly teaching that the Holy Spirit was divine, because that title was reserved to God. Further, the title "giver of life" obviously connects the Holy Spirit with the act of Creation, i.e., with the divine act of creating the world. The bishops of Constantinople included the phrase "Who proceeds from the Father" so as to exclude the idea (which some were holding) that the Son created the Holy Spirit. However, the most unambiguous claim for the divinity of the Holy Spirit by the fathers of Constantinople was the phrase "with the Father and the Son He is worshiped and glorified." Entitled to the same adoration as Father and Son, the Holy Spirit could not but be equal in being with the Father and Son.

In effect, the young Nicenes, who fought for this language, were able to establish the equality of the Holy Spirit with the Father and Son without insisting on the use of the term *homoousios* for the Holy Spirit. Why should they have fought such a battle when they had achieved everything they needed with the other phrases?

With these additions to the Nicene Creed, which eventually was known as the Nicaea-Constantinople Creed, the bishops of the second ecumenical council of the Church closed the book on the Arian controversy, which, beginning with a dispute about Christ, had led to significant (false) teachings on the Holy Spirit and the Trinity itself.

Of course, Arianism lived on. The missionary Ulfilas had translated the Bible into German to teach Christianity to the Germans. Unfortunately, he taught them an Arian version of Christianity, and so the Church was forced to continue to confront Arianism for another three centuries! Nevertheless, with the Council of Constantinople, the teaching of the Church was clear, and the Arians did not attempt to offer any further alternate formulas to the text of the Nicene-Constantinople Creed.

Arianism

This heresy, originating with the priest Arius, held that Jesus, God's Son, was not one-in-being with the Father. According to this heresy, Jesus was not truly divine, but was simply the first and greatest of all God's creatures.

10

Apollinarianism

FROM ALMOST THE BEGINNING OF THE ARIAN CONTROVERSY, THE PROBLEM turned on the relationship of the Son to the Father because Arius had said that the Son was created and therefore not equal or one with the Father. But if the Son were created, then he is not divine, not God from God, as Nicaea said. Not only does the Arian position raise the question of the relationship between Father and Son, it also questions the reality of the Incarnation. In other words, Arius not only denied that the Son was one-in-being-with-the-Father, he also denied what Nicaea had affirmed about the Incarnation: that God became man.

For the Arians, the Son of God, the *Logos*, is less than the Father and was created. Therefore, the *Logos* is not divine. For the Arians, the *Logos* took the place of the human soul in Christ. In Christ, there was no human soul. The human soul was replaced by the *Logos*. In modern terminology, in this Arian viewpoint, Christ was a human body united with a non-divine person or spirit, the *Logos*. There was only one nature in Christ: the nature created by the union of the created *Logos* with a human body.

While the question of the humanity of Christ did not surface in the first phases of the Arian controversy, it was addressed in the later stages of the struggle against Arianism. Hilary of Poitiers and others insisted that Christ possessed a complete humanity: a human body and a human soul. Without both a human body and a human soul, Christ would not have been truly man; without both a human body and a human soul, Christ could not have died, because death is the separation of body and soul. Furthermore, only what was assumed by Christ could be redeemed. If he did not have a human soul, then human souls are not redeemed, only human bodies. But this is impossible because human beings, body and soul, are redeemed.

Apollinaris of Laodicea

Apollinaris of Laodicea had difficulties with the idea that Christ had assumed human nature completely. For Apollinaris, it was impossible that one being, Christ, could possess both a divine nature and a complete human nature. Apollinaris thought that two natures could not exist together. Inevitably, he argued, the two natures would conflict with each other.

Further, Apollinaris argued, it is possible for human beings to sin especially because of the weakness of the flesh. In order for Christ to have been sinless, He could not have had a human mind and a human free will because with these human powers, He could easily have succumbed to sinful temptations. Apollinaris seems to have made a distinction between spirit and soul. (St. Paul seems to validate this distinction. See 1 Thessalonians 5:23.) For Apollinaris, the human soul had only the sensible (animal) and vegetative powers. The rational powers, the powers of mind and will, were the spirit of man. Apollinaris suggested that Christ did not have a human spirit. Rather the human spirit was replaced in Christ with the *Logos*. Therefore, Apollinaris could admit of a human soul in Christ (as he understood soul), but not a human spirit. Therefore, a divine spirit — the Son of God, i.e., the *Logos* — took the place of a human spirit in Christ.

Apollinaris's position is very close to the Arian viewpoint. However, there are important differences:

1. Apollinaris accepted Nicaea and the one-in-being-with-the-Father statement. This differentiated him from the Arians.

2. Since the one-in-being-with-the-Father *Logos* took the place of a human spirit in Christ and was united with a human body and a (vegetative and sensible) soul, the resulting union formed one nature (as the Arians said), but it was the union of the truly divine (spirit) and the partially human (body and soul) — what the Arians would not admit. It is difficult to talk of one nature with the divine *Logos* and a human body and soul. However, for Apollinaris, the *Logos* substituted Himself for the absent human spirit and thus completed the incomplete human nature of Christ. In Christ, there was one nature, but it was a mixture of the divine and human. Apollinaris does not seem to have questioned how the *Logos* could unite with human nature and not unite His own divine nature with the human body and soul. This was not a problem for the Arians because they did not accept the teaching that the *Logos* was divine. Therefore,

Christ was divine because His spirit was divine (the very point the Arians were at pains to deny).

3. Apollinaris, unlike the Arians, could admit of a human soul in Christ (as he understood soul), but not a human spirit.

Still, even with all these differences between the Arian position and that of Apollinaris, the problems are clear. Without a complete humanity, Christ could not have redeemed all of man. Christ would not have been fully man and therefore the Incarnation would have remained incomplete.

The Council of Constantinople repeated the 377 condemnation of the Apollinarist position by Pope Damasus (366-384). However, far more than Arius, Apollinaris was genuinely searching for a solution to a very difficult theological problem. He did have followers who persisted in accepting his opinions, but by 420 most of these had returned to the Church. The conflict over Apollinarianism was minor compared to the Arian controversy. Nevertheless, Apollinaris's ideas were important in the later discussions concerning the mystery of the Incarnation.

> ## Apollinarianism
> This heresy held that Jesus had an incomplete human nature, i.e., he lacked a human mind and a human will.

11

⤐⁕⤏

Donatism

A Serious Threat to the Church

ARIANISM WAS NOT THE ONLY MAJOR CONFLICT AFFLICTING THE CHURCH IN the fourth century. While not as geographically widespread as Arianism or as complicated from a doctrinal point of view, Donatism seriously threatened the structure and organization of the Church in North Africa for almost the entire fourth century.

Towards the end of Constantine's reign (d. 337), there were two hundred and seventy Donatist bishops present at a synod in Carthage. In 418, there were still thirty Donatist bishops available for a meeting and they ordained more Donatist bishops. It was indeed a powerful threat to the Church.

Donatism was driven by a relatively uncomplicated idea. The fundamental notion was that the validity of the sacraments of the Church depended on the holiness of the individual minister of the sacrament. The Donatists argued that the Church was the pure and unblemished bride of Christ and that no sinful minister could efficaciously celebrate a sacrament. The Donatists taught that the sinfulness of the minister prevented him from being an effective representative of God and the Church and a channel of grace for the Church.

The Donatist movement began in the aftermath of the Diocletian persecution. (Diocletian was Emperor from 284 to 305 and his persecution of the Christians was begun in 303.) One of the edicts issued by Diocletian against the Christians decreed that the clergy had to turn over to the government the sacred books of the Church. The reason for this measure was that the absence of books would make Christian worship difficult, if not impossible.

Under severe pressure from the imperial government, many clergy complied with the decree and were then labeled as *traditores*, literally, "those who handed over." Following some of the lines of thought suggested by Tertullian (also from North Africa), continued by some of the North African opponents to St. Cyprian, and in the footsteps of Novatian, the Donatists held that the *traditores*, "those who had handed over" (the books), could not validly celebrate the sacraments.

Rival Claimants to the See of Carthage

A disputed episcopal election in Carthage in 312 brought the issue to a head. A deacon named Caecilian was made bishop in Carthage, but another group held out for their candidate. Those opposing Caecilian pointed out that he had been ordained a bishop by a *traditor* and therefore could not possibly be a legitimate claimant to the bishopric of Carthage because he was not truly a bishop.

A synod of some seventy bishops declared against Caecilian and gave the bishopric first to Majorinus and then in 313 to Donatus, the man who gave his name to the entire movement. Constantine, as self-appointed protector of the Church, intervened.

Constantine first responded to a suggestion by the Donatists to convene a council of bishops from Gaul (modern-day France) to decide between the rival episcopal claimants in Carthage. The council decided in favor of Caecilian, but Donatus contested the ruling. Another synod was convened, and that also failed to resolve the issue.

Constantine then decided to use force and to exile Donatus and his followers. This policy failed because it made martyrs out of the Donatists, and so in 321 Constantine abandoned his persecution of them. The Donatist bishops were allowed to return to their sees. As a result, there were usually two bishops in each see: a Catholic and a Donatist. In effect, there was a schism. The doctrinal dispute had resulted in a jurisdictional dispute between the Donatists and the Catholics. The Donatists and the Catholics were contesting for control of the Church in North Africa.

The Schism Grows

The Donatists were able to build up the structure of the Donatist Church and to attract converts from Catholicism. Donatus built chapels, churches, and even basilicas. Catholics were attracted to the movement not only by Donatist doctrines, but also because the Donatists were usually of the middle and upper classes. They were socially more acceptable than the Catholics, who were generally associated with the poorer members of society. Catholics were also enticed to join the Donatists because Donatus was able to relax some of the requirements. In effect, the Donatists became a rival Church, a schismatic group of Christians.

In the case of Donatism, a heretical idea spawned a schism that lasted for over one hundred years. Arianism did not give rise to a schism in the same sense for a number of reasons. First, Arianism was spread over a much wider geographical area and so it was much more difficult to unite all the adherents in a Church organization. Second, Arianism always faced a strong opposition which never rested. Initially, Donatism did not face such opposition.

In effect, Donatism became widely popular in North Africa partly because the core Donatist belief had been erroneously believed by many North African Christians since Tertullian's time. Catholics in that region were reduced to a minority and for most of the fourth century were unable to challenge the Donatists effectively.

Not only were the Donatists a majority, but they also had the most effective leadership. Throughout most of the fourth century, the Catholics of North Africa failed to produce a charismatic leader who could effectively challenge the Donatist bishops. This situation changed with the advent of St. Augustine of Hippo (354-430), who became bishop in Hippo in 395.

Third, Arianism split very early into different parties and groups. While, as we shall see, there was a division in the Donatist party, it came after the Donatist Church was well established and it did not produce any further divisions. It was easier for the Donatists to retain a unity among themselves than it had been for the Arians.

From 321 until 347, the Donatists were able to grow and prosper to the point that Bishop Donatus of Carthage thought it might be a good idea to unite the relatively weak Catholic Church with his vibrant, growing Donatist Church. He applied to the Emperor, who sent delegates to survey the situation. But the representatives of the Emperor offended the Donatists when they made overtures to the Catholics. (How else were they to determine what possibilities there might be for a union of the two organizations?)

The Circumcellions

In 347, imperial representatives, traveling through one of the provinces of North Africa accompanied by Roman soldiers, were attacked by the Circumcellions, a group associated with the Donatists. (The Circumcellions were fanatical about martyrdom. They saw themselves as fighting the opponents of the faith as the early Christian martyrs had. They actively sought martyrdom.)

One of the Donatist bishops, Bishop Donatus of Bagai (not to be confused with Bishop Donatus of Carthage) had called on the Circumcellions to attack the Romans. The Donatist attack on the imperial representatives failed. Bishop Donatus of Bagai and the Circumcellions were killed.

Another Donatist bishop, Marculus, was executed after annoying the imperial delegates by trying to defend what had happened. The Emperor, irritated by the attack, issued an edict in the same year, 347, ordering that the Donatists and Catholics be united under the Catholic bishop of Carthage. Many Donatist bishops were sent into exile. But there were also those who were not able to face the imperial penalties and followed the law. Ironically, the Donatist Church itself had its sinners! This forced union lasted until the accession of the Emperor Julian the Apostate in 361.

In the years between 347 and 361, the weakness of the Catholic Church and its leaders in contrast with the Donatists is particularly striking. Little was done to try to heal the division. Of course, the Arian heresy was taking the time of some of the bishops in this period, but more could have been done from the Catholic perspective. The Donatists, even without their bishops, were able to build a large church dedicated to Bishop Marculus, whom the Donatists regarded as a martyr because he had been executed by imperial representatives.

Julian the Apostate

With the accession of the Emperor Julian, who wanted to foster divisions within Christianity to weaken it so that the old pagan Roman religion could be restored, the Donatist persecution ended. A period of peace for the Donatist Church existed between 361 until 372 when the Donatists in Mauretania, the western Roman province of North Africa (including present-day Morocco), joined a revolt against the Romans led by Firmus, a tribal leader.

The next year, the Romans forbade Donatist worship, and some

Donatist leaders were exiled. But by 377, even though the decrees against the Donatists were still in force, they were all but a dead letter because Flavian, the Roman responsible for enforcing the decrees, was himself a Donatist. This situation continued until the 390s, when opposition to the leading Donatist bishop, Primian, resulted in his deposition.

Maximian, Primian's own deacon, led the opposition to Primian, but Primian called on Roman authority and was able to regain his position. Many Donatists resented Primian's high-handedness and his victory over Maximian, but even worse were the actions of the Donatist Bishop Optatus, who in the 390s used the Circumcellions as his personal terrorist troops, especially against the Catholics. However, in a fatal mistake, he united himself with Gildo, a Roman military official in North Africa, who revolted against the Emperor.

Gildo was defeated and Optatus killed. Although many of the Donatist faithful saw Optatus as a martyr, the bishops and leading Donatists knew better. With the heavy-handed rule of Primian, the division with Maximian, and the ill-advised policies of Optatus, the Donatists lost prestige and status.

Augustine of Hippo

At about this same time (395), Augustine became bishop of Hippo. The Church in North Africa now had a true leader in both a pastoral and intellectual sense. Further, he appeared on the scene when Donatism had more or less been disgraced and did not have any leader comparable to Augustine. Augustine at first wanted the Catholics to approach the Donatists with a carrot rather than a stick.

Pastorally, he tried to make it as easy as possible for Donatists to become Catholic. Donatist priests and bishops, who wanted to become Catholic and had either not practiced re-Baptism or who wanted to join the Catholic Church together with their people, could now be received as clergy. (Previously, Donatist bishops and priests could only become Catholics as non-ordained laymen.) Doctrinally, Augustine urged dialogue and conversation. He urged everyone in conversation with the Donatists to point out that in their own schismatic division between those following Primian and those following Maximian, the Donatists had accepted as valid the sacraments of the Maximianists, the ones who had followed Maximian in his opposition to Primian.

If they accepted the sacraments of the Maximianist sinners, how could they not accept the sacraments of others who had sinned and yet celebrated the sacraments? In other words, by their own practices in the case of the Maximianists, the Donatists had not followed the core of their beliefs.

A meeting of Donatists and Catholics was called in 403, but the Donatists refused to attend and launched a new wave of attacks against the Catholics and particularly against the former Donatists who had converted. At this point, Augustine and the Catholics invoked the power of the Emperor, and a decree against the Donatists was issued.

The anti-Donatist measures of this decree remained in force until 410, when a new Roman official, the pagan Macrobius, came to North Africa. He issued a decree of toleration which was quickly withdrawn after the protest of the Catholics. In successfully protesting Marcobius's policy of toleration, the Catholic bishops asked for a dialogue between the Donatists and the Catholics.

A meeting was held in 411 between the Donatists and the Catholics. Augustine dominated the meeting, which was chaired by a Roman senator. After some days, the decision was in favor of the Catholic position. After the Emperor ratified the decision in January 412, any Donatists who resisted the reunion of the Donatists with the Catholics suffered sanctions. These included fines, confiscation of all the property of recalcitrant Donatists, and the now-common religious penalty for clergy: exile.

Although there were a few remnants of the Donatist movement between the years 412 and 430, Donatist structure and organization as well as effective Donatist opposition to the Catholics ended after the imperial decree of 412. While the work of Augustine was a *sine qua non* in the Catholic victory, the Donatists did not help their cause in their associations with the Circumcellions and those revolting against the Roman government.

Donatist Errors

The fundamental doctrinal mistake of the Donatists was to make the sacraments depend on the one celebrating the sacrament. This position ignored or weakened the role of the Holy Spirit in the sacramental life of the Church. By separating the gift of grace given through the sacrament from the moral character of the one administering the sacrament, Augustine was able to point out that the Holy Spirit confers the grace which is given when the sacrament is celebrated properly. Thus, the holiness conveyed by the sacrament (i.e., grace) is the work of the Holy Spirit, not the work of the celebrant of the sacrament. Therefore, the holiness of the celebrant is not relevant to the gift the sacrament imparts to the one receiving it.

In addition, the Donatists had an erroneous idea of Church. They believed that the Church in the world had to be pure and undefiled. But the members of the Church are men and women existing in the world. Some members are saints, others are sinners. Further, there is a mixture of holiness and sin within each member. The pure and undefiled body of the faithful will only exist in heaven at the end of the world. It is impossible to demand that the Church, as it exists in the world, be as pure and undefiled as those in heaven will be at the end of the world. However, this is precisely what the Donatists demanded.

Augustine believed that it was the Holy Spirit Who united all the members of the Church, even those who were sinners. The serious sinners in the Church still enjoyed a union of faith and hope even if they were not holy. Since they were in union, they could benefit from the activity of the Holy Spirit by the grace given in the sacraments. Those members of the Church who were in the state of grace and were striving for holiness would also benefit from the sacraments all the more.

In effect, Augustine distinguished between membership in the Church on earth, a membership that embraced both saints and sinners, and membership in the communion of saints in heaven. The two communities are not in all respects interchangeable. In failing to make this distinction, the Donatists did not see that their definition of the Church made it impossible for many people to be members. Further, the Donatist position would make the Church exist only for the saints, when it is actually for all of us sinners who need salvation. "And the scribes of the Pharisees, when they saw that he was eating with sinners and tax collectors, said to his disciples, 'Why does He eat with tax collectors and sinners?' And when Jesus heard it, He said to them [that], 'Those who are well have no need of a physician, but those who are sick. I came not to call the righteous, but sinners.' " (See Mark 2:16-17.)

Donatism

This heresy taught that the validity of the sacraments depended on the holiness of the minister of the sacraments. If the one celebrating the sacrament was a heretic, the sacrament did not achieve its effect, i.e., the gift of grace.

12

Pelagianism

Pelagius

AUGUSTINE NOT ONLY DEFENDED THE CHURCH AGAINST MANICHEISM AND Donatism, but he was also actively engaged in opposing another heresy named after its founder, Pelagius.

Pelagius moved from Britain to Rome in 390 as the Donatist heresy had almost run its course. While not a member of a monastic community, Pelagius lived a deeply committed Christian life. By example and by his spoken as well as written words, he suggested that such a Christian life was possible for all Christians.

Pelagius juxtaposed his view of a true Christian life with that lived by many lax and even average Christians in the large Christian communities of his day — Rome, for example. Some of these Christians believed that Baptism was sufficient for salvation and it was not necessary to make the effort to follow the moral teachings of the Church, including the ten commandments. Others believed that a true moral life was impossible, or that it could be expected only of certain heroic Christians who wished to embrace such a life. The idea that a Christian life was impossible in this world and the distinction between average Christians and those called to a more austere life had shades of Manicheism and some of the other dualistic heresies.

The lack of enthusiasm among many Christians of the fourth century can be attributed in part to the phenomenal growth of the Church. With the ending of the persecutions, the Church not only enjoyed official imperial toleration, but even imperial support. For the first time since the apostolic age, the Church could function in peace. This situation not only meant that the Church's missionaries could preach the Gospel freely, but it also meant that individual Christians no longer were in peril of severe penalties simply because their Christian faith made them criminals.

With imperial toleration and support, it no longer required heroic virtue simply to become Christian. There were fewer demands placed on converts to Christianity than there had been. Obviously, in this situation, many Christians of the fourth century were more comfortable in their Christianity than those of the previous centuries. It had almost become fashionable to be Christian. From a merely political viewpoint, this was true. From Constantine I (d. 337) through Theodosius I (379-395), except for the years 361-363, it was certainly better, if one wanted to curry imperial favor, to be Christian.

With great numbers converting to Christianity and fewer sacrifices demanded of them, with imperial support and cultural approbation of Christianity, many Christians of the fourth century were much less ready to make sacrifices than Christians of the previous centuries. It would have been surprising if a certain laxity had not been the norm among some fourth-century Christians. Of course, there were notable exceptions, like St. Jerome living in a cave in the Holy Land translating the Scriptures.

We also cannot rule out the *perception* of laxity by some who wished for the "good old days" when it truly meant something to be a Christian. This attitude of wishing for the days when it took heroic virtue to be a Christian can be seen in the Circumcellions of North Africa, who, as we have seen, were associated with the Donatists. They thought of themselves as the true heirs of the early Christians because they esteemed martyrdom and stood ready for it. (As we have already mentioned, the Circumcellion view of martyrdom was unhealthy and even suicidal. The Church has always taught that martyrdom is not to be sought!)

A Church of Saints

Opposing these ideas, Pelagius taught that all Christians can live a moral life, faithful to the Gospels and the teachings of the Church. Such a life is possible through the natural human powers of intellect and will. Human beings can know good from evil in their minds and then through their wills choose to do good and avoid evil. If one acts rightly, choosing the good through the powers of human nature, then salvation is assured.

Pelagius was reacting to the laxity among the Christians around him. He was trying to reestablish a stricter norm for Christian society. In a way, his efforts were an attempt to recreate the circumstances of the past centuries of Christianity. Instead of the pressure of imperial persecution necessitating a certain heroism in all Christians just to be Christian, now the pressure to live heroic lives would come from the moral norms of the Gospel.

Pelagius wanted all saints in his Church, no sinners! He wanted a Church of martyrs, not by Christians actually risking martyrdom, but by their living according to the moral norms as he defined them. Essential to his efforts was the idea that everyone, every Christian, could live up to the moral standard as he saw it with just a little effort.

Doctrinal Implications

While Pelagius fundamentally advocated an upright moral life, there were important heterodox doctrinal implications in his teaching:

Pelagius had a very optimistic view of human nature. For him, original sin did not harm the human mind or the human will. Even after sin, human nature remained whole and intact. Original sin was Adam's sin and the only negative effect it had on Adam's descendants was the effect of bad example.

Pelagius held that grace was the good example of Christ and the saints, not a supernatural gift present in the soul which transforms all those who have it.

Since there is no original sin in the sense of an inherited sin from Adam and Eve's original disobedience towards God, Baptism washes away personal sins, not original sin. Salvation is achieved through an upstanding moral life, which every human being can lead by using his or her mind and free will. Baptism is not a necessity for salvation. Clearly, this position calls into question the practice of infant Baptism. If Baptism only washes away personal sins, then infants and young children should not be baptized because they are not guilty of personal sins.

Finally, for Pelagius only good moral behavior is essential. Pelagius thus questioned the need not only for Baptism, but for prayer and all the other sacraments as well.

At first, the implications of Pelagius's teachings were not clear. Further, he appeared to be advocating an upstanding Christian life which had always been at the heart of the Gospel. But as it became clear that Pelagius was denying the propriety of infant Baptism, complaints were lodged.

Celestius

In 411, an accusation was filed with the bishop of Carthage against the Pelagian view of infant Baptism as defended by Celestius, an enthusiastic follower of Pelagius. (Celestius wanted to be accepted as a candidate for the priesthood in the diocese of Carthage.)

A synod was convened, and Celestius was examined. Failing to satisfy the synod on infant Baptism, Celestius was condemned. Of course, with the case of Celestius, the views of Pelagius became known in North Africa.

Augustine, the greatest figure among the Christians in North Africa at the time, responded with sermons, speeches, and written works against the movement. But even with the strength of Augustine's arguments, Pelagianism was given new life when a Palestinian synod rehabilitated Pelagius in 415. (Pelagius had gone to Palestine in 412-413.)

In the next year, two synods in North Africa reaffirmed the condemnation of Celestius. With North Africa on one side and Palestine on the other, the North Africans appealed to Pope Innocent I (401-417), who decided against Pelagius and in favor of the North African position.

Pelagius appealed, and with Innocent I dead, the next Pope, Zosimus (417-418), eventually confirmed Pope Innocent's decision. In addition, the Emperor issued an edict in 418 banning the teachings of Pelagius and his followers.

Pelagius was banned from Rome and Palestine, and he probably died in an Egyptian monastery. Celestius continued to defend the Pelagian ideas together with Bishop Julian of Aeclanum.

Julian was especially critical of St. Augustine's writings and accused him of Manicheism. According to Julian, Augustine's defense of the teaching that original sin wounded human nature was Manichean because Augustine was teaching that human nature was sinful. No one was persuaded by either Celestius or Julian. The condemnations against Pelagianism stood, and the movement gradually disappeared in the 420s.

Doctrinal Errors

Pelagius had an overly optimistic view of human nature, claiming that through the natural human powers all human beings can live saintly lives and achieve salvation. In order to maintain this optimistic view of humanity, Pelagius had to deemphasize original sin and its effects. With his understanding of original sin, Baptism had also to be questioned as well as all the other sacraments. They were unnecessary for salvation. The only thing necessary was an upright moral life.

The fundamental problem with the Pelagian view of Christianity is that without original sin and its effects, we do not need a Redeemer. Christ and the cross become unnecessary. Even Christ's mission of Revelation is called into question because if our natural powers of mind and will are not weakened by the effects of sin, we can know what we need to know — the moral law — without the necessity of Revelation.

Further, since the moral law is all we need to know, the mysteries of the faith revealed by Christ which we cannot know through human reason, such as the Trinity, are unnecessary. Therefore, Christ is unnecessary. If Christ is unnecessary, then the Church is unnecessary.

It is interesting to note that Pelagius never established an organized Church structure. There were no Pelagian churches or dioceses; there were no members of a Pelagian Church; there were no deacons, priests, or bishops. Unlike the Donatists, Pelagius did not establish a rival Church organization to the Catholic Church. Partly, this lack of organization among Pelagians is attributable to the implications of Pelagianism: the Church was not necessary.

But Pelagius also did not construct a rival Church structure because at the beginning he saw himself working within the Church to renew the life of its members. His theories were a response to the laxity in the lives of the Christians he saw around him.

In contrast, the Donatists began, not by trying to renew the Church, but rather by challenging one of its practices and the belief that was the foundation of that practice: the inherent validity of the sacraments independently of the moral character of the minister of the sacrament. Further, from the beginning the Donatists were challenging the Church structure because the Donatist movement began with a disputed succession to the bishopric of Carthage. In opposing the Catholic bishop, the followers of Donatus could not help but set up a rival Church structure to the Catholic Church.

The Church's Response

In response to Pelagius, Augustine defended the need for a Redeemer and grace by insisting on original sin and quoting Scripture. He argued that every member of the human race suffered from the effects of original sin because it was transmitted by Adam to all his descendents. (Of course, Christ, as God the Son, did not suffer the effects of original sin and, as the Church teaches, neither did Mary.)

For Augustine, the effects of original sin in us are an alienation from God and a loss of grace. This alienation from God — i.e., from Love Itself — caused in all human beings (except Christ and Mary) a disordered love of self. This selfishness inherent in fallen human nature resulted in almost a contempt for God. Grace was essential if this disordered love of self was to be transformed into a love for God and others. But grace can absolutely never be earned. For Augustine, grace is absolutely essential for human beings to live according to Gospel norms and come to salvation, but it is always and in every case a totally gratuitous gift from God.

Pelagius had overvalued human nature and thereby undermined the need for Christ and his life-giving grace. In other words, Pelagius had touched one of the central questions of Christianity: the relationship between grace and nature. If we are self-determining and can choose our own acts, then and only then are we truly free agents. In claiming that by knowing the good and choosing it, human beings work out their own salvation without God's help, Pelagius clearly was maintaining the notion that every human being is the source of his or her own salvation. Thus, he denied God's role in our own salvation.

Augustine, on the other hand, clearly taught the necessity of Christ and grace if human beings were to act according to Gospel norms. For Augustine, it was next to impossible for a human being to act properly without God's grace. But if it is only by the grace of God that we are able to act as Christ did, what happens to human responsibility and human freedom?

St. Augustine's viewpoint, if pushed too far, could deny all human responsibility and lead to a deterministic view of predestination: God chooses who will receive His grace and who will not. Those who receive it come to heaven by the power of God without any responsibility on their part, and those who do not receive it, do not come to heaven. Of course, this view goes too far in affirming the role of grace and denying human responsibility in salvation. Nevertheless, certain remarks Augustine made in the effort to counter Pelagianism and to solve what is fundamentally a profound mystery had suggestions of a deterministic divine predestination.

Augustine's teaching on grace and free will, developed in response to Pelagianism, came to the attention of some monks at the monastery of Hadrumetum in North Africa. They were more than a little disturbed by Augustine's views. They argued that if free will had no role to play at all in the working out of one's salvation, what could be said of the Church's teaching on the Last Judgment? In other words, if everything was attributable to grace, how could the Lord judge us according to our works? Did we feed Him when He was thirsty, etc.? (See Matthew 25:31-46.) Further, if everything is attributed to grace, what good was monastic discipline or correction? Of course, the monks had touched on the central problem of the dispute.

Augustine responded with two works. In one he clearly maintains that grace always operates in conjunction with free will. In other words, grace is absolutely necessary to salvation, but it never forces or even less suspends the human will. In the second work, Augustine argued that the decision to sin is not an act of freedom, but of slavery. Further, he maintained that grace insures freedom. (This same point is made today in slightly different language: grace cooperates with fallen human nature so that the human will is able to operate as it should — in freedom.)

In addition, Augustine argued that the grace of final perseverance — the blessing of dying in the state of grace — was a totally gratuitous gift from God, but if it is granted, the person will infallibly come to heaven. Therefore, Augustine taught that the number of those who will come to heaven is determined by God.

John Cassian and Semi-Pelagianism

This second work, addressed to the monks at Hadrumetum, came to the attention of Abbot John Cassian (c. 360-435) of St. Victor at Marseilles and Vincent of Lerins (d. before 450), a monk of the monastery on the island of Lerins off the coast of Marseilles. They opposed Augustine's teaching on grace because they argued that it left no room for human responsibility. Especially troubling to Cassian and Vincent were two of Augustine's ideas: that even the initial attraction to God was a gratuitous grace from God; and that the grace of final perseverance was a divine gift.

John Cassian suggested that the initial attraction to the faith was often attributable to human free will and that one could persevere in grace through the natural human powers. Cassian also believed that while grace can never be merited, human nature has a certain claim to grace. Of course, given these ideas, Cassian disputed Augustine's idea that the number of souls in heaven was predetermined.

Cassian's views are known to history under the name Semi-Pelagianism. Not denying original sin, the necessity of grace or the sacraments as Pelagius had, the Semi-Pelagians did attribute too much to human nature and human free will.

Augustine's Response to Semi-Pelagianism

Late in life, Augustine responded to Cassian. The bishop of Hippo insisted that all grace was totally gratuitous and unmerited. Therefore, even the initial stages of coming to faith must be a gift of grace, because otherwise the gift of faith would depend on a human act — coming to faith — and would not be totally gratuitous. He argued in the same way about the grace of final perseverance. Final perseverance could not depend on mere human nature, because then the grace of salvation would at least in some sense be earned or merited and this is impossible. Augustine also argued in this late work that since no one has a claim on God's mercy, the denial of grace to some is perfectly just.

Synod of Orange

Despite the work of Augustine's disciples after he died, Cassian and Vincent continued to argue their position. Semi-Pelagianism was influential in Gaul (modern-day France) for most of the fifth century. It was not until the Synod of Orange in 529 (in southern Gaul) that Semi-Pelagianism was condemned as heresy. The Synod of Orange taught that even the initial attraction to the faith was under the influence of grace; that all graces, including the first grace of faith and the grace of final perseverance, were entirely and completely gratuitous and could never be merited or earned; and that fallen human nature was incapable of meritorius acts without the influence of grace.

The teachings of the Synod of Orange were confirmed by Pope Boniface II (530-532) in the next year. It should be noted that the Synod at

Orange did not make any remarks about predestination to heaven or about the number of those destined by God for heaven. In other words, the synod confirmed Augustine's fundamental insights about grace, but obviously viewed some of his more pessimistic conclusions as his own private opinions. Nevertheless, private opinions or authoritative teachings of the Church, the ideas of Augustine on grace and its relationship to free will would give rise to some very intense controversies throughout the centuries.

Fundamentally, since the issue touches on the mystery of God's will, it can never be definitively solved. However, the Church has always taught that grace builds on nature. Grace never overpowers or forces humanity. Grace gives us the strength to do what we freely choose to do as Augustine did argue. Unfortunately, many have wanted to probe deeper into this mystery, and the attempt usually has given rise to controversy.

Pelagianism

This heresy taught that salvation could be achieved solely by upright moral behavior which was possible for every human being, even without grace. This heresy called into question the sacraments, the Incarnation, and the doctrinal teachings of the Church.

Semi-Pelagianism

This heresy taught that human nature had a certain claim on the grace of coming to believe and the grace of final perseverance. Its adherents believed that these graces were not entirely gratuitous, but rather in a sense "owed" by God to man.

13

Nestorianism

Theodore of Mopsuestia

WHILE DONATISM AND PELAGIANISM DISTURBED THE CHURCH, THE EFFECTS of these heresies were mostly felt in the West. In the East in the fifth century, the problem of the relationship of Christ's divinity to His humanity, raised by Arius and then by Appolinaris, continued to be discussed.

The Arians had denied the divinity of Christ by claiming that the *Logos*, not equal to the Father, had united with humanity and formed one nature. Appolinaris had denied the full humanity of Christ. The response to both these heresies resulted in an emphasis on both the humanity and the divinity. Lacking precise terminology, the theologians did not have the proper tools to try to express the divine and human united in an unbreakable bond in Christ. By emphasizing both the divine and the human, there seemed to be two persons in Christ.

Though at pains to defend the unity in Christ, the theologians were caught in a dilemma: if one talks about two realities, there are two realities, no matter how much one emphasizes that they are united. To some, reading Theodore of Mopsuestia (d. 428), it seemed that the unity in Christ was almost like that of the union of husband and wife in marriage. Theodore suggested this image by using the word "conjunction" for the union of the human and divine in Christ.

The difficulty with a dualist notion of the union of the divine and human in Christ is that if God the Son united Himself with an existing human person, then it is impossible to claim that God cried (at the death of Lazarus) or even that God died (on the cross). These acts would be those of the human person, not of the *Logos*. If God did not die on the cross, then we are not redeemed because the Redemption is precisely the death of God, i.e., God's sacrifice of Himself for us so that we might again experience the love of God. To be fair to Theodore, while using certain dualistic terms, he constantly held that what was said of the man Christ could be said of God.

Nestorius

Theodore of Mopsuestia represents a theological point of view associated with Antioch in Syria. Another direction was taken by those associated with the see of Athanasius, Alexandria in Egypt. Nestorius, who became bishop of Constantinople in 428, was of the Antiochean school. In other words, he was attached to the more dualistic tradition represented by Theodore. (It must be noted that Theodore died as a Catholic and was never accused of heresy until more than one hundred years after he died.)

When Nestorius became bishop of Constantinople, there was a discussion in his diocese about whether the Blessed Virgin could be given the title "Mother of God." Nestorius denied that Mary could be properly called the Mother of God and preferred the term "Mother of Christ." Nestorius argued and vigorously defended his view that Mary could not be the Mother of God because that would imply that the divine nature was born, suffered, and died.

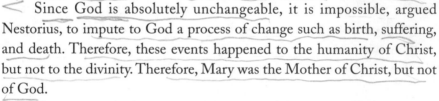

Since God is absolutely unchangeable, it is impossible, argued Nestorius, to impute to God a process of change such as birth, suffering, and death. Therefore, these events happened to the humanity of Christ, but not to the divinity. Therefore, Mary was the Mother of Christ, but not of God.

Nestorius took the suggested dualism of Theodore and some others of the school of Antioch to an extreme. While most followers of Antioch had always maintained a unity between the human and divine (while having great difficulty explaining how this was possible), Nestorius abandoned the unity in Christ in favor of a complete dualism. For Nestorius, what was attributed to the humanity could not be attributed to the divinity and vice-versa. However, as we have seen, this view clearly holds that God did not die and then, of course, we are not redeemed.

Since Nestorius represented the school at Antioch, it was not unexpected that Alexandria reacted to his teachings. St. Cyril, who was bishop of Alexandria from 412 to 444, heard of Nestorius's views and immediately wrote letters to the bishops and monks of Egypt defending Mary's title as Mother of God. He also wrote Nestorius requesting a clarification of what Nestorius taught regarding Christ and the Blessed Mother.

Nestorius responded to Cyril with an admonition for Christian restraint (meaning that Cyril should not have intervened) and also with a campaign to advance his own ideas. This campaign included contacting Pope Celestine I (422-432). Cyril also contacted Rome. The Pope ruled in favor of Cyril and ordered Nestorius to affirm publicly what he had denied. If he failed to affirm the faith of the Church within ten days, he would suffer judgment against him. Cyril was charged with the implementation of the Pope's decision.

Council of Ephesus

In the same year, 430, the Emperor Theodosius II (408-450) sent an invitation to the bishops to meet in a general council on Pentecost (431) at Ephesus. The Emperor also sent an invitation to Rome and to Hippo, but Augustine had already died.

The Pope appointed Cyril as the papal vicar for the council. Although some bishops were delayed in arriving at the council, Cyril, on his own authority, decided that the council would be opened on June 22. Nestorius refused to attend the council until all the bishops arrived. Obviously, the bishops who agreed to attend the council on June 22 were more or less the ones who supported Cyril. The council confirmed the judgment against Nestorius which the Pope had given and Cyril had tried to implement.

When the absent bishops arrived, they convened their own meeting and deposed Cyril. The Emperor intervened and declared that the decisions of both councils were null and void. Although the Pope had appointed Cyril as the papal vicar, he also sent representatives who were instructed to follow Cyril's judgments. When these representatives arrived at the beginning of July, the majority of the bishops, who had already met on June 22 under Cyril's leadership, met again. With the papal legates present bringing a letter from Pope Celestine, the bishops ratified their previous decisions, i.e., the condemnation of Nestorius and his views.

Unfortunately, Nestorius and his followers did not accept the decisions of this second meeting any more than they had accepted the decisions of the first. They made the claim that they were waiting for the imperial representative. When the imperial representative arrived, he made known the decision of the Emperor in favor of the deposition of Nestorius, but he also ordered the deposition of Cyril. (The Emperor was clearly attempting to remove the two antagonists in the dispute in order to end it.)

After lavishly distributing gifts to influential people (in order to curry favor with the Emperor), Cyril secretly left Ephesus before a successor could be appointed for his See. Nestorius was not as fortunate. His diocese, Constantinople, was closer and it was easier for the Emperor to arrange a successor to Nestorius. Nestorius returned to his monastery at Antioch, but eventually retired to the Libyan desert. Cyril, of course, remained the bishop of Alexandria.

The council ended without a reconciliation between the two parties. However, the Emperor was anxious for an agreement. With Nestorius deposed and banished, the head of the party he represented, the party of Antioch, was John of Antioch. Cyril of Alexandria continued to represent the other side. After long and difficult negotiations, an agreement was reached in 433 with an exchange of letters between Cyril and John. Antioch accepted the judgment against Nestorius and acknowledged that his doctrine was not in accord with the true faith. Cyril accepted the formulation of the creed as drafted at Antioch. This creed used Cyril's formula of a union of the two natures in Christ rather than the word "conjunction," which was preferred by Nestorius and some of the Antiochenes. However, the creed also added "without confusion." Therefore, the language read that in Christ two natures were in union without confusion.

The without-confusion phrase was a concession by Cyril, and it also represented his agreement not to insist on his own formulations. Although this concession may seem today to be minor, it created some problems for him among his followers. Of course, the use of the word union rather than conjunction created problems among the followers of John of Antioch, the Nestorian party.

The two sessions of the Council of Ephesus — that is, the two meetings of the bishops under the leadership of Cyril — definitively set the Nicene Creed as the norm for the faith. Anything not in conformity with the Nicene Creed was not to be accepted. Until Ephesus, the finality of the Nicene Creed as a statement of the Catholic faith had not been absolutely established.

Theotokos: the Mother of God

The bishops also definitely established that the Blessed Virgin Mary is properly called *Theotokos*, the Mother of God, denying the radical dualism in Christ posited by Nestorius. The same denial of Nestorian dualism can be seen in the decision by the bishops at Ephesus to affirm that it was proper to say that God cried and God died. In other words, what happened in Christ's humanity happened to the *Logos*, the second Person of the Blessed Trinity.

The denial of the dualistic approach to the union of the divine and the human in Christ was decisive because it set the foundation for future reflections of the Church on the mystery of the Incarnation. Even though Ephesus did not perhaps answer with total clarity the question Nestorius was trying to answer (how is it possible to maintain both the human and divine in Christ?), it did clearly reject the Nestorian answer. Even though the progress made at Ephesus in Christology was negative — that is, the bishops rejected the wrong answer — it still was progress, because now the Church would move from the wrong answer to a further search for the right one.

Different Approaches, Personalities, and Vocabularies

The dispute between Cyril and Nestorius was partly a clash of strong personalities. In addition to the personality clash, there was also the rivalry between Antioch, represented by Nestorius, and Alexandria, represented by Cyril. Although this rivalry has been overemphasized in the past by some writers, the two schools had completely different approaches to the mystery of the Incarnation.

Alexandria emphasized the divinity of Christ, while Antioch was more concerned (but not exclusively so) with Christ's humanity and the question of the union of the divine and human in Christ. Nestorius and Cyril also were struggling with the lack of precise terminology. When Nestorius and Cyril wrote or spoke, they used the same words, but with different shades of meaning.

Although the young Nicenes had tried to clarify certain terms like *hypostasis* and *ousia*, these terms were still not used with the same meanings by everyone. Further, new terms were introduced. For example, Theodore of Mopsuestia wrote of the *prosopon* of Christ. *Prosopon* meant a manner of appearing, not person, as we would translate it today.

Theodore said that in Christ the divine and human resulted in the one *prosopon* of Christ. Another representative of the Antioch school also used the word *prosopon*, but he posited two *prosopa*, one divine and one human, in Christ. Clearly, words used were not precisely defined and everyone in the discussion, while using the same words, meant something different. No wonder Cyril and Nestorius and their followers had difficulties!

Nevertheless, while Nestorius can certainly be faulted for maintaining his position once the Church decided in favor of Cyril, still Nestorius did propose a solution. Without his proposal, the Church would not have been able to move as rapidly or as clearly in defining the union of the two natures in Christ. Even the meeting of the bishops opposing Cyril contributed to the eventual resolution of the issue. At their counter-meeting, these bishops suggested a statement of faith to the Emperor which acknowledged Christ as one Son, one Lord, and allowed the title of Mother of God to the Blessed Virgin.

This confession of faith on the part of those opposed to Cyril — made by those of the Antioch tradition — was the basis for reconciliation between John of Antioch and Cyril in 433. Needless to say, this confession of faith certainly demonstrates that there was truth on both sides and also shows how close the two sides actually were. Still, it must be remembered that Nestorius seems to have embraced a much more dualistic approach than this confession of faith: "one Son, one Lord." But the future was not to lie in Nestorian's dualism.

Nestorianism

This heresy taught that Mary was not the Mother of God because the divine cannot be born, suffer, or die. These acts (being born, suffering, and dying) cannot be attributed to the divine nature. If Christ is both divine and human, and birth, suffering, and dying cannot be attributed to the divine nature, then it must be attributed to the human nature. But it is not just a nature that is born, suffers, or dies, but a person. Nestorianism seems to hold that Christ was a human person. But since He was also divine, He had to be a divine person as well. Nestorianism seems to teach that there were two persons in Christ, a divine person and a human person.

14

The Monophysites

Eutyches

SINCE THE DUALISM OF NESTORIUS WAS REJECTED BUT THE FUNDAMENTAL question of exactly how the two natures of Christ were united in the one divine Person was not answered, with total clarity there was plenty of room for continued difficulties. (Ephesus and the exchange of letters between John of Antioch and Cyril had merely affirmed that the human and divine were united without confusion in the one Son, one Lord of Christ and that what was said of the humanity could be said of the divinity [God died, God cried, etc.].)

The entire issue resurfaced in 446 when an elderly abbot, Eutyches, in Constantinople affirmed that there were two natures before the union created in the Incarnation, but only one after the union. In other words, he affirmed that in Christ there was only the divine after the union. In making this claim, Eutyches was trying to follow Cyril, but took an extreme interpretation of Cyril's words. Further, Eutyches rejected the formula agreed to by Cyril and John of Antioch in their exchange of letters in 433. For Eutyches, Christ had only one divine nature. His humanity was totally absorbed by the divinity. Since Eutyches was abbot of over 300 monks in the capital of the eastern Empire, and because he was the godfather of one of the most influential advisors to the Emperor, his views became widely known.

Synod of Constantinople

Eutyches's views were attacked by Theodoret of Cyrrhus and also by Eusebius of Dorylaeum. In fact, at a synod at Constantinople in 448, Eusebius brought charges against Eutyches. After some delaying tactics and attempts to impress the synod with his following of monks and his court connections, Eutyches was asked whether he accepted the formulation of the two natures in Christ. When he refused to acknowledge the two natures in Christ, he was deposed as abbot and forbidden to exercise his priestly office. His teachings were also condemned.

The "Robber" Council

Appealing through his godchild, the advisor to the Emperor, Eutyches managed to have the Emperor call a council to meet at Ephesus on August 1, 449. Theodoret of Cyrrhus was to be excluded from the council, but Dioscorus of Alexandria, the successor to Cyril at Alexandria, was asked to bring twenty Egyptian bishops with him to the council. (Dioscorus of Alexandria together with Eutyches represented the extreme wing of the school at Alexandria.) In other words, the critics of Eutyches were to be excluded, and his supporters were not only included but as many as possible were invited.

Pope Leo I, the Great, was also invited and even sent legates. However, Dioscorus presided over the synod and refused to allow the letter of Pope Leo I, which came to be known as the *Tome of St. Leo*, to be read. (This was the Roman statement formulated by Pope Leo regarding the Christological problem.)

Eusebius of Dorylaeum, one of the opponents of Eutyches, was not allowed to be heard at the council. In fact, he was shouted down, but Eutyches was permitted to present a very biased report on the synod which had condemned his views. One hundred thirteen of 140 bishops present at the council affirmed the orthodoxy of Eutyches and condemned Flavian of Constantinople (who had taken the position that Eutyches's views were not in conformity to the faith) and Eusebius of Dorylaeum. Theodoret of Cyrrhus, Domnus of Antioch, and Bishop Ibas of Edessa, all Antiochenes who questioned the orthodoxy of Eutyches, were deposed. With this action, the Antiochenes were totally defeated and the agreement of 433 between John of Antioch and Cyril was set aside.

This council of Ephesus was never acknowledged as a legitimate meeting of the bishops of the Church because of their flagrant disregard of the papal legates. When Pope Leo I heard of the acts of the council, he said that the bishops had engaged not in a judgment, a *judicium*, but rather in a robbery, a *latrocinum*. Of course, this was a play on Latin words, but ever since that papal remark, the council of Ephesus which met in 449 has been known in history as the "robber" council of Ephesus.

What gave the acts of the "robber" council their effect was the imperial authority behind the council's decisions. The deposed bishops were banished because the troops of the Emperor enforced the decrees. Flavian of Constantinople and Theodoret of Cyrrhus appealed to Rome. Pope Leo at a synod in Rome condemned the acts of the "robber" council and at the suggestion of Flavian asked the Emperor to call another council. The Emperor met these requests with silence, but the entire situation changed when the Emperor died in the summer of 450.

Council of Chalcedon (451)

After the death of the Emperor, his sister, Pulcheria, immediately took up the reins of power. Four weeks after her brother's death, she married Marcian, who became Emperor. Eutyches's imperial protector was tried, convicted, and sentenced to death. The bishops deposed at the "robber" council were allowed to return to their bishoprics (except for Flavian, who had died).

The project of a new council was accepted by Pulcheria and the new Emperor, Marcian. The Pope also agreed to the project, but insisted that his legates would preside at the council, that the deposed bishops would be restored, and, most importantly, that his letter to the previous council, the *Tome of St. Leo*, be incorporated into the decision of the council. The council met at Chalcedon in October 451.

Three hundred fifty bishops participated in what was at that time the largest gathering of bishops in the history of the Church. Dioscorus, refusing to ask pardon for his condemnation of Bishop Flavian at the "robber" council (as others who had participated in that condemnation had done), was deposed. Dioscorus was exiled, and the decree was enforced by the Emperor.

Regarding the doctrinal issue, the bishops were very much agreed that the Nicene Creed, the statement of Constantinople (381), the letters of Cyril to Nestorius, the agreement reached between John and Cyril in 433, and the *Tome of St. Leo*, adequately expressed the faith. In fact, the bishops acclaimed the *Tome* as the statement of Peter through Leo. The bishops were very reluctant to formulate a new statement of the faith, believing that the existing statements were sufficient. But the Emperor insisted, and so a formulation of the faith including the *Tome of St. Leo* was issued by the council.

The statement of Chalcedon in a sense closes the period of the Church's initial reflection on the Incarnation after four and a half centuries of debate. It represents in a definitive way the Church's teaching on the Incarnation. For that reason, it deserves to be quoted:

"Hence we follow the holy Fathers and unanimously teach that the Son, our Lord Jesus Christ, is one and the same. The one and same is perfect in His divinity and perfect in His humanity, true God and true man, consisting of a rational soul and a body. The one and the same is equal in substance to the Father in His divinity and equal in substance to us in His humanity; He became like us in all things, except sin (See Heb. 4:15). He was begotten of the Father before all time in His divinity; in the latest epoch, however, the same was born for us and for our salvation of Mary the Virgin and Mother of God in His humanity.

"We confess one and the same Christ, the Son and Lord, the only-begotten, Who exists in two natures, without admixture, without change, without division, without separation. The difference of natures was never annulled through the union; rather the special property of each nature is preserved as the two come together into person or *hypostasis*.

"We confess, not one separated and mutilated into two persons, but one and the same only-begotten Son, the divine Word, the Lord Jesus Christ."

As is apparent from the above quote, the fathers of Chalcedon combined their sources into one statement without changing anything or making any new statements. In the Chalcedonian formula, one sees Nicaea, Constantinople, the letters of Cyril to Nestorius, Ephesus, the formula of 433, and the *Tome of St. Leo*. It is nothing short of remarkable that, beginning in the 300s with massive confusion both in ideas and in the meanings of words, a rather precise formulation of the faith could have been worked out by 451.

Post-Chalcedon Monophysitism

Unfortunately, despite the decrees of the council of Chalcedon, the Monophysite movement remained very strong. Egypt, especially, remained predominantly Monophysite. The Church in Syria was also greatly influenced by the teachings of Eutyches, the founder of the Monophysites.

With the continued strength of the Monophysites, various nuances appeared. In one form, Monophysitism closely resembled Docetism. It may be recalled, Docetism was the position taught by Valentinus in the early third century which held that matter was evil and so God, the ultimate Good, could never have united Himself with matter. Therefore, Christ's humanity was merely a vision, a projection. God the Son did not truly assume human nature. The Monophysite position is different because the Monophysites did not hold that the material world was evil. However, they did hold that in Christ the human nature was absorbed or subsumed into the divine nature.

Eutyches had the notion that the divine nature was like an ocean and the human nature like a drop of water. The humanity, while there, was totally engulfed (to continue the ocean metaphor) by the divinity. In the Monophysite view, the humanity could not be a source of activity separate from the divinity, any more than it is possible to separate the drops of water in the ocean. The obvious conclusion is that there can be no true and actual perception of Christ's humanity because Christ's humanity was absorbed by the divinity. Therefore, the Apostles did not see or in any way sense Christ's body. What they saw and sensed was an appearance, a vision, because Christ's body (and the rest of his humanity) was absorbed in the divinity.

One sect of the Monophysites came to this conclusion and said that the body of Christ was a phantom. While arriving at this conclusion from a different starting point, the result is the same position taken by the Docetists. Another sect of the Monophysites taught that Christ's body was incapable of suffering and was incorruptible because it belonged to the divine nature. Clearly, these conclusions directly assail the teaching on the Redemption accomplished through Christ's passion and death. If Christ's humanity were totally absorbed by the divinity or if His body were incorruptible, the sacrifice on the cross would have been impossible.

Other versions of the Monophysite position directly attacked the teaching on the Trinity. Some Monophysites taught that all three Persons actually became incarnate. This conclusion flows from the (false) idea that there is only one nature in Christ, the divine nature. If that is true and if the divine nature is one and the same in all three Persons of the Trinity, then it is obvious that if the humanity is absorbed into the divine nature, it is absorbed by the divine nature belonging to all three Persons.

In fact, some Monophysites even went so far as to say that the Trinity was the one "Who was crucified for us." Of course, this view is very similar to the Sabellians or Father-sufferers of the early third century, c. 200. The difficulty with this point of view is not that it destroys the distinction of the three Persons in God because the claim is not, as it was with the Sabellians, that the three Persons were really just separate names for the same individual being. Rather, the claim is that because Christ's nature was divine and His humanity had been absorbed by that nature to which all three divine Persons were united, all three joined to the single divine nature had absorbed the humanity! Clearly, this view contradicts the constant teaching of the Church that the Word became man (John 1:1) and not the Father and the Holy Spirit.

A different attack on the Trinity occurred when some of the Monophysites taught that each divine Person had a distinct divine nature and that the divine nature of the Son absorbed the humanity. The problem with this view is that it destroys the Trinity because if each Person has His own nature, there is no unity in the Godhead and there are in effect three gods. Clearly, the only formula which preserves intact the revealed truth is that of Nicaea-Constantinople-Chalcedon: in the incarnate Second Divine Person there are two natures, divine and human. The acting agent is the Second Person, and He can act in and through only His humanity (as when He ate, or cried), only in His divinity (as in His divine knowledge of the universe), or in both at once (as in the miracles).

The Monophysites remained very strong, partly because they were appealing to tradition, the tradition of St. Cyril. Cyril, who died in 444, was a hero to the Christians in Egypt because he had led the fight against the Nestorians at the Council of Ephesus in 431. For the Monophysites, Cyril's formula of one *physis* (one nature) in Christ, was the touchstone of the true faith. According to the Monophysites, when Chalcedon spoke of two natures in Christ, it abandoned St. Cyril's position and caved in to the Nestorians.

Further, the Monophysites had a martyr. Their bishop, Dioscorus of Alexandria, had been exiled. The deposition and exile of Dioscorus, as the successor of St. Cyril and the defender of Cyril's teaching, was a repudiation of Cyril and his theory. Also, the fall of Dioscorus was an insult to Alexandria and the Christians of Egypt.

Also aiding the Monophysite position were the previous struggles in the eastern Church. As we have seen, council after council, synod after synod had been undone by continued struggles. The "robber" council of Ephesus had been undone by Chalcedon. From recent history, was it not at least possible that the Monophysites, if they continued to struggle, could undo what had been done at Chalcedon? After all there did not seem to be an authority that could definitively settle an issue.

Into this equation one must also place the famous *Tome of St. Leo*. As an intervention of the Pope, this was seen in some circles as an interference in the eastern Church by a western bishop. In some quarters it was resented. Far from representing a definitive statement by the successor of St. Peter, some saw the *Tome of St. Leo* as an unmitigated seizure of unwarranted authority by the bishop of Rome. Without the acceptance of a definitive voice that could speak authoritatively — a council or the Pope — the Monophysites embraced an ecclesiology which allowed them to continue to hope that their views would eventually prevail.

An additional factor in the Monophysite opposition to Chalcedon was the famous Canon 28, which gave Constantinople a preeminence in the East over all the other sees. Given this organizational and disciplinary canon of Chalcedon, it was not unnatural that the bishops of Constantinople (and the imperial authority also located there) would support Chalcedon, and that the sees of Alexandria (Egypt) and Antioch (Syria) would oppose it. (Actually, there was some opposition in Syria, but the Monophysites were strongest in Egypt.) One also has to understand that the Chalcedonian position came to be imperial policy. As such it became a political issue. The bishops supporting Chalcedon appeared to be political hangers-on of an imperial political position. Since this imperial policy was supported by imperial authority, including the police and the army, the supporters of Chalcedon hardly appeared to be interested in fundamental truths of the faith. Rather, they could be seen as echoing imperial policy for political gain.

This was hardly the case for many if not most of the Chalcedonian bishops, but these bishops were open to this charge against them. From this point of view, the other side looked more heroic and more pure, especially since the Monophysite movement was in a large part carried by the monks — part of the tradition that began with Eutyches, who was an abbot.

All these factors contributed to the surprising and lasting strength of the Monophysite position. Even with the full extent of imperial power, it was impossible to impose Chalcedon on Egypt. In fact, the imperial power gave up trying to maintain the Chalcedonian bishop in Alexandria between 482 and 537.

The Henoticon

The imperial policy was to try to bring peace to the Empire. The Emperors, since Constantine, had almost always striven to unite the Church so that the Empire would not be rent by religious disputes, leading to political and civil problems. In an attempt to settle the religious controversy, the Emperor Zeno in 482 issued what came to be know as the *Henoticon*. This document affirmed Nicaea, Constantinople, and Ephesus. It accepted the exchange of letters between John of Antioch and Cyril in 433.

There was no mention of Chalcedon, of the one-nature formula of Cyril, or of the *Tome of St. Leo*. Neither the Monophysites nor the Chalcedonians accepted this document (*Henoticon*). The Monophysites would not accept anything that did not condemn Chalcedon and restore the one-nature formula of St. Cyril (even though he himself had accepted a compromise position on this very point in 433). The Chalcedonians would not accept anything that did not affirm Chalcedon and the *Tome of St. Leo*. The *Henoticon* was doomed almost before it was issued. Nevertheless, from 482 until 519, the Emperors tried to impose this document on the eastern Church. It was not heretical. Rather, it tried to state the faith in pre-Chalcedonian terms that would be acceptable to everyone.

Acacius, the Patriarch of Constantinople, probably wrote the *Henoticon*, but he soon became unacceptable in Rome. There was a dispute between two rival claimants to the bishopric of Alexandria, and Acacius took the part of one while Pope Felix III (483-492) took the part of the other. Acacius was excommunicated by the Pope in 484 and the Acacian schism (484-519), one of the most important breaks between Rome and Constantinople before 1054, began. The policy of promoting the *Henoticon* became entangled with the politics of the schism. Of course, Rome was a bit suspicious of the *Henoticon* because it did not mention the *Tome of St. Leo.*

Nevertheless, the *Henoticon* was not heretical and it did represent a valid attempt to find a formula acceptable to both the Chalcedonians and the Monophysites. Unfortunately, it was not received well by either side and was abandoned in 519 by the new Emperor, Justin I, the uncle of the great Justinian.

Justinian and the Three Chapters

The Emperor Justinian (527-565) is remembered in history as the Emperor who almost reunited East and West, creating again one government for many of the lands washed by the Mediterranean. The attempt at reunification was a magnificent failure. Justinian's troops were able to re-conquer North Africa, and an attempt was made in Italy, but the years of Roman dominance of the entire Mediterranean were gone forever.

Justinian is also remembered for his codification of Roman law. However, in the history of Catholic dogma and teaching, Justinian is the Emperor of the Three Chapters, a further attempt to appeal to the Monophysites and to reconcile them with the Chalcedonians. Of course, it is important to remember that the Monophysites believed the Chalcedonian formula to be tainted with Nestorianism and therefore refused to accept it.

The Three Chapters named the works of three theologians whom some regarded as Nestorians. These three men lived and worked in the first half of the fifth century when Nestorianism was disturbing the Church. The first text of the Three Chapters was a letter of Ibas of Edessa. In this letter, Ibas expresses a somewhat unfriendly attitude towards Cyril of Alexandria (therefore it has Nestorian leanings) and also refuses to condemn Theodore of Mopsuestia who, as the reader will recall, proposed that the union of the divine and human in Christ might be described as a "conjunction."

This view represented a dualistic approach and was, as some said, the source for Nestorius's ideas. As a result, by the middle of the sixth century, Theodore of Mopsuestia was considered in some quarters to be the founder of Nestorianism. (As we noted above, Theodore was never accused of heresy during his lifetime and died a Catholic in good standing with the Church.)

The second text of the Three Chapters was the work of the same Theodore of Mopsuestia.

The third text of the Three Chapters was the work of Theodoret of Cyrrhus. Theodoret wrote against some of the condemnations which Cyril of Alexandria had hurled against people Cyril regarded as Nestorians. In other words, Theodoret was anti-Cyril. Chalcedon had accepted Ibas as well as Theodoret, and Theodore of Mopsuestia had not been accused of heresy, even though Cyril had tried to have Theodore condemned posthumously.

Probably no one would have ever referred to the letter of Ibas, the works of Theodore of Mopsuestia, and the writings of Theodoret together if Justinian had not issued a decree condemning the Three Chapters. The text of the decree is lost, but it was issued between 543 and 545.

In condemning the Three Chapters, Justinian was attacking theologians who were perceived as Nestorians and as opponents of St. Cyril. Clearly, though, in issuing a decree against the Three Chapters — that is, against the writings of theologians who had been approved by the Church and two of whom had been explicitly accepted by Chalcedon — Justinian was attacking Chalcedon. Of course, that was precisely Justinian's purpose because he wanted to placate the Monophysites in order to reunite the Church in his Empire.

Although there was some resistance among the bishops, most of the bishops of the East signed the condemnation of the Three Chapters. Justinian did not give them much of a choice.

It should be noted that while the predecessors of Justinian had often meddled in Church matters, they usually worked through the structures of the Church: synods and councils. A meeting of the bishops would agree on a statement of faith and an imperial decree would follow the synod. Justinian, however, simply issued his decree without even the formality of a council or synod. The lack of proper Church procedure demonstrates Justinian's assumption of power over the Church. This exercise of imperial authority over the Church is also demonstrated by Justinian's letter to the bishops simply commanding them to sign the condemnation of the Three Chapters in place of allowing the bishops a discussion – or even the sham of a discussion – at a synod or council.

Those in the West were generally opposed to Justinian's decree against the Three Chapters. The bishops of the West were following the lead of Pope Vigilius (537-555).

To secure the cooperation of the bishops of the West, Justinian had to have Pope Vigilius's approval of the condemnation of the Three Chapters. The cooperation of the bishops of both East and West was essential because Justinian was intent on restoring the political unity of the East and West under his authority as Roman Emperor.

In 547, Justinian commanded Vigilius to come to Constantinople. After the Pope's arrival in Constantinople, he initially refused to bow to imperial pressure and did not sign the condemnation of the Three Chapters. He also broke with the Patriarch of Constantinople, who had signed the condemnation. However, after some months in the imperial city, the Pope issued a document — his *Judicatum* (Judgment) — which embraced the imperial position, at least in part. In other words, the Pope bowed to the continued political pressure applied by Justinian and his ministers.

The western bishops strongly disagreed with the Pope's *Judicatum*, and an African synod of bishops even excommunicated the Pope. (A question of Church law immediately arises: Do bishops, even a synod of bishops, have the authority to excommunicate a Pope? Obviously, with the later developments in the understanding of Church law, the answer is a resounding "No," but at that time the issue was not as clear as it would be later.)

Under pressure from both sides, the Pope told the western bishops that he had been forced to issue his *Judicatum* and withdrew it. Justinian permitted the Pope to abandon his support for the imperial policy and agreed that the issue should be settled by a synod. But the price Justinian extracted for this limited concession was that the Pope would work diligently to have the synod condemn the Three Chapters and that nothing would be done without Justinian's agreement. This agreement between the Emperor and the Pope was secret.

Nevertheless, through this agreement Pope Vigilius had surrendered the initiative and had almost become an agent for Justinian. Justinian issued another condemnation of the Three Chapters in 551, but this act was more than the Pope could tolerate. He was under some pressure again from the western bishops.

Vigilius demanded the withdrawal of the new condemnation of the Three Chapters and fled his lodgings in the imperial city, seeking asylum.

Justinian sent the imperial police after Vigilius, who was forced to defend himself physically. Finally yielding to Justinian on the promise of his own personal safety, he returned to his former residence in Constantinople only to have Justinian break his promise.

Justinian now treated Vigilius as his prisoner. The Pope managed to escape again. This time the Pope fled to Chalcedon. Justinian again tried force, and then promises, but the Pope would not return to Constantinople. In Chalcedon, the Pope deposed the Patriarch of Constantinople, but Justinian did not want an open break. (It will be remembered that Justinian's entire purpose in the question of the Three Chapters was to unite the Empire. To have an open break with the Pope and therefore with the western bishops [if not some of the eastern bishops as well] was not in the imperial interest.)

Justinian arranged an apology to the Pope from the Patriarch, and with that the Pope felt free to return to Constantinople. Shortly after these events, in 552, the Patriarch died. The new Patriarch of Constantinople was loyal to the Pope and it was agreed that a synod should decide the issues.

The synod or council, known as the Fifth Ecumenical Council, met in Constantinople in 553. The Council had 166 bishops, but only a few came from the West. The Pope refused to participate, deciding to make a judgment on the council after it issued its decisions. Since almost all the eastern bishops present at the council had already signed the condemnation of the Three Chapters, it appeared that Justinian would finally achieve his goal. However, at this point, Pope Vigilius issued a *Constitutum* which was also signed by some western bishops as well as a few eastern bishops. In this document, the Pope did condemn sixty different propositions from the works of Theodore of Mopsuestia, but did not condemn Theodore himself. The Pope also refused to call the Ibas letter or the work of Theodoret into question. The council decided to ignore the Pope's *Constitutum* and condemned the Three Chapters.

Seemingly, Justinian had won. But the Monophysites did not yield. The entire effort had been made so that they could be reunified with the Church within the Empire. They did not see their understanding of the human and divine in Christ sufficiently reflected in the condemnation of the Three Chapters.

The bishops of the West had not agreed to the conciliar decrees because most of them were not present at the council. Justinian needed their signatures. But to obtain the assent of the bishops of the West, Justinian needed the cooperation of the Pope. Under pressure, Vigilius agreed to the condemnation of the Three Chapters and issued another *Constitutum* (in 554) which condemned the letter of Ibas. With this document, Justinian allowed the Pope to leave and return to Rome. However, the Pope died while returning to Rome.

Pelagius, an advisor to Pope Vigilius (not to be confused with the Pelagius of the Pelagian heresy), had repeatedly supported Vigilius's opposition to Justinian, but after Justinian imprisoned him and following the death of Vigilius, Pelagius yielded to the Emperor. Since Justinian's troops now controlled Rome, Justinian was able to make Pelagius (555-561) the new Pope.

Facing strong opposition to the imperial policy from Roman Church circles, Pelagius abandoned the condemnation of the Three Chapters. In other words, he abandoned Justinian's policy, probably because of the pressure from the Church in the West. Unfortunately, some of the western bishops broke with Rome over the Three Chapters and unity was not restored in the West until 581.

It is difficult to explain the actions of Vigilius. If a politician today acted in this way, we would say he "flip-flopped." Vigilius "flip-flopped" not once, not twice, but actually three times: (1) He was against imperial policy when he first came to Constantinople and then in the *Judicatum*, he was supportive of imperial policy. (2) In the first *Constitutum*, he reverted to his opposition to Justinian, (3) but in the second *Constitutum*, he supported the Emperor. It is very difficult to understand these varying statements.

One must remember the pressure placed on Vigilius by Justinian and by the western bishops opposing Justinian's policies. Further, there was the language problem. The various decrees regarding the Three Chapters were all in Greek, and Vigilius was from Latin-speaking Rome. He was not sufficiently familiar with Greek to discern all the theological nuances contained in the writings that he was to judge. In addition, it must be remembered that the discussions regarding the Three Chapters were complicated by other ecclesiastical issues and personalities.

In the entire period between Constantine and Justinian (and even after Justinian), there was almost never a significant doctrinal opinion or idea advanced which did not become complicated with other issues, such as rival claimants to the same bishopric. In other words, there was hardly a time in this whole period when matters of the faith were able to be discussed in a pure way, without other political considerations. In Vigilius's case, some of these other side issues can partially explain some of his actions.

From Justinian's point of view, the whole effort of condemning the Three Chapters had as its purpose the unifying of the Empire. But this goal was impossible from the very beginning because the Monophysites were never willing to accept the condemnation of the Three Chapters as a sufficient repudiation of Chalcedon.

They demanded nothing less than the acceptance of their understanding of St. Cyril's formula. Those who remained faithful to Chalcedon found in the condemnation of the Three Chapters an attack on Chalcedon which was unacceptable. Justinian hoped for some middle ground that both the Monophysites and the Chalcedonians could accept.

Unfortunately, the condemnation of the Three Chapters never could satisfy the Monophysites or be accepted by the Chalcedonians. Justinian put a considerable effort into what another man might have seen as impossible from the beginning. In this instance, Justinian's effort to reconcile the Monophysites was not only a total failure, but it was hopeless even before it was launched.

Despite Justinian's failure, attempts to satisfy the Monophysites did not end with him when he died in 565. Justinian's successor, Justin II (565-578), issued another *Henoticon*. This document again condemned the Three Chapters and granted amnesty to the Monophysite bishops who had remained in exile (since they refused to be reconciled to the Church after the conciliar decrees against the Three Chapters of the Fifth Ecumenical Council that met in 553).

Again, the Monophysites refused to see in this *Henoticon* a sufficient softening of Chalcedon. A persecution followed to force them to accept the *Henoticon*. However, Justin lapsed into insanity, and Tiberius took control in 574 succeeding Justin II on Justin's death in 578. Tiberius ended the persecution.

When the Persians attacked the eastern provinces of the Empire during the reign of Heraclius (610-641), the Monophysites, populating in some cases entire provinces, were not much in a mood to fight for the Empire (which had persecuted them). A discussion over doctrine on the natures of Christ had led to persecution which in turn had led to political disunity which now, with the military pressure of the Persians, resulted in serious defeats for the Empire.

Heraclius was able to defeat the Persians and reconquer the territory in the East overrun by the Persians. But his work was far from finished. Somehow, the Monophysite disunity had to be addressed or another enemy might be able to dismember the Empire.

Monoenergism and Monotheletism

In this situation, the Patriarch of Constantinople, Sergius, issued a statement that suggested that Christ had one energy. The Patriarch of Alexandria, Cyrus (appointed by the Emperor and so the orthodox bishop of Alexandria, the bishop not of the Monophysites, but of those loyal to Chalcedon in Alexandria), took Sergius's formula and constructed a series of nine statements which he thought might form the basis of unity between the Chalcedonians and the Monophysites. (Obviously, as the orthodox bishop of Alexandria where there were many, many Monophysites, Cyrus had a special motive in seeking a basis for unity!) This pact was issued in Alexandria in 633 and used the formula for Christ "one energy."

There were those opposed to this formula. Sophronius, the Patriarch of Jerusalem, invoked Aristotle's principle that energy flows from nature. Since there were two natures in Christ, one could not speak of one energy. However, Sophronius did agree that one could speak of Christ as a single Operator — one operating principle, i.e., one operating person. Sergius of Constantinople agreed with Sophronius's formula. The Pope also agreed, but suggested that instead of introducing new terms — one energy and one Operator — it was preferable to speak of one will in Christ.

The Patriarch of Constantinople, Sergius, was pleased with the Pope's suggestion and Heraclius issued a decree in 638, the *Ecthesis*, decreeing that the formula "one will" was to be used. But in 640 Maximus Confessor from North Africa objected. He was able to organize resistance to the *Ecthesis* in North Africa. (This series of events is now familiar: the Emperor and the Patriarch try to achieve a union with the Monophysites in the East only to face disunity from the West.)

The new Emperor, Constans (641-668), issued a decree forbidding all discussion of "energies" and "wills" in Christ. In this decree, Constans also abrogated the *Ecthesis*. Of course, few, if any, paid attention to the decree of Constans. Maximus turned to the new Pope, Martin I (649-655), who convened a synod at the Lateran in Rome. The synod rejected the *Ecthesis* as well as the decree of Constans. The synod taught that Christ had two wills and excommunicated the Patriarch of Constantinople, Sergius, and Sergius's successor, Pyrrhus, as well as Cyrus, the Patriarch of Alexandria.

The Emperor reacted by forcibly taking Pope Martin to Constantinople, where he was tried for treason because he had cooperated in allowing the Exarch of Ravenna, a Byzantine official in Italy, to declare himself Emperor. Pope Martin was sentenced to death, but this punishment was commuted to banishment. He never returned from exile, dying in 655. (At his trial, every attempt to mention the question of the nature of Christ, the real reason for the Pope's arrest, was quashed.)

Maximus was also arrested and tried. Suffering mutilation in the hands and tongue as well as exile, Maximus also died without returning. With the death of Constans in 668, the intensity of the discussion lessened. (Those who had initiated the discussion and had participated in the heat of the controversy had died.) In 680-681, after a preparatory synod in Rome, the Sixth Ecumenical Council was called at Constantinople and declared that in Christ there were two wills. The Monothelete heresy (one will in Christ) had ended.

It is interesting to note that the Monophysites were not in the least attracted to the discussion of one Operator. Once the formula of "one energy" was abandoned, the issue of nature disappeared (because, as Aristotle taught, energy flowed from nature). With the formula of "one energy" gone, it seemed to the Monophysites that they had prevailed. With the "one energy" language abandoned, they had no interest in the discussion. The only formula which would satisfy the Monophysites was their own formula: "one nature." They would not abandon this position.

Obviously, however, the formula of one will in Christ also points to one nature. One might ask the question: Why were the Monophysites not interested in the formula of one will, which also suggests one nature — the Monophysite position? What was the difference between the one-energy formula and the one-will formula, since both pointed to one nature?

The most likely reason that the Monophysites did not see in Pope Honorius's formula of "one will" a teaching they could accept is that Pope Honorius intended with his one-will formula to indicate that Christ's human will sought always the divine will, not that Christ only had one will. Since the human will and the divine will in Christ always acted in unison, the one-will formula did not necessarily mean that there was only one nature. Therefore, the Monophysites did not see in the Honorian formula anything that they could accept.

The formula of one will was not unambiguous. If will is taken to mean what Christ actually chose, there is only one will in Christ because in His actions, Christ's human will was always united to His divine will. In this sense, Honorius's formula is true. However, if will is taken to mean the power to choose, i.e., the ability to make choices, then Christ had two wills: one belonging to His divine nature and one to His human nature. In this sense, Honorius's formula of one will is not true. Honorius proposed the one-will formula in the orthodox sense, i.e., that will meant what Christ actually chose.

Maximus the Confessor, while admitting that Honorius's formula of one will (*una voluntas*) was orthodox (when properly understood), objected to those using the Greek terms for one will because he believed those using the Greek denied the existence of Christ's human will. The confusion results from a twofold problem which we have seen before in the discussions on the natures in Christ. First, there is an imprecision in the terms used. Does will mean the decision to act (in which case the one-will formula is orthodox because in Christ's acts His human will was always in perfect unity with the divine will) or does will mean the power by which we choose (in which case the formula of one will is not orthodox)? The second problem was one of translation from Latin to Greek (and Greek to Latin) and an inability on the part of both sides to understand the other completely. In Honorius's formula of one will (*una voluntas*), the Latin can easily mean one choice or one decision. However, Maximus understood the Greek formula used by Sergius and Heraclius (supposedly a translation of the Honorian *una voluntas*) to mean only one power to choose.

The confusion caused by differences between Latin and Greek terms — in addition to the imprecision of the terms themselves (in either language) — was a major factor in the entire controversy. In fact, the language problems probably played a greater role in this issue than in any of the previous ones we have discussed.

But there was more to it than doctrinal discussions. During this entire period, Islam was attacking the eastern provinces of the Empire. By 646, Syria, Palestine, and Egypt had fallen to the Muslims. Of course, these provinces were the strongholds of the Monophysites who were disaffected with the Empire. Relieved of the persecution of the Empire, they almost were pleased to be dealing with the Muslims, who might just give them better terms than the Emperor. Under these circumstances, why should they bother with discussions about the natures of Christ which had proven fruitless for almost two centuries?

Under Islam the Monophysites could exist as a tolerated minority without undue interference. After all, the Muslims would not care to engage in a discussion about the two natures in Christ, since they rejected Christ's divinity.

Monophysitism
This heresy taught that Christ's humanity was totally absorbed by His divinity so that His human nature disappeared into the "ocean" of the divinity. For the Monophysites, Christ had only one divine nature.

Monotheletism
This heresy taught that in Christ there was only one power to choose, Christ's divine will.

15

Iconoclasm

Influences on Iconoclasm

THE MONOPHYSITE CLAIM THAT THE HUMAN NATURE OF CHRIST WAS SUB-merged or absorbed in the divinity so that in Christ there was only one nature had serious implications, as we have seen. One of those implications was that the representation of Christ in paintings and sculptures was improper.

If Christ had no human nature, then obviously the depicting of His humanity, i.e., his physical features, was tantamount to a false teaching: the representation of the Lord's humanity in art conveyed the idea that Christ had a human nature.

This Monophysite argument was one of the defenses used for Iconoclasm by some elements of the eastern Church. Iconoclasm literally means image breaking, and it was a heretical movement which disturbed the Church in the eighth and ninth centuries.

Iconoclasts also drew support from the Nestorians. The Nestorians had divorced the divine and human in Christ. Some followers of Nestorius even posited two persons (*prosopa*) in Christ. Since an artist could not represent the divine (because it was not composed of matter) in art, a picture or sculpture only showed Christ's humanity and yet purported to represent the whole Christ. Christians were supposed to be devoted to images of the Lord because of the divine, yet the image could only represent the human. Therefore, from this Nestorian point of view, the cult of images should not be allowed.

The dualistic tradition represented by Manicheism and other heresies also opposed the representation of Christ and the saints in art. The dualistic heresies suggested that there were in fact two gods. One god had created the material world and was evil. The other god had created the spiritual world and was good. In the dualistic view, Christ's body and all other human bodies were evil, the creation of the anti-god.

Some of the dualistic heresies even went so far as to deny the existence of Christ's body. (In this view, they came very close to the Monophysite position.) Clearly, dualistic thought would resist the depiction of Christ's body (or, for that matter, any human body) in art. The art failed on two accounts: first, it attempted to represent something inherently evil, i.e., the human body; and second the art used paint and stone, material things, which were in themselves evil. From this point of view, it was not only representations of Christ which were questionable, it was any image of the human body — including images of the saints.

Another influence on Iconoclasm, at least at the beginning, could have been a heretical sect known as the Paulicians. The Paulicians, so named because they followed the "little Paul" (though we do not know who the "little Paul" was), were dualists. They believed in an anti-god who created the material world and the true God who created human souls. Only the true God should be adored.

They rejected the Old Testament (a Marcionite influence) and accepted the Gospels and some Epistles. They believed that Christ was an angel sent into the world by the true God.

The Paulicians rejected images, the sacraments (clearly because the sacraments used material things), and the hierarchy of the Church. A certain Constantine, calling himself Silvanus, seems to have been the first one to preach the Paulician doctrines in Armenia in the 650s. Through the Paulicians, who preceded Iconoclasm by about a half century, the dualistic tradition may have influenced the first Iconoclasts.

The Muslims also rejected images. Since the middle of the seventh century, Muslims were conquering some of the eastern provinces of the Empire and interacting with Christians. Since through this interaction each side became more acquainted with the ideas of the other, Islamic teachings against images have been cited as influences on Iconoclasm. There was even a decree by an Islamic Caliph forbidding Christians in his jurisdiction from employing images. (This decree was pretty much of a dead letter even at the time it was issued.)

There was a long tradition within the Church itself opposed to the use of images. Some believed the cult of images was a departure from the purity of worship in the early Church. Of course, it should be noted that even if the Christians of the first centuries wanted to have a cult of images, it would have been almost impossible because the Church suffered persecution. Without much of a chance for the Church to function openly with public worship and gatherings of the faithful, it was difficult to have a cult of images. The lack of churches through much of the first three centuries meant, to put it quite simply, that there was no place to put images permanently. Whatever was used in worship had to be moveable, taken to wherever the faithful were called to gather on a particular Sunday.

Some therefore saw in the cult of images a lack of simplicity and purity which had characterized the first Christian devotions. Further, there was a sense that images of Christ and the saints led to idolatry. After all, said some, *the* image of Christ was the Eucharist, His very own Body and Blood. Further, since it was impossible to represent holiness through art — and holiness was what was honored in the saints — images of the saints were at the very least questionable.

Whether reacting to Monophysite, Nestorian, dualist (Paulician), and Islamic influences or responding to the long-felt unease toward images, some bishops of Asia Minor (modern-day Turkey) approached the Patriarch of Constantinople, Germanus, in the 720s and asked him to limit or even forbid the cult of images. Germanus refused, but the bishops went home and in their own dioceses, under their own authority, began to remove the images and forbid their veneration.

Leo III

In 726, The Emperor Leo III (717-741), perhaps having seen the bishops when they visited Germanus or having heard of their actions against the images, urged the people to rid themselves of the images and icons. Leading the way, the Emperor had a popular icon of Christ removed from one of the gates of the palace. A riot followed and some of the soldiers who were carrying out imperial orders in trying to remove the icon of Christ were killed.

The Emperor did not institute a persecution, but he did punish those who had rioted against his wishes. Germanus, the Patriarch, discreetly disagreed with the imperial actions, but suffered no consequence as a result of his dissent from the imperial will.

Leo III was committed to the anti-image policy and, despite the opposition of the Patriarch, he issued a decree on January 17, 730, against the images.

This date represents the beginning of the official campaign against the images, the beginning of the heresy of Iconoclasm. Further, this decree of Leo represents an important departure from previous imperial policy. When Emperors in earlier centuries intervened in doctrinal matters, it was always to restore unity to the Church in the East and with Rome so that there would be unity in the Empire. Although Leo III might argue that the bishops of Asia Minor, who had instituted a policy against the images in their own dioceses, had raised a question creating disunity, there had been no significant reaction by the people to the bishops' policies. Nor had Iconoclasm spread beyond Asia Minor. In other words, at the time the Emperor issued his decree, there was no significant disunity in the Empire resulting from doctrinal disputes.

Certainly, there was no split in the Empire such as the Arians, Nestorians, and Monophysites had caused. In fact, it was Leo III's removal of the icon of Christ which caused the problem: a riot in Constantinople.

The decree against the images also alienated Rome and was one of the factors in the papacy's turn towards the Franks (culminating in the coronation of Charlemagne by Pope Leo III – not to be confused with the Emperor, Leo III – on Christmas day, 800). In other words, the Emperor had every reason not to bring this issue to a head if he were to follow previous imperial policy of trying to promote unity with Rome and internal unity in the East.

But the Church in the East was changing. The role of the Emperor more and more included responsibility for the Church, not just in secular matters like finances and buildings but also in doctrinal issues. The decree of Leo III against the images is a step in the development of Caesaro-papism in the East. (Caesaro-papism is the name for a political system in which the secular authority also governs the Church.)

Germanus, the Patriarch, continued to oppose the imperial policy and resigned. Unlike some of his predecessors and even Popes who had opposed Emperors in the past, Germanus was allowed to retire in peace. After the decree took effect, there was a persecution of those supporting images and some even died for their support of the images. With imperial policy making the claim that the images were idolatrous and applying pressure rather heavy-handedly, those supporting the images needed a rational defense for their position.

St. John Damascene provided the theological defense of the icons, arguing that opposition to them amounted to accepting the Monophysite position that Christ's humanity had been absorbed into His divinity or the dualistic position that matter was evil. Neither position represented the authentic tradition of the Church, and therefore the images were legitimate.

Constantine V

Leo III died in 741 and was succeeded by his son, Constantine V (741-775). Opposing the theological defense of the images offered by St. John Damascene, Constantine took the theological position that it was impossible to represent the divine in Christ and therefore images of the Lord should be forbidden. (Of course, in the past the Emperors had offered their theological positions and even forced them on councils as well as on the people under their jurisdiction.) With two rival theological positions proposed, only a council could settle the theological dispute.

A council of the Church was called in 754, but the Pope and the Patriarchs of Antioch, Jerusalem, and Alexandria were not present or even represented. Still, there were some 338 bishops who attended. The council began its deliberations in February and sat until August — a very long time for a council of antiquity. The decree of the council embraced Iconoclasm: it proscribed the making and honoring of icons. The only proper image of Christ was the Holy Eucharist. With these decrees, Iconoclasm now rested not just on an imperial decree, but on a teaching of the Church promulgated in a conciliar decree. Still, the council did not wish the wholesale destruction of existing works of art. Icons should not be destroyed, but at the same time, they should not be honored. They were to be considered art treasures, but not objects of devotion.

Most of the monks of the East were attached to the icons. The monks resisted the decree of the council — which, of course, was tantamount to resistance to the imperial will. Constantine reacted with increasing wrath against the monks opposed to his theological policies. The Emperor suppressed monasteries where there was opposition, forced the monks into the army, and turned their monasteries into barracks. Even torture, banishment, and the death penalty were inflicted on those defending the images. The full weight of the imperial persecution did not fall on the monks until about 764 — about ten years after the council. By this time, Constantine had become more and more extreme in his view, even forbidding relics and the very mention of the saints. This attack against relics and the invocation of the saints went beyond the initial opposition to the images.

Those suffering persecution, chiefly the monks, did not remain inactive in the face of the oppression. Pamphlets appeared defending the icons and attacking the Emperor. Of course, in the sees which had not been represented at the council of 754 (and did not acquiesce in its decrees) and where imperial power did not reach — Rome, Antioch, Jerusalem, and Alexandria — the campaign against the images did not have any effect. In these areas, the cult of the icons continued as before.

When Constantine died in 775, his son, Leo IV (775-780) succeeded him. Leo continued his father's iconoclastic policy, but did not enforce it to the same degree. He allowed the monks to return from exile and allowed the intercession of the saints, although towards the end of his short five-year reign, Leo began to take steps against those who cultivated image-worship in the imperial palace. But this attempt was short-lived.

Irene

When Leo died, his wife, Irene, became the regent for her underage son, Constantine VI. With Irene, not only did the persecution end, but there was active support for the images and for the monks. Monasteries were allowed to accept new vocations, and new monasteries were founded. Still, the decrees of the council of 754 remained in place. For there to be a restoration of the images, these decrees would have to be nullified by another council.

Irene and the new patriarch of Constantinople, Tarasius, approached Pope Hadrian (772-795) and suggested the calling of an ecumenical council of the Church to take up the question of the images. Pope Hadrian agreed to the council, sent a letter stating his faith in the cult of images of Christ and the saints, appointed two papal representatives to attend the council, and affirmed his right as Pope to ratify the decrees of the forthcoming council. Without the patriarchs of Antioch, Jerusalem, and Alexandria (they had been invited, but because they were under Muslim rule, they were unable to attend — although it seems that Antioch and Alexandria had at least some representatives present), the Second Council of Nicaea met on September 28, 787.

The council was attended by more than 300 bishops. At the beginning there were fewer, but the numbers grew as the council continued. Monks and abbots were also in attendance and were permitted to vote — an unusual provision which was probably granted to the monks because of their unfailing support of the images. Numerous bishops attending the council had been appointed while the imperial iconoclastic policy was in place. Many of these had submitted to the will of Leo III and Constantine V regarding the images. They could not all be excluded from the synod because their numbers were too great. There would have been hardly any bishops left to deliberate at the council! Therefore, only those who refused to renounce their previous iconoclastic views and policies were refused admittance to the council.

A few bishops who had persecuted those adhering to the images were deposed. At any rate, it is apparent from the deliberations of the council that the iconoclastic party did not make a very strong showing. Maintaining a silence, they did not even make their former arguments against the cult of the images. This silence was in spite of the call for a free exchange of ideas. Of course, as we have noted, Iconoclasm at its beginning was more the result of imperial thought (i.e., the ideas of Leo III) than it was the result of pastoral or theological reflections by bishops and theologians. Perhaps it is not surprising that the Iconoclasts did not have a spokesman: Leo III and Constantine V were both dead!

Unfortunately, those supporting the cult of images did not have an outstanding theologian who could argue for the images. In the place of sound theological thought, weight was given to legends and miracle stories. One might attribute this devotional aspect of the council to the influence of the monks, but the more important cause of this theological superficiality was the absence of an adequate theological spokesman in the party of those supporting the images.

St. John Damascene's writings might have offered some grounding for the cult of the images, but these were not used. The council did employ the letter of Pope Hadrian, which represented the fruit of western developments in support of the images. Given the weakness of those supporting the images, it was well that the Iconoclasts did not make much of a defense of their position!

In the end, the council condemned Iconoclasm as a heresy. It also held that images — those of Christ as well as of the saints — were to be venerated, but not adored. Adoration was reserved for the Trinity alone. Veneration was to be shown through candles and incense as marks of honor for the person (Christ or a saint) represented by the image.

The previous arguments about the impossibility of representing the divine in an image of Christ (Monophysite), or purporting to represent the whole Christ through an image of only His humanity (Nestorian), or about the intrinsic evil of all material things, were not explicitly addressed. However, by restoring the images, the fathers of the Second Council of Nicaea implicitly rejected these arguments.

Since dualism, Nestorianism, and the position of the Monophysites had all been previously rejected by councils of the Church, it was unnecessary to revisit old ground. The rejection of the arguments against the images was consistent with previous Church teachings.

Leo V

It might have appeared after the decrees of the Second Council of Nicaea that Iconoclasm was dead. In fact, the major theological arguments had been made and the decrees embraced the now traditional theology concerning Christ and the saints permitting the cult of the images. However, despite the theological resolution of the problem, there was a further attack on the images. Continuing Muslim incursions in the eastern provinces had forced refugees to flee. Many came to Constantinople, and many of these were Iconoclasts (because they came from the areas where Iconoclasm had been strongest). Further, they blamed Irene and other supporters of images for their difficulties because it was under the pro-image imperial administrations that the condition of the Empire had deteriorated and victories had been won by the Muslims. Of course, the support of the images had nothing to do with the success or lack of success of Byzantine armies. Nevertheless, the Empire had been blessed when Iconoclasm was flourishing and it had not been blessed when the images were restored. In the minds of many, the will of God was that the images be suppressed. (This is a clear case of the logical error of *post hoc ergo propter hoc* — one event happens after another event and people conclude that the first event caused the second without there being any necessary or logical connection between the two events.)

Some members of the upper classes as well as influential soldiers and ex-soldiers were also pushing for a suppression of the images. The Emperor had to deal with this political situation, and so in December 814, Leo V (813-820) removed the same image of Christ that his namesake predecessor, Leo III, had removed in 726. Leo's next move was to call a synod of bishops, which met at Easter. Many of the bishops who supported images were left off the invitation list!

The synod deposed the patriarch of Constantinople, a pro-image prelate, and reinstated Iconoclasm. The bishops present who did support images were literally beaten into submission.

Now Leo V had synodal decrees to reinforce his Iconoclasm. But while many images were destroyed as in the previous period of Iconoclasm (a great loss of sacred art), there was no widespread persecution. The theological defense of Iconoclasm in this second period was weak compared with the arguments used in the previous century.

The Iconoclasts defended their anti-image policy with reference to the Bible. Since there was no mention of a cult of images in the Scripture, they felt it must be wrong. Further, the Iconoclasts renewed the argument that an image could not represent holiness.

Others opposed to the Iconoclasts clearly demonstrated the long tradition of the cult of images in the Church, and they had no difficulty with the holiness argument because it was either dualistic or Monophysite. The pro-image position had the better side of the argument, but compared to the earlier period of Iconoclasm, the theological arguments on both sides were relatively weak. In spite of his iconoclastic tendencies, Leo V did not institute a widespread persecution. If those who supported the images kept a low profile, they were left undisturbed.

The opposition to the imperial policy came from the monks, but not to the same degree as in the first period of Iconoclasm. In this second period, there was stronger opposition to the imperial policy from the bishops. The pro-image bishops were in many cases former monks who had been advanced because of the strong stand they had taken.

The monasteries were therefore deprived of their most vehement pro-image leaders and were (in comparison to the first period of Iconoclasm) weaker in their support of the images than previously.

Leo V was assassinated in 820 and was succeeded by Michael II (820-

829), who ended the mild persecution and allowed those exiled to return, but he continued the iconoclastic policy of his predecessor. Still, he desired unity and issued a decree forbidding discussion of the whole issue of the images — which, of course, was observed by no one.

However, Michael was not able to devote much attention to the question of the images. His reign was troubled by the revolt of Thomas the Slav, who had himself crowned Emperor by the patriarch of Antioch and who was even able to lay siege to Constantinople. Although Thomas was allied with the Muslims, Michael was able to suppress the revolt. (It should be noted that through this alliance with a disaffected Byzantine, the Muslims were again drawn into a struggle with Byzantium and were able to do some harm to the Empire.)

At Michael II's death in 829, his son, Theophilus (829-842), became Emperor. Under Theophilus and the iconoclastic patriarch of Constantinople, John VII (837-843), persecution of those supporting images intensified, especially against those monks who supported the images. Still, it seems that the campaign against the images was not as important an imperial policy under Theophilus as it had been under Leo III and Constantine V because the Empress, who apparently supported the images and had a personal attachment to some of them, was allowed to retain them.

Michael III

With the death of Theophilus in 842, the images were restored. The new Emperor, Michael III (842-867), was only three, and his mother, the former Empress (wife of Theophilus) became regent, supporting the cult of the images. More importantly, her advisor, Theoctistus, was very much in favor of the images, and he was able to implement a program favorable to the icons. The patriarch of Constantinople, John, abdicated and a new patriarch, Methodius, was appointed. A synod met in 843 and reaffirmed the veneration of images.

After 843 Iconoclasm as imperial policy and widespread movement was never to trouble the eastern Church again. It died somewhat abruptly. One reason for its death is that in the second period of Iconoclasm (814-843) the Empire suffered some reverses. In other words, the political argument used in favor of Iconoclasm at the beginning of the second period was turned against the Iconoclasts at the end of the period.

The Iconoclasts did not seem entirely convinced of their own policy, because it was not pursued vigorously. Another reason for the demise of Iconoclasm was that in the second period, it had been strongly influenced by Paulicians, Islamic as well as Jewish elements, and Monophysites. These influences were represented at the imperial court and were resented as a foreign influence.

In the 840s, there was an attempt to excise this foreign element from the court and from the Byzantine world. Further, the victory for the images can be partially attributed to the weak theological defense of Iconoclasm offered in the second period on the one hand and the better theological arguments of the supporters of images on the other. In addition, the pro-image party was more organized and united in this second iconoclastic period than in the first one. Further, it had the support of the Pope. Its members, especially the monks, had experienced a leadership role and had a certain confidence in themselves gleaned from experience. In other words, they were veterans who knew how to fight and win.

Finally, the pro-image party had also won a certain esteem and respect from the people through its suffering in the persecutions, especially in the first period, and through its initial victory in the first restoration of the icons in 787.

Effect of Iconoclasm: Separation of East and West

The struggle with the Iconoclasts clarified a very important doctrine of the Church: images are venerated, and only God is adored. But the initial struggle between 726 and 787 was one of the factors that turned the West away from the East.

As early as 751 (that is, in the midst of the first iconoclastic period), Pepin the Short, the Mayor of the Palace of the Franks, had asked the Pope to allow him to depose the last descendant of Clovis and assume the kingship.

In 754, the Pope anointed Pepin substituting the sanction of the Church for the lack of royal blood in Pepin's Carolingian line. Iconoclasm was one of the factors influencing the papacy to look away from the East and towards the Carolingians. Even though in 787, the Second Council of Nicaea had involved the West and the Papacy in its decrees, the trend towards a greater and greater separation of the two branches of the Church was clear.

When Charlemagne was crowned Holy Roman Emperor on Christmas Day 800 by Pope Leo III (795-816), the break between East and West became more acute. One sign of the separation is that lack of involvement of the Papacy in the decrees of the synod of 843. Of course, at this time in the West, there were internal wars and external attacks (from the Muslims, Vikings, and Magyars), but in 843, there was not even an attempt made in the East to involve the Pope or western bishops in their decisions.

With the Papacy allied with the Carolingians and the eastern patriarchies under Muslim rule, Constantinople turned in on itself attempting to settle its own problems. Iconoclasm was a stepping stone in the gradual separation of the "two lungs" of the Church—a separation which would become permanent after 1054.

Iconoclasm
This heresy taught that it was contrary to the faith to represent Christ and the saints in art because it was impossible to show Christ's divinity or the saints' holiness.

Conclusion to Part II

EXCEPTING ICONOCLASM, DONATISM, AND PELAGIANISM, THE HERESIES DIS-
cussed in this lengthy part were on the question of the Incarnation: Was
Jesus "God from God, light from light, true God from true God, begotten,
not made, one in Being with the Father," as the Nicene Creed affirmed, or
not? If He was not (the heretical point of view), then reconciling this belief
with the Redemption and other teachings of the Gospel was essential. This
was one of the burdens felt by those holding the heretical positions.

If Christ was what the Nicene Creed proclaimed Him to be, then the
question arose: how is He both human and divine? By the end of the period
discussed in this part, the Church had arrived at a formula which continues
today to represent the belief of the Church, i.e., that Christ is only one
Person, the second Person of the Trinity, God the Son, Who possessed two
natures, the divine nature from all eternity and a human nature assumed in
time.

The Church had also rejected certain implications of the heretical
positions, like Iconoclasm. While others throughout history would question the union of the divine and human in Christ, the answers given by the
Church would always be those given in the years between 325 and 843. As
should be obvious to the reader, the answers did not come easily!

PART III

Sacraments and Grace: Heresies from 843 to 1789

We believe in the Holy Spirit, the Lord, the giver of life,
who proceeds from the Father and the Son.
With the Father and the Son he is worshiped and glorified.
He has spoken through the prophets.

IT IS NOT SURPRISING THAT FOLLOWING THE DIFFICULTIES REGARDING THE Incarnation there would be questions concerning the sacraments and the mystery of grace.

After the questions regarding the Trinity — in the first three centuries — and the questions regarding the mystery of the incarnate Christ — in the next period, 325-843 — there were questions regarding the activity of the Holy Spirit. The progression of issues should not have been unexpected because the chronological order of issues followed the order of the Nicene Creed — the Trinity, the Incarnation, and the activity of the Holy Spirit in the world. And there was a logical order to the questions. The mystery of the Trinity needed to be clarified before the activity of the Son (Redemption through the Incarnation) and the Holy Spirit (sanctification through the gift of grace in the sacraments) could be put in proper perspective.

Further, the work of the Holy Spirit (sanctification) clearly depends on the work of Christ, and so the questions regarding the Incarnation had to be settled before the work of the Holy Spirit could be considered. Therefore, after the questions about the Trinity and the Incarnation, there arose in the period between 843 and 1789 questions regarding the mystery of the sacraments and grace. The Eucharist, the "source and summit" of the Christian life (according to the well-known phrase from the Second Vatican Council), was the first sacrament to be discussed in the 843-1789 period.

16

Debating the Holy Eucharist

Ninth-Century Eucharistic Discussions

IN THE FATHERS OF THE CHURCH, THERE WERE TWO TRADITIONS OF THOUGHT regarding the Holy Eucharist. Following the thought of St. Ambrose (c. 340-397) there was an emphasis on the change of the bread and wine into the body and blood of Our Lord. Those in the tradition of St. Augustine (354-430) emphasized the Holy Eucharist as a sacrament — as an outward sign, a symbol.

These two positions are not contradictory, but rather complementary, because the Holy Eucharist is simultaneously symbol — outward sign or sacrament — and truly the body and blood of Our Lord. However, when this issue first arose in the ninth century, neither the ideas nor the vocabulary existed to make the accurate distinctions necessary to explain the Eucharist both as symbol and reality.

Eventually, by the thirteenth century, the ideas and vocabulary necessary for a coherent theology of the Eucharist had been developed so that St. Thomas Aquinas (1225-1274) was able to construct a theology of the Eucharist synthesizing the two traditions represented by St. Ambrose and St. Augustine.

In the meantime, however, people struggled. In the mid-ninth century, Paschasius Radbertus (786-860), abbot of Corbie, wrote a treatise on the Eucharist. He believed the Eucharist to be in all respects the same body of Christ which was born of Mary, died on the cross, and rose from the dead. In other words, Radbertus overemphasized the real presence to the point that the sacramental presence of Christ was identical in every way to His physical presence on earth.

Radbertus's work did not attract much attention at first because he wrote it to explain the Eucharist to his fellow monks. However, when he sent it to Charles the Bald (840-877), one of the grandsons of Charlemagne

(768-814) and ruler of the west Franks (who lived mostly in what is modern-day France), it elicited a response from Rhabanus Maurus and the Saxon monk Gottschalk.

Gottshalk was a student of Ratramnus, also a monk. Rhabanus Maurus, Gottschalk, and Ratramnus stressed more the sacramental meaning of the Eucharist. Rhabanus Maurus taught that the Eucharist united all those who took communion with Christ into one body of faith, a sacramental effect of the Eucharist. Gottschalk argued that the presence of Christ in the Eucharist was like the union of the two natures in Christ so that the outward appearances of bread and wine in the sacrament were as important as Christ's presence.

Ratramnus argued against Radbertus that the Eucharist was not the same body of Christ which was born, suffered, died, and rose from the dead. He suggested that Christ's presence in the Eucharist was somewhat like the working of the Holy Spirit through the baptismal waters. Clearly, this view emphasizes the sacramental nature of the Eucharist if only because the image used is that of another sacrament.

The works of Radbertus, Rhabanus Maurus, Gottschalk, and Ratramnus are perhaps interesting in themselves to a historian, but to few others. Even in the ninth century, there was a very, very small circle of people who followed these discussions. (The number was small even for that world, when very few people could read or write.) It should be noted that none of the ideas proposed by any of these four authors was called into question by any synod or council. In other words, none of these ideas was judged to be contrary to the faith. Further, there was no widespread movement defending and embracing any of these ideas. There was no imperial pressure to accept or reject the teachings of any of these authors. In effect, the work of these four theologians on the Eucharist represents proposals which today might be made in a professional academic journal. However, since some of these ideas found their way into later discussions about the Eucharist, they do have an importance beyond their own time.

Berengar and Lanfranc

Two centuries later, there was a controversy between Berengar of Tours and Lanfranc. Berengar was the master at the cathedral school in Tours from about 1030 until he died in 1088. Lanfranc was born in the town of

Pavia in Italy about 1010 and died as the archbishop of Canterbury (in England) in 1089. During his long life, Lanfranc studied law in Italy, probably at Pavia, and became a lawyer. He traveled north of the Alps and taught at Avranches and then entered the monastery of Bec, where he founded a school. He entered the controversy with Berengar while at Bec. In 1070, William the Conqueror nominated him to be the archbishop of Canterbury.

Berengar began the controversy about 1047 by questioning the teachings of Paschasius Radbertus, the Carolingian theologian representing the realist position. Radbertus's teaching had come to be the dominant viewpoint on the Eucharist in the intervening centuries. Admittedly, Radbertus's formulation that the Eucharistic body of the Lord was in all ways identical to His physical body was not nuanced at all. Berengar opposed the ultrarealism of Radbertus and suggested that after the consecration the substance of the bread and the substance of the wine remain, but the body and blood of Christ are also truly present —however, Christ's body and blood are present only in a spiritual or intellectual sense.

After he made his view known, Berengar's teaching on the Eucharist was condemned by three different synods held in 1050 and 1051. The three synods were held at Rome, Vercelli (an Italian town), and Paris. Pope Leo IX (1049-1054) was present at the Roman synod and confirmed the judgment against Berengar.

At another meeting at Tours (in France) in 1054, the papal representative (a legate of the pope), Hildebrand — the future Pope Gregory VII (1073-1085) — accepted Berengar's formulaton. Hildebrand seems to have found Berengar's affirmation that Jesus' body and blood were truly present in the Eucharist as sufficiently in accord with the doctrine of the Church. The question of how Jesus' body and blood were present seems to have been avoided at this meeting. The previous synods had difficulty with Berengar's idea that Jesus' body and blood were spiritually present, but in 1054 the mode of the presence of Jesus' body and blood does not seem to have been discussed.

In any event, Berengar's affirmation of the presence of Christ's body and blood in the Eucharist was judged sufficiently orthodox. However, this did not end the difficulties. At a Roman synod held in 1059 in the presence of the Pope, Berengar was asked to sign a statement of faith which followed the realist tradition of Radbertus. Berengar signed the statement, but later repudiated it.

In the following years, Berengar moved away from his initial belief that the body and blood of Christ were spiritually present. Instead, he suggested that the bread and wine remained bread and wine (the same thing he had said in his earlier formulation), but that after the consecration, the bread and wine became the sacrament of Christ's body and blood, yet one could not speak of the presence of Christ's body and blood in the Eucharist. Berengar's viewpoint was the result of the application of the "old logic" to the words of consecration: "This is my body" and "This is the cup of my blood."

The "Old Logic"

The "old logic" is the name given to the rediscovery of two works of Aristotle and one each of Cicero and Porphyry as translated by Boethius (480-524). Gerbert of Rheims (Pope Sylvester II, d. 1003) was master of the cathedral school in Rheims and was dissatisfied with the manuals of logic that had been in use since Carolingian times. Turning to the translations of Boethius (480-524), Gerbert introduced into the schools of the late tenth and eleventh century the study of systematic logic as found in two works of Aristotle and the ones by Cicero and Porphyry.

Gerbert was the first man since Boethius to master and understand these works. Gerbert's work began the development which would lead to the twelfth century renaissance in learning. His mastery of the works of Aristotle available to him began the trend in theology and other fields which would find its highest development in the flowering of learning during the twelfth and thirteenth centuries.

After retracting his statement made in 1059, Berengar applied the "old logic" to the problem of the presence of Christ in the Eucharist. Berengar argued that the word "This" in the words of consecration that the priest says at Mass to change the bread and wine into the body and blood of the Lord — "This is my body" and "This is the cup of my blood" — refers to the bread and to the wine.

Since the word "This" refers to the bread and the wine, the bread and the wine must be present. Berengar was applying the new methods of dialectic (logic and careful reading of texts) to matters of the faith. "This" must mean what it says. Therefore, the bread remains bread and the wine remains wine. That is what the Lord meant when He said, "This is my body" and "This is the cup of my blood." Of course, without knowledge of Aristotle's complete system, Berengar did not fully understand the terms he was using.

The Church always taught and teaches that the bread and wine are no longer bread and wine after the consecration. The bread and wine disappear and the body and blood of Christ are present. The outward appearances of bread and wine are present, but bread and wine are not present. (Of course, we must remember that the language we use is the fruit of centuries of reflection and work. Berengar and Lanfranc did not have the precise language we do, at least not until the very last years of the controversy.)

Lanfranc opposed Berengar's interpretation. Also using dialectic and logic, Lanfranc employed the distinctions between substance (what a thing is in itself) and accident (what a thing looks like). We might say that substance is the "inside" of things and accident (or appearances) is the "outside." Color, weight, and shape are all appearances (or accidents) — the outside. Bread and wine, human being, and grass are all substances — the inside. By introducing these distinctions, Lanfranc began the development of the Church's understanding of the Eucharist that resulted in the standard teaching on the Eucharist used today.

Berengar's essential mistake was to presume that the language which expressed the mysteries of the faith meant exactly what the words said, nothing more and nothing less. In this view, the dialectical analysis of the words and of the sentences would reveal the meaning. In revealing the meaning of the words, one would know the mystery of the faith expressed by the words. Therefore, reason using the dialectical method would reveal all the mysteries.

Berengar (and others after him) failed to note that the mysteries of the faith could not be expressed fully in human language. Words are simply signs for our thoughts. Since human thought can never fully comprehend the mysteries of God, words that express those thoughts can never fully contain the mysteries of the faith. This key mistake led Berengar to deny that any mysteries exist. He believed that all the mysteries of the faith could be explained if reason were used properly.

Further, Berengar rejected any argument from authority. He rejected the authority of the Church and the authority of the Scriptures. Arguments from authority were an affront to human reason. (Of course, the error Berengar makes is thinking that all knowledge comes through our own direct experience. Through our reason, we know things, yet how we come to know things differs. Some things we know through our own experiences. Other things we know because God teaches them to us through the Church and the Scriptures.)

Lanfranc did not make the mistakes Berengar made. First of all, he acknowledged that words expressing the faith did not completely contain the mysteries. He was therefore content not to try to understand everything. Second, he did not have a problem with the authority of the Church.

Still, far from rejecting the new intellectual tools represented by the "old logic," Lanfranc accepted the use of dialectic and logic. Lanfranc was as schooled as Berengar and knew the tools of dialectic. The difference between the two men was not that one rejected reason and the other embraced it. Both used reason in the tradition of Gerbert. However, they used it differently.

Substance and Accident

One difference was that the two understood the terms "substance" and "accident" in different ways. (However, Lanfranc, like Berengar, did not have a complete understanding of the Aristotelian terms he was using. Of course, this lack makes Lanfranc's accomplishment in suggesting terms to use in a theological discussion of the Eucharist all the more impressive.) Another difference was the emphasis each placed on different elements of dialectics. For Berengar, the analysis of words, such as the word, "This," was of much more importance than for Lanfranc.

Finally, in 1079, Pope Gregory VII, the former Hildebrand who had accepted Berengar's position on the Eucharist at Tours in 1054, summoned Berengar to Rome for another synod and asked him to sign a statement of faith on the Eucharist which affirmed that at Mass the bread and wine were substantially converted into the body and blood of Christ. Thus, the statement made use of some of the ideas of the "old logic" and while remaining in the realist tradition of Radbertus, it avoided his ultra-realism. Berengar submitted and the controversy ended. Fundamentally, the Church had accepted Lanfranc's formulation and, except for some later refinements, the Church continues to teach the mystery of the Eucharist in the terms Lanfranc first suggested.

Lanfranc was a monk and was much more willing to accept arguments from authority than Berengar was. In this regard, Lanfranc reflects the monastic and more conservative tradition. Berengar was the intellectual grandson of Gerbert (he was taught at Chartres by Fulbert of Chartres — Fulbert had been a student of Gerbert's) and was a master at Tours. Coming from the cathedral-school tradition, he was much more ready to rely exclusively on the use of reason and to reject authority than Lanfranc. Further, in the controversy the "old logic" (the fruit of Gerbert's work) played a very important role, even though both Lanfranc and Berengar were hampered because the "old logic" only gave a foretaste of Aristotle's thought.

More of Aristotle's thought would be discovered during the next 150 years. Still, even with the few tools available, a new understanding of the Eucharist emerged. This view immensely enriched the Church.

Effects of the Berengar-Lanfranc Controversy

The controversy between Berengar and Lanfranc cannot be compared in its effects to the ancient heresies of Arianism, Nestorianism, and Monophysitism. Those ancient heresies rocked the Church for decades and caused countless disruptions in the life of the Church and even in civil society. The eleventh-century Eucharistic controversy did not affect very many people. However, the Berengar-Lanfranc difficulties had greater effects than the debate on the Eucharist between Radbertus, on the one side, and Gottschalk, Maurus, and Ratramnus on the other. The difference lies in the fact that Berengar was judged a number of times to be out of step with the teaching of the Church. In the end, in a definitive way, the Church rejected his view of the Eucharist. This decision by the Church qualifies his views as heretical. However, unlike other intellectuals who have suggested false teachings, Berengar, in the end, accepted the judgment of the Church.

The controversy arose out of an effort to understand the Eucharist in a more systematic way by applying newly available intellectual tools. Without such an effort, the Church would never have been able to come to a better understanding of its teaching. What hampered Berengar (and to a certain extent, Lanfranc) was that the intellectual tools they had were barely adequate for what they were trying to do. Thus, Berengar's efforts led to a net gain for the Church, and he himself is to be judged not so much by the false ideas he proposed as by his acceptance of the judgment of the Church in 1079.

Hildebrand (Pope Gregory VII)

It is interesting to note the activity of Hildebrand (Pope Gregory VII) in the controversy between Berengar and Lanfranc. Best known to history as the protagonist in the famous Investiture struggle with the Holy Roman Emperor, Henry IV (1056-1106), he is usually portrayed as an unbending defender of papal privileges. But in the Eucharistic dispute, Hildebrand treated Berengar with what seems to be extraordinary patience and kindness, accepting Berengar's statement of faith in 1054 and agreeing to a formula of the faith which Berengar could accept in 1079.

Far from unyielding or rigid, Pope Gregory VII emerges on the Eucharistic issue as a flexible figure who sympathizes with the efforts of Berengar to find a formula which would maintain the faith and yet not lean too far towards the realist position. Whenever a discussion of Pope Gregory VII arises, his stance on the Eucharistic controversy of the mid-eleventh century should be remembered.

Berengar's Eucharistic Heresy

This heresy held that Christ's body and blood were not truly present in the Eucharist, that the Eucharist is only the sacrament (sign) of Christ's body and blood.

17

The Cathars

Medieval Dualism

WHILE NO ONE IN THE EUCHARISTIC CONTROVERSY OF THE ELEVENTH CEN-
tury thought that matter was evil, this issue re-surfaced in the twelfth and
early thirteenth centuries through the Catharist heresy. Resurrecting the
dualist tradition represented by the Manichees and others, the Cathars were
described in a letter written by a certain Everwin, provost of Steinfeld (which
is near Cologne), to St. Bernard of Clairvaux (d. 1153) in 1143. Everwin's
letter is the first mention of the Cathars known to history. Twenty years
later, in 1163, Eckbert of Schoau preached a series of sermons against the
Cathars and described their beliefs.

The Cathars held that there were two gods: a god of light or truth and
a god of darkness or error. The god of light was the Christian God and was
identified with the New Testament. The god of darkness was the evil god
and was identified with the Old Testament. There was a constant struggle
between these two gods which was played out on earth through the un-
ceasing conflict between spirit and matter. All matter had its origin in the
god of darkness and was evil while all spiritual entities were associated with
the god of light and were good. Spirit and matter, good and evil, were
opposed to each other. Of course, the human body, as matter, was evil. But
the human soul, a spiritual entity, was good. Soul and body were therefore
in opposition to one another, and for good to win, evil (i.e., the body) had
to lose. The purpose of life, for the Cathars, was to free the spirit from
matter, that is, free the soul from the body.

As a result of the Catharist belief that physical bodies were evil, the
Cathars believed that sexual intercourse was especially evil. First of all, this
act amounted to the union of two physical bodies, each of which were evil
in themselves. The physical union only united two evils, creating a third
and greater evil. Second, this union resulted in new human life, i.e., an-

other body—another evil—in the world. Therefore, sexual intercourse was especially to be avoided. But this view of the physical expression of love was extended by the Cathars to animals.

Logically, if all physical life was evil because it was composed of matter, animals were evil as well. Since animals were the result of a sexual union, even the sexual union in animals was evil. Since practice should follow belief, the Cathars taught that one should abstain from all foods which resulted from a sexual union. Not marrying and not eating meat or milk (given through a living body which came into the world through a sexual union) represented a very austere and difficult life. It could not be lived by everyone.

Of course, the sacraments were also evil because they employed material things, e.g., water, bread and wine, oil. The Cathars substituted the laying on of hands for the physical signs of the sacraments. (Of course, there is an inconsistency here. If the body is evil, how can the laying on of hands be good? But the Cathars could not totally reject the sacramental system of the Church if they hoped to attract people to their sect.)

Since the Church promoted the sacraments and was in the world while not trying to free itself from the world, the Church in the eyes of the Cathars was the agent of the god of evil! Of course, the Cathars rejected the Incarnation. Christ only seemed to have a human body. After all, if He is God the Son — the Son of the god of light — how could He possibly have united Himself with evil — with matter in the form of a human body? The Cathars rejected images of Christ or the saints and the use of vestments (because vestments were material things and therefore were evil). The use of the crucifix was especially offensive to the Cathars because these images suggested that suffering in the body was somehow redemptive. How could that possibly be true (because the body was in itself an evil thing and nothing good can come from evil)?

Perfect and Hearers

As a result of the austere demands of the Cathars, they were divided into the perfect and the hearers. The perfect were the pure ones. (In fact, the name "Cathar" comes from the Greek term for the pure, *katharoi*.) The perfect abstained from meat and milk and lived as celibates. The hearers were those who were not bound to strict adherence to the prohibitions on food and marriage. They lived in ordinary society, but aspired to the state of the perfect.

One became perfect through the laying on of hands, which was called the *consolamentum* (consolation). Once the *consolamentum* was received, the new member of the perfect was bound absolutely to live out the beliefs of the Cathars. There was no forgiveness for any deviations from the rules. If one did fall, one could receive the *consolamentum* again, but in this case, the perfect one did not have any claim on the hearers. For these reasons, the *consolamentum* was often not received until a hearer was close to death.

A later development found a solution to any weakness in someone who had just received the *consolamentum*. If there were doubts that a new perfect one could live up to the demands of his new position, his friends would ceremonially kill him through suffocation. This was called the *endura*. The hearers thought of themselves as followers of the perfect and were required to receive any of the perfect (at least those who had not fallen and received the *consolamentum* a second time) who might be visiting and to offer them a solemn reverence called the *melioramentum*.

Origins of the Cathars

The origin of the Cathars is not entirely known. However, the notion of two gods, one the god of evil and the other the god of good, is a simplification of Christianity. It also has the advantage of explaining the origin of evil. That dualism would occur to people in the twelfth century is not totally implausible. The twelfth century in Europe was an age of population growth and expanding agricultural production. These developments allowed a growth of schools. The students and teachers in the new schools were intellectually stimulated by some works of Aristotle, previously unknown in medieval Europe, which arrived via Arabic Spain in Latin translations. There were developments in art and architecture and in other fields as well. In fact, historians speak of the renaissance of the twelfth century.

It is in this cultural context that new ideas were often welcomed. Some enthusiastic-minded men created genuine, long-lasting beneficial communities. But there were others who preached various versions of the Gospel which were in fact contrary to the faith and even dangerous. At times, it was difficult to tell the difference between the saint and the overly enthusiastic but wrong-headed individual. In the light of the intellectual and religious ferment in twelfth-century European culture, it is not surprising that some-one might suggest that there were two gods: a god of good and a god of evil.

However, there seem to have been some dualistic influences on twelfth-century Europe from the East. Dualistic traditions had survived in Bulgaria, and through the increasing trade of the twelfth century, these traditions could have found their way westward and influenced medieval Europe. Further, in the middle of the twelfth century, the Byzantine Empire began a persecution against certain dualistic ideas, and many of the people who accepted these ideas emigrated westward to Europe. With the crusades and especially the crusader states in the Holy Land (founded after the First Crusade of 1095), there was more interchange between Europe and the East, and this could have been the conduit for the conveyance of the eastern dualistic ideas to the West. Naturally, if the twelfth-century intellectual and religious ferment in Europe did not produce the dualistic ideas, still that same culture would have been able to receive these ideas with a certain excited curiosity.

The Church and the Cathars

It was difficult for the twelfth-century Church to react to movements contrary to the Gospel. The Gregorian reform movement of the late eleventh century had emphasized that the Church should have priests and bishops who were not tainted with simony. This goal, laudable in itself, gave people a reason to distrust the institutional Church. If one had a problem with a particular bishop or priest, it was possible now not to follow his lead with the cry that he was not holy or was guilty of this or that breach of canon law.

The goal of the Gregorian reform — to strengthen the institutional Church by insisting that its clerics follow certain rules — led to the use of those rules (even when there had been no violation) against the clergy, especially the higher clergy. With the widespread distrust of the bishops, it was difficult for the institutional Church to discipline those who were promoting notions contrary to the Gospel.

Coupled with this problem, the institutional Church had not yet established a canonical procedure for the correction of heretics. At the same time there was the phenomenal growth in religious orders, such as the Cistercians, Premonstratensians, Carthusians, and a host of others. The combination of a religious reform movement expressed through the foundation of numerous new orders and a distrust of the hierarchy as the (unintended) legacy of the Gregorian reform allowed numerous individuals who were enthusiastic about religious matters to preach their own versions of Christianity. Without significant opposton from the Church, the Cathar movement grew. Whether indigenous to Europe or arriving via eastern influences (or a combination of both), by the 1160s the dualism of the Cathars was widespread in Europe.

Geographical Dispersion of Cathars

By the 1160s the Catharist heresy had followers in Germany (near Cologne), in France (especially southern France), in Italy, and even in England. The numbers and the geographical diversity of the Catharist heresy distinguish it from other heretical ideas promoted by individual clergy who were never able to attract many followers, like Henry of Lausanne (d. c. 1145) and Peter of Bruis (d. c. 1139). (Henry and Peter both show that the religious and intellectual ferment of the twelfth century permitted, and to a certain extent welcomed, new, even extravagant, ideas.)

The greatest number of Cathars lived in southern France and in Lombardy. In the south of France, they were called the Albigensians. This name was taken from the town of Albi, where the Cathars were very numerous. In Lombardy, northern Italy, they were known as *Patarini*. (It is interesting to note that the name *Patarini* was the one used for the allies of Pope Gregory VII in Lombardy during the last quarter of the eleventh century. However, there does not seem to be a connection between the earlier movement and the Cathars.)

In Lombardy and in southern France, the Cathars had achieved the status of an organized religion challenging the Church. One Cisterican remarked that the Catharist heresy had infected over a thousand cities and that it could have misled the faithful in all of Europe had it been allowed to grow and develop. In other words, the Cathars were a definitive threat to the Church. Nothing comparable to the Cathars had rocked the Church since the Iconoclasts in the eighth and ninth centuries.

Pope Innocent III

Unless the Church was to concede large geographical areas as well as souls to the Catharist heresy, an active campaign against its errors was essential. Pope Innocent III (1198-1216) was adamant against heresy. For him heresy was an attack against the Church equivalent to the crime of treason against civil government. A heretic was a Christian who was disloyal to the Church, the institution which had imparted to the heretic the truth and the means to live according to the truth. The heretic, in accepting the gifts of the Church, had bound himself to the Church just as a citizen had bound himself to the state from which he accepted protection and other benefits. Heresy, like treason, was ingratitude. But more than that, heresy was the acceptance of untruth, of lies. In a sense, the heretic had allied himself with the prince of liars, the devil, the enemy of the Church. Like the treasonous citizen who allied himself with the enemies of the state, the heretic had thrown in his lot with the enemy of the Church, the devil, even if the heretic did not fully realize what he was doing.

Pope Innocent III therefore sanctioned the same penalties against heretics as the state imposed for those who committed treason: confiscation of property and disinheritance of offspring. Of course, the Church did not have the means to impose these penalties, but the state did. Therefore, Innocent looked to the Catholic princes to enforce the penalties against heretics. Despite these strong views, Pope Innocent III also believed that the best approach to heretics was to try to persuade them of the truth they had abandoned. Therefore, Innocent's first effort toward the Albigensians was to convey to them the truth they had rejected, with the hope that they might be persuaded to abandon their errors and again embrace the Gospel as preached by the Church.

The preaching mission to the Albigensians began when Bishop Diego of Osma (Spain) was sent to southern France together with a young companion, an Augustinian canon, Dominic of Caleruega, in 1207. The bishop had an interesting idea: he suggested that he and Dominic should travel among the Albigensians very simply attired. In other words, they should appear to be as simple and pure as the pure ones.

The bishop and the Augustinian canon were joined by a group of Cistercians. The mission had some success converting some of the Albigensians. The work continued through the summer of 1207 but could not be extended beyond that time because the bishop and the Cistercians needed to return to their diocese and monasteries, respectively. Dominic, however, continued the work, but he was alone, and there is no question that the Cathars were still a significant force in the south of France. Even Dominic, working alone, was not able to win enough converts to substantially weaken the Cathar dominance.

Given Pope Innocent's views on heretics, there was no question that if gentle persuasion and preaching did not significantly alter the situation in the south of France harsher measures would be used. After asking the French king, Philip Augustus (1180-1223), to eliminate heretics from his realm in 1204 and 1205, he repeated the request in 1207. (Obviously Innocent, while willing to try the preaching mission, had prepared for its failure through his requests to Philip.)

The Crusade Against the Cathars

The difficulties in southern France were exacerbated by the murder of the papal legate, Peter of Castelnau, in 1208. Pope Innocent offered to those who would campaign against the Albigensians the same privileges and exemptions granted to those who fought in the crusades against the infidel in the Holy Land. In other words, Innocent III launched a crusade against the Albigensians. This was the first time that a papally sanctioned crusade had been used against Christians, even heretical Christians. Even though King Philip Augustus continued to resist the blandishments of Innocent, a sufficient number of lesser nobility and even bishops agreed to participate in the crusade.

The crusade began in 1209. Beziers and Carcassone, both towns in the south of France, fell in that year. Many of the inhabitants of Beziers were massacred, and the citizens of Carcassone were forced to flee the city. Raymond VI of Toulouse, accused of at least sympathizing with the Cathars (although this was probably not true), was under some difficulty after the fall of Beziers and Carcassone. He had joined the crusade against the Albigensians after the murder of Peter of Castelnau, but with the influx of Cathars from Carcassone and Beziers into his lands, it was difficult for him to participate in their suppression.

Simon of Montfort became the governor of the lands conquered (Carcassone and Beziers, among other holdings) as well as the champion of the Catholics against the Albigensians. With Raymond's somewhat lukewarm stance towards the effort to suppress the Albigensians, a war broke out between Simon and Raymond. Raymond was defeated in 1213 at the battle of Muret by Simon, even though Simon had the smaller force. By 1215, Simon held most of Toulouse, formerly Raymond's lands, as well as Beziers, Carcassone, and other holdings near those cities.

Two abbots traveling with the crusade had been made bishops of Narbonne and Carcassone. Another Catholic had been appointed bishop of Toulouse. A persecution of the Cathars was launched, especially of the perfect ones. In Avignon in 1209, each parish was required to have a priest and at least two laymen who had taken an oath to report heretics. Once reported, if the heretics persisted, they were subject to death by burning. At Minerve, Casses, and Lavaur, there were a number of perfect ones who were burned for their beliefs.

The persecution did not win over the majority of the people. In some respects, in fact, it hardened them in their resistance. Many non-Cathar Catholics were not willing to denounce fellow citizens as heretics. With this opposition and Simon's strained resources, he could not impose his rule throughout the region. Simon managed to control a few centers, but resistance to his rule was significant.

St. Dominic

To win over the people, it was necessary to sponsor a preaching mission — a mission of gentle persuasion that would demonstrate why the ideas of the Cathars were contrary to the Gospel as revealed by Christ. Bishop Fulk, the Catholic bishop of Toulouse, found the person to undertake this mission: Dominic, the man who together with Bishop Diego of Osma had conducted the first preaching mission to the Albigensians in 1207.

Dominic came to Toulouse in 1215 to begin this second and much more extensive effort of preaching the Gospel. Of course, this mission saw the beginnings of the Order of Preachers, the Dominicans. (It is interesting that the Dominicans still have the charism of preaching the Gospel, carrying on the original work that Dominic pursued in the south of France in the thirteenth century. The initials of their order are still O.P., for Order of Preachers.)

The followers of Dominic not only preached the faith; they also lived it by example, not owning property and begging for their maintenance and sustenance. Together with the Franciscans, the Dominicans were the mendicants, the beggars. It was very important for the success of their mission to live simply so that they could be authentic witnesses to the faith and not be unfavorably compared with the perfect or pure ones.

Still, there was resistance. After Raymond of Toulouse had been defeated, the Fourth Lateran Council (1215) met and issued certain decrees (canons) regarding heretics, including the confiscation of their lands. (This act confirmed Pope Innocent III's existing policy.)

There was a reaction to the council. The war was renewed, and Simon de Montfort was killed in 1218. Simon's son, Amaury, succeeded him, but by 1224 the son of Raymond VI of Toulouse (d. 1222), Raymond VII, had successfully taken possession of most of his family's former holdings. Most of the other southern nobles had also regained their former positions.

With the return of the southern nobility, the Cathars made a reappearance. The pure ones were seen again in the south. In 1226, the French king, Louis VIII (1223-1226), agreed to undertake a crusade. But King Louis died before there could be a decisive encounter with Raymond VII. However, Raymond recognized the need to settle the issue and entered into negotiations with the monarchy. In the Peace of Paris of 1229, Raymond recognized the large holdings of Beziers and Carcassone as royal possessions and agreed to marry his daughter to a member of the royal family.

The Albigensian crusade, together with the preaching of the Dominicans, was successful. While some pure ones and some hearers remained, they were reduced in number and had to seek refuge in a small number of strong points. By the middle of the thirteenth century, even these succumbed to the unrelenting pressure. In Italy, partly because of the tensions between the Holy Roman Emperor and the Pope, the Cathars were able to survive longer. However, the Inquisition, instituted as a procedure to defend the Church against the Cathars, began to have an effect even in Italy.

Long-Term Effects of the Campaign Against the Cathars

The Inquisition was born as a response to the Albigensian heresy. A second outcome of the Albigensian heresy was the expansion of the royal domain (the lands directly under the control of the king of France). The crusade devastated the south of France so that it lost its position as one of the dominant geographical areas of the western Mediterranean. Finally, this crusade set a precedent of using a crusade in western Europe against Christians. Formerly, the holy war was officially prosecuted only against infidels, or non-Christians.

The Catharist Heresy

This heresy taught that there were two gods: a good god who created the spiritual world and an evil one who created the material world. Each human being was to try to free his or her spiritual powers from the evil of the material world, e.g., one's own body.

18

The Waldensians

Peter Waldo

ABOUT THE TIME THE CATHARS WERE ATTRACTING FOLLOWERS IN THE SOUTH of France, a certain Peter Waldo, a rich merchant of Lyons, wanted to embrace poverty and preach the Gospel. His devotion to poverty prefigured *Il Poverello,* St. Francis of Assisi, but his teaching gradually came to prefigure the Reformation.

About 1174, Waldo, after providing for his wife and daughters, gave away all his property and had the New Testament and some books of the Old Testament translated into his own mother tongue. He began to preach and was joined by others who were attracted to his preaching and lifestyle.

Waldo sought permission of Pope Alexander III (1159-1181) at the Third Lateran Council, convened in 1179. The Pope agreed to allow Waldo and his followers to embrace a life of poverty, but refused to allow Waldo to preach except with the permission of bishops and pastors. The difficulty with accepting Waldo's preaching apostolate was that he was untrained and only knew the Bible through vernacular translations. (Of course, at this time, the only official Bible in the Latin West was the Latin Vulgate.) Waldo probably had not learned Latin — in effect, then, he was officially illiterate — because he had been a merchant and did not need anything except the vernacular.

With the permission of Pope Alexander, Waldo and his followers returned to Lyons and came to be called the Poor Men of Lyons. Although initially loyal to the Church, they continued to preach despite not having obtained the proper permissions. In effect, they declared their independence from the Church. Further, irritated by the refusal of the necessary permissions, they began to preach against priests and bishops, delineating the sins of the Church's pastors. They were expelled from Lyons for preaching without permission and condemned as an heretical sect at a synod held at Verona (Italy) in 1184.

Rather than curbing the Waldensians, the condemnation of the council of Verona seems to have encouraged them. Waldensian preachers appeared in towns throughout France, and a group was founded in Milan. The new society held the preachers of their group in great respect, not only because of their work but also because the preachers embraced poverty.

In this respect, they resembled the Albigensians. Just as the Albigensians had two classes of members, the perfect and the hearers, so the Waldensians had the preachers and the believers. The devotional life of the Waldensians revolved around the vernacular Scriptures.

Waldensian Attacks on Church Beliefs and Practices

The emphasis on the Scriptures led the Waldensians in directions which will again be seen in the Reformation. They rejected the Church's teaching authority, the hierarchy, Tradition (the transmission of what Christ said and did in and through the life of the Church), the sacraments (especially the sacrament of Reconciliation), as well as the veneration of saints, images, and relics. They also rejected praying for the dead, indulgences, oaths, tithes, military service, and the death penalty. Peter Waldo ordained bishops, priests, and deacons, creating his own hierarchy. Nevertheless, their example of the apostolic life gained them many converts.

Thus, the Waldensians attacked doctrine, the devotional life of the people, and even civil society. In rejecting the Church's teaching authority and renouncing the hierarchy and Tradition, the Waldensians attacked doctrine. Of course, Peter Waldo did not intend this rejection at the beginning. He wanted to preach the Gospel according to the vernacular Scriptures. Since the hierarchy refused permission, if he wanted to continue to preach he had to reject the Church's authority to refuse permission. Further, in order to make Scripture the sole touchstone of his preaching, he had to eliminate Tradition.

Waldo attacked Catholic devotional life in his rejection of the full sacramental life, in his rejection of the practice of praying for the dead, in his objections to indulgences, and in his refusal to acknowledge the veneration of saints, images, and relics. Presumably, these practices were not sufficiently grounded in Scripture. Even the practices of civil society came under fire.

When Waldo called into question oaths, tithes, military service, and the death penalty, civil society was threatened because medieval society was founded in a large part on the taking of oaths — on the promises made by one man to another, like the promise of a vassal to the lord. Similarly, the paying of tithes and the owing of military service for a certain number of days in a year were at the heart of the "glue" of the medieval European world. The death penalty was recognized as a legitimate punishment for those guilty of capital crimes.

The Church's Response

Since the Waldensians emphasized preaching, they were trying to make converts to their beliefs. In other words, like the Cathars, they posed a threat to the Church. Therefore, they could not be ignored. Through his conciliatory policy towards those who had rejected Church teaching, Pope Innocent III was able to reconcile some of the Waldensians to the Church in 1207 following a disputation at Pamiers in the south of France.

Durand de Huesca and some of his followers reunited with the Church and even founded a society in the Church called the Catholic Poor. However, many Waldensians continued to preach doctrines and devotions contrary to the Church's teaching. But in the course of the thirteenth century, with the preaching of the Dominicans and the Franciscans, the crusade against the Cathars (which also was used against the Waldensians in the south of France), and the beginnings of the Inquisition, the Church was able to lessen the impact of the Waldensians as well as that of the Cathars. It should be noted that the Inquisition was instituted as a procedure against heretics. Its purpose was to identify those who taught doctrines contrary to the faith and try to persuade them to renounce those teachings and return to the Church. Prior to the late twelfth and early thirteenth centuries, the Church had no institutionalized means of dealing with those who rejected its teachings. Most of the punishments were light, not involving the death penalty or indefinite imprisonment.

It must be remembered that it is inappropriate to apply modern standards to past centuries. By our standards, the Inquisition is difficult to justify. But when severe punishments were commonplace in civil law, the Inquisition appeared almost benign — at least in most cases. Nevertheless, the Waldensians, unlike the Cathars, were able to continue to exist, if not flourish.

Existing in various localities all over Europe, many of the Waldensians eventually merged with the Protestant Reformation Churches, demonstrating the undeniable similarity in doctrine and devotion between the Waldensians and the Churches born from the Reformation. Other groups continued to exist independently and survive even to our own day. However, the Waldensians ceased to be a threat to the Church after the thirteenth century.

The Waldensian Heresy

This heresy held that preaching was the privilege of any Christian, regardless of the approval or disapproval of the Church. Insisting on preaching, the heresy attacked the Church's authority, doctrines, sacraments, and the veneration of images of the saints and of the Lord.

19

Joachim of Fiore and the Flagellanti

The Twelfth-Century Renaissance

BOTH THE CATHARS AND THE WALDENSIANS DEVELOPED IN THE LAST HALF of the twelfth century and were very strong in the south of France and in northern Italy. Both heresies had a two-tiered membership, with the elite called to heroic virtue. Both extolled a simple life for the elite, with the Waldensians emphasizing apostolic poverty. Both attracted a large following and represented a significant movement contrary to Church teaching, devotion, and discipline.

Obviously, many saw in these movements values which were not as strongly mirrored in the Church. Certainly, the simple life with an emphasis on poverty contrasted with the official Church. The twelfth century was the era of the beginnings of the great Gothic cathedrals, representing a vast investment of wealth. Older monasteries were often very well endowed with vast tracts of land which had been donated over the centuries. (If land were given to a monastery, it remained with the monastery forever because the monastery never ceased to exist. In effect, the land was taken out of "circulation." The longer a monastery had existed, the more lands it had. Many monasteries were in fact quite wealthy. On the other hand, lands held by individuals were transmitted to their heirs and remained in "circulation.") Newer monasteries were founded throughout Europe in the twelfth century, particularly Cistercian monasteries. They eventually became wealthy through work and particularly gifts. In many respects, the Church was well established and enjoyed a very comfortable existence.

Added to this "established" Church was a stirring ferment of activity on many fronts. There was the academic excitement of the "new learning" fueled in large part by the works of Aristotle entering Europe via Arabic-Latin translations often done in Muslim Spain. Further, there was an expansion of lands under cultivation as well as a population increase. New schools and universities were founded and towns were developing, particularly in Italy and the south. The growth of towns both reflected and in turn was the cause of the growth in trade. More and more merchants were engaged in trade. The amount of money in circulation increased. In short, the twelfth century saw a renaissance. It was a time of change and development, and while the Church was part of the changing scene, it also was very much part of the establishment. No wonder, given this cultural climate, that the Cathars and the Waldensians found a market for their ideas.

But the Church responded to the new cultural situation through the mendicant orders: the Dominicans and the Franciscans. Embracing poverty and often located in the towns, the Dominicans and Franciscans were able to make an appeal similar to the Cathars and the Waldensians. Particularly, the devotion to poverty of the Franciscans and the commitment of the Dominicans to preaching would have appealed to those who might have flirted with the Cathars or the Waldensians.

The common thread behind the mendicant orders as well as the Cathars and the Waldensians was a demand to imitate Christ. (Of course, the mendicants were within the Church and lived this demand authentically, whereas the Cathars and the Waldensians rejected some fundamental Church teachings and therefore were not truly following Christ.)

This demand of imitating Christ was perceived more and more as pertaining to all Christians — not just monks and members of religious orders. The concept of a personal call to imitate Christ, if carried to an extreme, could easily eliminate the need for an institutional Church, especially if that Church were not viewed as a true reflection of its founder. In other words, some thought that the true (institutional) Church should be abandoned in favor of a union of the faithful, each of whom was following the Lord according to his or her lights.

Joachim of Fiore

Since it was the Holy Spirit who guided the individual in this search to follow Christ, there emerged in the early thirteenth century an emphasis on the Holy Spirit. The leading figure in developing a constellation of ideas regarding the Holy Spirit was an abbot, Joachim of Fiore (d. 1202).

Joachim developed a theology of history. His basic concept was that the Old Testament represented the age of the Father. The New Testament was the age of the Son. These two ages were to be followed by a third one: the age of the Holy Spirit.

The age of the Father, of the Old Testament, was represented by the worldly married man. The age of the Son, of the New Testament, was represented by the worldly cleric. But the last age, the era of the Holy Spirit, would be represented by the monk and the mystic.

Pushed to its extreme by some of Joachim's followers after his death, the age of the Holy Spirit, the era of the monks, would be one without a visible Church, without sacraments and external worship. Joachim held that the Church of Peter was to be replaced in favor of the Church of John. The last age was to be characterized by a spirit of poverty which would result in peace. Further, in this third age, the Scriptures would be interpreted in a spiritual way. At root, Joachim's ideas were the vision of a perfect society within history With the concept that society would be perfected within history, Joachim introduced a new idea into Christianity.

In some ways, Joachim's ideas were exciting and gave the people a new framework to interpret history. Joachim's thoughts encouraged a climate of excitement about religious ideas, but also an intensification of the criticism of the official Church which was involved in political struggles, was relatively wealthy, and seemed to some to neglect the pastoral needs of the people.

Despite the rejection of some of Joachim's ideas by the Fourth Lateran Council (1215), they were spread far and wide, particularly after his death. He had founded two monasteries, but by 1250, less than fifty years after his death, there were fifty houses following the order he had established at Fiore. However, 1250 was the high point for the order founded by Fiore.

Joachim's ideas, especially with the emphasis on poverty, were very influential in the new order founded by St. Francis (c. 1210). John of Parma (the Father General of the Franciscans from 1247 to 1257) was particularly influenced by Joachim's ideas. Even the noted Franciscan theologian and successor to John of Parma, St. Bonaventure, seems to have been slightly influenced by Joachim.

For the most part, Joachim found acceptance among the Spirituals of the Franciscan order. (The Spirituals were the members of the Franciscan order who took the most radical notion of poverty. While all Franciscans took the personal vow of poverty, the Spirituals believed that Franciscan poverty required the order itself not to own anything, not even houses, or friaries where the Franciscans could live.)

The Apostolics

In 1260, the year that Joachim had designated as the beginning of the age of the Holy Spirit, the Apostolics of Gerard Segarelli of Parma were formed. They proclaimed that the age of the Holy Spirit had dawned, demanded the practice of apostolic poverty by everyone, and condemned the Church and the clergy (because the Church and clergy belonged to the second age).

The Church also came under fire for its wealth and for its exercise of almost governmental authority. The Apostolics also rejected anything like rules that limited the freedom of the Holy Spirit. They preached penance and poverty, marching through town and country, often beating themselves in acts of penance. These were the first of the flagellant processions.

It is difficult for our age to understand a movement that advocated self-inflicted pain. However, the Apostolics believed that the "official" Church had embraced the world to the exclusion of the simplicity and poverty of Christ. They were doing penance for these sins. Further, they sincerely believed that the final age of the world had dawned and that the end of the world was close at hand. Penance was one of the means of preparing for the second coming of Christ and for the Last Judgment.

Many thousands supported the Apostolics and their ideas, but the Church used the Inquisition as well as a crusade to end the movement. Joachim's ideas had fostered not just a new religious interpretation of history, but a social movement founded on an exclusive personal relationship with the Lord that precluded any notion of a visible Church. Such ideas, if followed to their natural conclusion, would have overthrown the social fabric of medieval Europe because members of that society were linked by many bonds, not the least of which was the bond of the visible Church.

The Apostolic Heresy

This heresy held that the year 1260 marked the beginning of the age of the Holy Spirit. This third age would be the age of the monk, would do away with the necessity of a visible Church, would be an age where all would embrace poverty, and would have an emphasis on penance as a preparation for the imminent end of the world.

❦

20

John Wyclif and John Hus

The Fourteenth-Century Church

THE CHURCH'S APPROVAL AND ACCEPTANCE OF ST. FRANCIS AND THE FRANciscan rule was a significant endorsement of evangelical poverty. In other words, by approving of the Franciscan movement, the Church acknowledged as never before that Christ modeled the life of a poor man, and that one path to holiness — one way to imitate Christ — was to embrace poverty.

Since the Church is a continuation of Christ's presence on earth, the continuation in a different way of the Incarnation, obviously, the Church as a whole should mirror Christ in every way possible. Therefore, if people are to see the face of Christ in the Church, it too should have an aspect of poverty.

Unfortunately, almost in an inverse relationship, as the emphasis on evangelical poverty grew through the Franciscan movement, the Flagellant movement, and some interpretations of the writings of Joachim of Fiore, the visible Church seemed more and more to be seeking worldly wealth.

First of all, unlike in previous eras, more and more appointments were made through the papal household. This centralization reached the point that the papal bureaucracy was at times overwhelmed and unable to handle the workload. One of the reasons for the centralization was that when an appointment was made by the Pope, the candidate appointed was responsible for paying one year's income from his new office to the papal household. The papacy, of course, needing money for the expanding bureaucracy, was highly motivated to reserve more and more appointments to itself.

Further, it was often the case that if a particular office was vacant for more than a year, a bishopric for example, the income from that office was to be paid to the papal household. With the expansion of the papal bureaucracy during the "Babylonian Captivity" — the era between 1309 and 1377 when the Popes lived at Avignon in the south of France — the necessity for money fueled more and more the desire to reserve more appointments to the Pope, and even at times to leave offices vacant in order to collect the income from those offices.

Theses tendencies increased dramatically in the next era, the years of the Great Schism — 1378-1415, when there was Pope in Rome as well as a rival Pope in Avignon, both claiming to be the legitimate vicar of Christ. In an even greater anomaly, a third Pope was elected by the Council of Pisa in 1409, and therefore for the last six years of the Great Schism — 1409 to 1415 — there were actually three claimants to the papacy: one at Rome, one at Avignon, and one called the Pisan Pope (after the council that elected him).

Aside from the difficulty in recognizing the face of Christ in the Church when there were three claimants to the papacy, each of the Popes had a bureaucracy that needed money. Each of the Popes (although the Pisan Pope never had much time to build a following) had kingdoms and principalities, dioceses and monasteries loyal to him. From these constituencies, each Pope made appointments, let offices remain vacant in order to collect the income from those offices, and generally tried to collect as much income as possible.

Throughout the Great Schism, the need for money simply to maintain the papal households and bureaucracies was insatiable. Christendom had struggled to maintain one papal household and bureaucracy; now it had to maintain three! This endless scrounging for money hardly enhanced the perception of the Church as a spokesman for the poor carpenter of Nazareth!

But it was not just the Popes who were grasping for money, position, and a comfortable lifestyle. Many prominent cardinals and bishops held more than one benefice or appointment. For example, a particular bishop might actually live in the papal household in Avignon and yet be the bishop of two different sees.

Many such bishops would hire a priest in each of their dioceses to take care of the administration of that diocese. The priest would do the work for a fraction of the total income of the diocese, which would be paid to the bishop living in Avignon. The bishop would be absent from his diocese(s) for most of the year.

The practice of holding more than one appointment in the Church is called pluralism. Obviously, pluralism led to the further evil of absenteeism, the practice of not living in the diocese or in the residence given with the appointment. How could one be in two dioceses at the same time? But absenteeism also existed when a man held only one appointment, but lived elsewhere, hiring someone else to do the actual work of the office. (Of course, the most obvious case of absenteeism was the Pope himself, who although bishop of Rome, lived in Avignon!)

In addition to pluralism and absenteeism, there was the practice of ecclesiastical officials appointing friends and relatives (who often paid for the favor) to various offices in the Church. With multiple incomes from more than one appointment, absenteeism, and the granting of appointment to those who were willing to pay for such favors (nepotism), the higher clergy could often live very comfortably.

It seemed to many that the clergy had much more concern about the present life than the life to come. In the fourteenth and fifteenth centuries, the visible, official Church did not reflect the poverty of Christ. In fact, as mentioned above, the more evangelical poverty was emphasized, the more the visible, official Church seemed to spurn that poverty.

The Church, at least as represented by the higher clergy, often failed to mirror much of Gospel values as traditionally understood. The surprising fact that no religious order founded in the fourteenth and fifteenth centuries had any influence on the Church or society comparable to the influence of the Cistercians in the twelfth century or of the Franciscans and Dominicans in the thirteenth century demonstrates that the vitality and spiritual life of the Church was not what it once had been.

The secular lifestyle of the higher clergy, the centralized administration, the insatiable need for money, and the concomitant practices of pluralism, absenteeism, and nepotism were certainly in part responsible for the waning spiritual life of the Church in the fourteenth and fifteenth centuries.

John Wyclif

As one might expect, there were many reactions to the visible, official Church. One theologian, John Wyclif (c. 1330-1384), severely criticized the official Church and the higher clergy for the lack of what he regarded as a sufficient witness to the poverty of Christ.

Born in England near York, Wyclif spent most of his life at Oxford earning a Master of Theology degree and then teaching there as a professor of theology. We know very little of the details of his life. He was ordained a priest while at Oxford, probably rather early in his career there. He wrote several works on Scripture and followed these with several treatises in theology regarding divine authority, civil authority, the office of the king, and the nature of the Church.

In 1377, nineteen articles were drawn from Wyclif's treatise on civil authority and criticized during an interrogation by the bishop of London. However, Wyclif was protected by very powerful figures, including John of Gaunt, the Duke of Lancaster, who was one of the sons of Edward III (1327-1377) as well as the father of Henry IV (1399-1413).

In 1378, at a conference at Lambeth, Wyclif offered a partial recantation of the nineteen articles, or as it is sometimes stated, an alternative interpretation. But his troubles were not yet over.

In 1382, Archbishop Courtenay of Canterbury (1381-1396) convened a provincial synod which found twenty-four of Wyclif's propositions either heretical or erroneous. In November 1382, Oxford approved the findings of Archbishop Courtenay's synod, and Wyclif was forced from his teaching position and retired to his parish, the benefice he had received while still a professor. He died on the last day of the year in 1384 while still at his parish. Apparently, he was able to escape any further punishment because of his powerful friends.

Wyclif's Teaching

Beginning with Scripture as the sole norm for the faith and for the structure of the Church, Wyclif saw no possible justification for the wealth and property of the Church. He proposed the ancient Church as the only proper model for the structure and the administration of the Church. In other words, he opposed, on the basis of Scripture, the wealth and lifestyle of many clerics as well as the pattern of Church administration which had emerged in the late thirteenth and fourteenth centuries.

It should be remembered that Wyclif lived and worked during the period of the "Babylonian Captivity" and the beginnings of the Great Schism. His views put him in direct opposition to the hierarchy of the Church, which accounts for some of his difficulties. In addition to his harsh criticism of the lives of the clergy and the wealth of the Church, he had some very harsh words for the monks. Since many monasteries had been in existence for centuries, they had acquired vast tracts of land through the generosity of the faithful. This vast monastic wealth was grist for Wyclif's mill of criticism that the Church did not sufficiently reflect the poverty of Christ.

But Wyclif did not stop with the attack on wealth. His view of Scripture as the sole norm for the faith led him to deny the confession of sins to a priest; that is to say, he denied the Sacrament of Reconciliation. Further, he criticized the cult of relics, the veneration of the saints, the existence of purgatory, and the practice of indulgences.

However, his most serious attack on the doctrine of the Church came on the Eucharist. Arguing from Scripture, he denied that the bread and wine were transformed into the body and blood of Christ at the celebration of the Eucharist.

Wyclif denied the Eucharist as the re-presentation of the sacrifice of Christ, as food for the grace life of the soul, and as Christ remaining with His people. In other words, Wyclif denied the presence of Christ under the appearances of the bread and wine. His objections to the real presence were in part based on his reading of Scripture, but it also seems that he found it impossible on philosophical grounds to believe that the substance of the bread and wine were no longer present after the consecration. Wyclif suggested that the substance of bread and wine cannot be replaced by Christ's body and blood.

There seem to be more profound trends in Wyclif's views. In denying the Eucharist, Confession, the veneration of the saints, the cult of relics, purgatory, and the practice of indulgences, Wyclif attacked the clergy and some of the sources of wealth for the clergy. If the Eucharist is not the body and blood of Christ, does one need a priest? If Confession is not necessary, are the clergy essential? If there is no purgatory, do offerings have to be made to the clergy for prayers for the dead? If people are not to venerate the saints or practice the cult of relics, those devotions and the priests who do them are unnecessary. Furthermore, the purchasing of statues and relics is unnecessary. If indulgences are not to be granted, can the Church attach indulgences to those who give alms to the Church or to the poor?

Clearly, Wyclif's attack on the Church's wealth is not inconsistent with his views against the sacraments of Reconciliation and the Eucharist, against the cult of relics and the saints, against purgatory and indulgences. Certainly, Wyclif's attacks were based on his notion of Scripture, but they were also rooted in his wish to re-create the ancient Church so that the medieval Church with all its faults (as he perceived it) would disappear.

Popularity of Wyclif's Teachings

Wyclif's theories did not remain simply theories. His attack on clerical wealth and privilege and on the papacy were popular. In England, there was resentment among the nobles towards the papacy, which attempted to exercise certain ecclesiastical rights within England. Wyclif's criticism of the papacy appeared to some to be a defense of English rights against a powerful foreign ruler (the Pope) who wanted to extract revenue from the English.

Further, many people were genuinely scandalized by the lifestyles of some churchmen. For these reasons, some men joined Wyclif and tried to spread his teachings. Since Wyclif downplayed the sacraments and other devotions, he emphasized preaching. He sent his followers to preach his teachings to all those who would listen.

Called Lollards and Poor Priests, these men spread Wyclif's teachings to the countryside. In addition to Wyclif's teachings, the Lollards promoted a program of economic and social reform. (Clearly, this was a companion program to the criticism of the Church's wealth. If the Church's structure were to be changed and its wealth administered by others, there would have to be massive social and economic changes, since the Church was such an essential component in the medieval economy and society.)

Through this social and economic program, the Lollards were associated with the Peasant Revolt of 1381 and were suppressed by the government. Wyclif remained aloof from the revolt of 1381 and was able to escape any consequences stemming from that social disturbance.

Wyclif has been called the "morning star" of the Reformation. With his harsh criticism of the Church, his emphasis on Scripture as the sole norm of the faith, his attacks on the sacraments, on the veneration of the saints, on the cult of relics, on pugatory and indulgences, he certainly prefigures most of the positions of the Reformers of the sixteenth century. He is best known for his insistence on evangelical poverty both for the institutional Church and its higher clergy, and for his denial of Christ's real presence in the Eucharist.

It is difficult to assess why Wyclif did not succeed in starting a movement as the Reformers of the sixteenth century did. Certainly, one reason is that his most widely known positions did not emerge until just a few years before he died. He did not have the time to father a fully matured movement. Further, while he had support from some very powerful nobles because the effect of his views matched their goals, there was no agreement on the underlying principles.

Wyclif's advocacy of a Church embracing evangelical poverty was too radical a social and economic change for the world of fourteenth-century England. One might also suggest that the theological views he advocated had to be promoted for a few years before they could find an adequate hearing. In other words, people had to hear these ideas a few times and for a few generations before they could be widely accepted. Society had to digest and absorb these ideas before they could be the basis of a new movement.

John Hus

Society did not have to wait very long after Wyclif's death to hear the same ideas promoted. The Englishman's thoughts and works became known in Bohemia and were taken up by the Reformers there. It might seem surprising that Wyclif's works should be known in Bohemia, but there was a lively scholarly exchange between England, especially Oxford, and Bohemia in the last quarter of the 1300s.

King Richard II of England (1377-1399) married Anne of Bohemia, and through this link the courts of England and Bohemia were in close communication. Students from Bohemia came to England to study, and there was an interchange of ideas. Wyclif's ideas fed the growing reform movement in Bohemia, stimulated by the same factors which influenced Wyclif — the worldly lifestyle of the higher clergy, the growing demand for money by the papal bureaucracies, as well as the practices of pluralism, absenteeism, and nepotism.

The Bohemian Reformers were centered at the University of Prague. As in England, where the criticism of the Church found a sympathetic hearing among those in the aristocracy who wished to limit papal influence in England, the Reformers in Bohemia found allies among those who wished to limit German influence in Bohemia. German and imperial authority — the authority of the Holy Roman Emperor —was linked in Bohemia with ecclesiastical authority. In other words, to criticize the Church and the higher clergy was tantamount to opposing German control of Bohemia.

One who promoted Wyclif's ideas was John Hus. John Hus was born in Bohemia about 1370. He studied at the University of Prague, receiving a degree from the arts faculty, but after his ordination to the priesthood in 1400 he devoted himself to the study of theology.

John Hus joined and became the leading figure in the Bohemian reform movement centered at the University of Prague. After his ordination, Hus was appointed by the Archbishop to preach a series of sermons in preparation for the biennial synod, a meeting of the clergy of the archdiocese of Prague. In addition, he was made rector of the university for the academic year 1402-1403.

Significantly influenced by Wyclif's teaching, Hus preached in the vernacular to lay people in the Bethlehem chapel in Prague, attacking the vices of the clergy. Hus also translated one of the works of Wyclif into Czech. While borrowing heavily from Wyclif, Hus was able to liberate Wyclif's teachings from the ponderous scholastic arguments used by the Englishman. Hus was also able to make use of Wyclif's teachings in a politically astute way, tying these ideas to the politically favorable Bohemian nationalist (anti-German) movement.

While Hus was favored by his own archbishop, the Roman Pope (the reader will recall that there were two claimants to the papacy at this time: one in Rome and one in Avignon), Innocent VII (1404-1406), asked the archbishop in 1405 to take measures against the teachings of Wyclif, particularly those on the Eucharist.

This measure threatened Hus because he had embraced Wyclif's ideas. Nevertheless, the archbishop continued to protect Hus. In 1408, the Roman Pope Gregory XII (1406-1415) issued another letter against the spread of Wyclif's ideas. This letter motivated King Wenceslaus IV (1378-1419) to look into the matter. As a result of this royal pressure, the university made efforts to clear itself of any charge of heresy. All Wyclif's writings were ordered to be turned over to the office of the archbishop of Prague for correction. Hus complied with this order.

Although Hus was guilty of heresy in promoting the ideas of Wyclif (which had been condemned), he had been protected by the archbishop of Prague against serious difficulties. But he had also obeyed the archbishop, especially in 1408 when he surrendered Wyclif's writings as the archbishop demanded.

However, in 1409 Pope Alexander V (it should be remembered that in this year yet another rival Pope was elected, the Pisan Pope, Alexander V) directed the archbishop of Prague to withdraw all Wyclif's writings and to forbid preaching except in cathedral, collegiate, parish, and monastic churches. This ban on preaching was directed at Hus, who had been given permission to preach in the vernacular to lay people in private chapels such as the Bethlehem chapel.

The archbishop called a synod and complied with the wishes of Pope Alexander V. Hus resisted, and the archbishop formally excommunicated him and his followers in 1410. Hus appealed to the new Pisan Pope, John XXIII (not to be confused with Pope John XXIII of the twentieth century), but John XXIII through Cardinal Colonna, after an attempt to dialogue with Hus, sustained the archbishop's excommunication.

Since King Wenceslaus wanted to recover his previous position as Holy Roman Emperor and he needed to show the world that his kingdom was well administered and free of heresy, he intervened. With the Pope (the Roman and the Pisan one), the archbishop, and the king against him, Hus had very little support. When in 1412 Hus preached against an indulgence proclaimed by Pope John XXIII for all who would donate to a crusade against the ruler of Naples, he irritated the Pisan John XXIII even more.

With this decision to defy the Pisan papacy, Hus lost the support of his fellow professors at the University of Prague. Hus left Prague, totally unreconciled to the Church or the university.

In fact, he wrote a work entitled, *On the Church*, which proclaimed Wyclif's teaching about the Church. Like Wyclif before him, Hus questioned the hierarchical structure of the Church and the requirement that Christians obey the Church. Clearly, there was an open break within Bohemia between Hus on the one side and the hierarchy of the Church and the civil authority (King Wenceslaus) on the other. Tensions were running high.

Council of Constance

The Emperor Sigismund, a brother to Wenceslaus, suggested that Hus attend the Council of Constance which Sigismund had announced (in consultation with the Pisan Pope and others). This council was called primarily to solve the problem of the Great Schism (which it did accomplish). Sigismund wanted Hus to be given a fair hearing so that the matter could be properly settled, and so gave him a safe-conduct.

The council met in November 1414. Hus arrived in Constance in that month. However, since Hus was already excommunicated and was considered a heretic, many were opposed to him. This party prevailed and Hus, despite the imperial safe-conduct, was imprisoned at the end of the month of November.

The authorities wanted to handle Hus's case with a committee, but Hus insisted on a hearing by the whole council. With imperial support, this was granted and in the first part of June 1415, Hus was allowed to address the council. While rejecting many statements falsely attributed to him, Hus refused to acquiesce in the council's condemnation of over three hundred articles of Wyclif. Despite the Emperor's attempts and those of others to persuade him to change his mind, even up to the last moment, he refused. With this refusal, he was condemned for formal heresy, given over to the secular powers, and burned at the stake.

There is no question that Hus took from Wyclif some of the ideas against the Church and the higher clergy. Still, there is no evidence that Hus adopted Wyclif's views on the Eucharist and other matters. But Hus refused to condemn Wyclif's ideas because he said that he had not defended them or he had not studied them sufficiently. Still, one has an obligation as a Catholic to acknowledge the truths as taught by the Church.

Hus should have acknowledged the truth of the judgments of the council, even if he had not studied the propositions to the point that he could honestly — from an academic viewpoint — agree. Clearly, matters of faith as taught by the Church, while not contrary to reason, are superior to reason and take precedence over reason. In other words, if the Church teaches as true a matter of the faith, even if one does not understand it or even "see" it intellectually, there is an obligation to accept it as a supernatural truth of the faith.

One should not argue, as Hus did, that before he could assent to a decree of the council, he needed to understand the decree. More than Wyclif, Hus seems to have become more insistent on his own position as the struggle intensified. For example, if he had not studied certain teachings of Wyclif (that is, if he did not hold these to be true), why not agree to the council's judgment that these statements were in error?

Hus probably refused because he had decided to oppose any attempt to wean him from his adherence to his mentor, believing that agreeing to even the smallest concession would simply lead to a wholesale surrender of everything he believed. To be precise, he became more and more entrenched in his own ideas, not even bending when, in an intellectual sense, he could have. In the end, he placed his judgment above that of the Church, even though he was probably more in agreement with the Church than Wyclif was!

Taborites and Utraquists

The condemnation of Hus and his death after he had received the safe-conduct from Emperor Sigismund were certainly considered by the Bohemians as a betrayal. In fact, even today, the death of Hus arouses strong feelings. Following the death of Hus, the Bohemians looked upon him as a martyr, spurned the reconciliation attempts of the Emperor Sigismund, and launched a rebellion against the Emperor which lasted from 1419 to 1434.

The rebellion only ended when the Hussites split into two groups: the Utraquists (named because they insisted on receiving both the host and the precious blood at communion) and the Taborites. (Taborites took their name from their custom of meeting on mountains. Tabor is a mountain in the Holy Land.) The Utraquists were willing to compromise with the Empire and the Church, whereas the Taborites were not.

The Council of Basel (1431-1437) granted minor concessions to the Utraquists, who then won a victory over the Taborites in 1434. With this victory, the political rebellion ended. But the heretical fruit of Hus's teachings continued in the group called the Moravian Brethren. Holding religious beliefs antagonistic to the Church, this group merged with the Protestant Reformers of the sixteenth century. Thus, while Wyclif did not begin a movement, Hus did. The second time some of these ideas were proclaimed, they launched the beginnings of a movement, a small stream. (The next time these ideas were proclaimed, they resulted in a tidal wave: the Reformation!)

The practices of the Church of the fourteenth and fifteenth centuries, as well as the diplomatic failure to find a way out of the problem of Hus short of burning him, contributed significantly to the small stream begun by the preaching and writing of John Hus. (It should be noted that in 1999 Pope John Paul II expressed his "profound regret" over the "cruel death" of Jan Hus: "On the eve of the great Jubilee, I feel the need to express a profound regret for the cruel death of Jan Hus and the consequent wounds— the sources of conflicts and divisions—which were opened in the spirits and the hearts of the Bohemian people.")

Wyclif

This Englishman denied the presence of Christ in the Eucharist, the Sacrament of Reconciliation, the veneration of the saints, the cult of relics, the doctrine of purgatory, and the practice of indulgences. Opposed to the traditional structure of the Church, he insisted that Scripture was the sole source of Revelation.

John Hus

This professor at the University of Prague adopted many of Wyclif's thoughts and refused to acknowledge as false those teachings of Wyclif condemned by the Church. He began a movement against the Church.

21

Luther

Luther's Early Life

MARTIN LUTHER WAS BORN AT EISLEBEN IN GERMANY IN 1483, BUT IN THE next year, his family moved to Mansfeld. In 1497, at age fourteen, Luther attended the school of the Brothers of the Common Life at Magdeburg, and then in 1498 he transferred to a school at Eisenach. He entered the University of Erfurt in 1501, earning a Bachelor's degree in 1502 and a Master's in 1505.

Luther's entire religious training from home through his early education was designed to instill a fear and awe of God. Certainly, Luther's early education was no different from the schooling of thousands of others of the same period. But some have seen the origins of Luther's later teaching in his personality and psychological makeup as shaped and formed by the way the faith was practiced and taught. According to this theory, what set Luther apart from other boys were radical changes in his emotional states.

From an early age, Luther knew he was subject to mood swings. He experienced emotional highs, but he was also subject to severe depressions which could last for months. Given this rather sensitive personal emotional structure, the teachings of the Church affected Luther in ways which were not commonplace.

In this period of the Church's history, the Church emphasized death and the afterlife in order to encourage its members to avoid sin and to embrace the commandments. The Church tried to instill a reverence and awe of God and promised the glories of heaven, but the Church also tried to foster fear of a sudden and unprovided death as well as an absolute abhorrence of hell. The Church held out the infinite mercy of God, which gave hope of eternal life, but the Church also encouraged an approriate fear — fear of death, fear of hell, and fear of the judgment of an all-just God.

Michelangelo's great fresco of the Last Judgment in the Sistine chapel captures the alternating messages rather well. The saints are brought to the glory of reigning with Christ in heaven (hope), but sinners are cast into eternal flames (fear). The more positive presentation of the teachings of the Church were part and parcel of Luther's emotional highs, but fear contributed to his depressions. Most were able to work out a *modus vivendi* — literally, a way of living, or a way of reconciling the seeming contradiction between the message of mercy and the message of fear. Some put the emphasis on mercy, confident and hopeful that the saints and the compassion of God would save them if they did their best. With confidence in God's mercy, the message of fear became less central and important in their lives. Others, succumbing to fear, followed the teachings of the Church because the alternative was unthinkable. Responding only to fear, these people were unfortunately unable to hear the message of mercy very clearly, but they were able to follow the teachings of the Church with fear as their chief motive.

It is hard for us to imagine how real religious truths were to the people of the sixteenth century. Without much control over their lives, the teaching of the Church about God, the all-powerful one who controlled everything, was simply awesome. When people were totally subject to the vagaries of the weather, not even knowing when rain would come, facing the real chance that crops might not grow, the authority and majesty of God — His power of control — were staggering. He had to be respected and feared. Further, the saints were not dead people whose souls had gone to heaven, they were daily companions who watched over the living. Heaven, hell, and purgatory were accepted with such conviction and faith that these were as real as the fields the farmers cultivated.

For whatever reason, according to this theory, Luther's psychological makeup with its alternate states of emotional highs and lows, prevented him from coming to a *modus vivendi*. He could not always embrace the message of hope, but he could not live with the fear. Eventually, he tried to limit the fear by assuring himself of salvation with his theological theories.

This view of Luther has much to recommend it, but it has problems as well. First of all, it is founded on a psychological analysis of someone who was dead centuries before the advent of modern psychology. It is very difficult to make an accurate assessment (let alone a diagnosis) of someone living. Can even a professional psychologist make accurate determinations about a person from that person's writings and the historical record alone?

Further, even if Luther's personality and psychological makeup were exactly as the above analysis suggests, there would have been others who experienced the same education and training who easily might have had similar tendencies. In other words, the theory does not completely account for the mystery posed by Martin Luther.

Nevertheless, even the objections to the theory pose difficulties. Everyone is different, and history is the study of decisions by particular individuals who have made particular decisions. Each decision and the reasons for it are unique to that person and ultimately can only be explained by that individual and by his or her personality. Clearly, Luther's psychological state is not irrelevant to an examination of his decisions. In addition, the historical record for Luther is so rich that it might just be legitimate to make some inferences about his personality, relying heavily on his own extensive and extant writings.

Luther's Early Theology

Still, Luther's teachings were founded on theological principles and cannot be understood without some reference to his theological career. This career began one day while he was journeying home for a vacation. Outside of Sotternheim, near Erfurt, on July 2, 1505, there was a thunderstorm, and lightning struck very close to Luther. Thrown to the ground, in fear for his life, Luther made a promise saying, "St. Anne, help me and I will become a monk."

Despite the opposition of his family, particularly his father, and his friends, he entered the monastery of the Hermits of Saint Augustine of the Observance at Erfurt only two weeks after he made the vow: on July 17, 1505. If one follows the psychological theory, Luther could not help but fulfill the vow, even though uttered in total fear of his life, because he would offend St. Anne and be lost for all eternity. Of course, Luther and a hundred other men of his age, faithful and trained, might have reached the same conclusion about fulfilling the vow, no matter what his or their psychological makeup was.

After entering the monastery of the Hermits of Saint Augustine, Luther was ordained a priest in 1507 — only two years after he entered the monastery and only one year after taking his vows as a monk (before the vows, there was a year of novitiate — a kind of probation during which the candidate had a chance to experience the life before definitively committing himself and the community had a chance to determine if the candidate had the proper qualifications to become a member of the community).

The influence of the faith as it was taught at the time on Luther's personality was clear at his first Mass. So awed by the terrible majesty of God was Father Martin Luther that he almost had to flee the altar before completing the Mass. He apparently could not absorb or understand the more positive aspects of the faith made clear in some of the texts of the Mass, e.g., *clementissime Pater*, "most merciful Father." (The phrase comes from the first line in the Roman Canon or first Eucharistic prayer of the Mass and is still used when the first Eucharistic prayer is said.) All he could see was the power and awesomeness of God, who was to be feared.

After ordination, Luther continued his studies, having been earmarked as a future professor of theology. He became a lecturer in moral philosophy at the University of Wittenberg in 1508, but continued his theological studies. Returning from Wittenberg to Erfurt in 1510, he had completed the requirements for the Master's degree in theology. In 1511, after a trip to Rome in the previous year (taken in part on behalf of the order to resolve some disputes within the Augustinians), Luther was assigned to Wittenberg again, but this time as a professor of Scripture.

In 1512, he was appointed as preacher in the Augustinians and became a doctor of theology. With the doctorate, Luther became the Scripture scholar at Wittenberg. In the next years, he lectured on the Psalms (1513-1515), on the Epistle to the Romans (1515-1516), on the Epistle to the Galatians (1516-1517), and on the Epistle to the Hebrews (1517-1518).

Between 1512 and 1518, during the period of the lectures on the Psalms, Romans, Galatians, and Hebrews, Luther reports an enlightenment, a mystical experience. He had always been inordinately frightened by the phrase in the Scriptures "the justice of God." To Luther, the justice of God meant that God as a just judge would punish the sinner for sins. There was no way to escape this judgment.

Since Luther had a keen consciousness of his own unworthiness and sinfulness (born partly of his depressions, reinforced by the aspect of the fear of God instilled through the way the faith was taught in those years), the certainty of divine justice and judgment must have hit him as a thunderbolt. He would have been impressed with the utter hopelessness of his plight, never able to avoid sin, but subject to divine punishment because of those sins. But in his monastic cell in the tower of the Wittenberg monastery, he was meditating on the phrase in Romans "the just man lives by faith" (cf. Rom 1:17) and it dawned on him that if justification (the "just man") occurs through faith, then we are made holy (justified) through faith. In other words, it is not what we do or who we are, but it is by faith that we are made holy.

This holiness (by faith) means that we are no longer subject to the punishment of God. For Luther, this insight (which he attributed to the Holy Spirit) gave him his *modus vivendi* between the mercy of God and the fear of God's awesome power. The mercy of God gives faith by which a man is justified (made holy). Through this holiness, one no longer has to fear the anger of God at one's lack of holy actions because the actions are not important; the justification (holiness) granted by God comes from faith.

If one imagines a man absolutely tormented by the knowledge that he can never live up to the demands of the all-powerful One no matter what the man does, but that the all-powerful One will punish the man for failing to live up to the demands, one has a dim sense of Luther's state of mind. He was absolutely tormented. He would confess his sins, sometimes doing it daily and at length, in the effort to render his actions more acceptable to God. He fasted, again sometimes for days. He strictly obeyed the rule. Nothing gave him relief because he could not shake the notion that whatever he did was not acceptable, or enough. In this context, the insight that holiness came from faith (justification by faith) was received as incredible relief.

With the insight into the meaning of justification by faith, we have the three major elements which explain Luther's subsequent theological development: the majesty and awesomeness of God; a tempering by God's mercy through the gift of faith; and a certain primacy of Scripture, which had been the means of the great insight relieving Luther's terrible suffering. (Scripture is the Revelation of God which, when properly interpreted, solves theological and even personal difficulties).

It is important to emphasize that all three of these points can be interpreted in a Catholic sense. Certainly, Catholicism does acknowledge the awesomeness of God. Faith is a gift of God's mercy and already involves a commitment to God by the one who has faith because the individual, in accepting faith, entrusts himself or herself to God at least to the extent of accepting what God has revealed as true. Further, there can be no doubt that Scripture contains God's Revelation of Himself and can solve theological and personal difficulties, and even that it has a certain primacy.

Indulgences

Luther's fundamental stance, one that he had taken since youth, was the emphasis on the awesomeness and majesty of God. This understanding of God was challenged by the Church's practice of granting indulgences. An indulgence is a gift by the Church to an individual. Through an indulgence, the Church substitutes the merits of Christ and the saints for specific acts of penance on the part of the penitent. For example, when a penitent commits a sin and confesses it in the sacrament of Reconciliation, the sin is absolved and the eternal punishment due to mortal sin (hell) has been removed. However, the penitent is asked to do a penance — to say some prayers or to do an act of kindness. This act of penance helps to remove the temporal punishment due to sin. But not all of the temporal punishment due to sin is always removed by the act of penance done after receiving the sacrament of Reconciliation. An indulgence substitutes the merits of Christ and the saints for additional acts of the penitent. The indulgence removes all or part of the temporal punishment remaining from the sins of the penitent.

The theological ground for the doctrine of indulgences is that Christ and the saints have done acts infinitely pleasing to God. From this infinite treasury of merit, the Church — since the Church has the powers of the keys of the kingdom of heaven — can grant to penitents a full or partial remission of the temporal punishment which their sins have caused them to accumulate. An indulgence relieves the burden of paying the debt of temporal punishment from the shoulders of the penitent.

Indulgences are attached by the Church to certain acts which the Church wishes to encourage, e.g., prayers and devotions. However, indulgences can be attached to the giving of alms or to acts of fasting and other penitential works. Further, indulgences can be gained for oneself or for others. They can be gained for the souls in purgatory — not for the saints in heaven because they do not need such help, and not for the souls in hell because they are beyond any help. Nevertheless, the gaining of an indulgence is not automatic. It involves a prayer offered to God by the Church that He would graciously accept the merits of Christ and the saints and remove all or part of the temporal punishment a particular person has incurred through sin. It should also be noted that the indulgence is always attached to a particular act — a prayer, devotion, or gift — and that act must be pleasing to God.

As such, the act in itself (even without the indulgence) does remove part of the temporal punishment due to sin if the one acting is in the state of grace. With the indulgence, however, the Church adds to the act from the treasury of merit, so that more of the temporal punishment due to sin is removed. A partial indulgence removes some temporal punishment, and a plenary indulgence removes all the temporal punishment.

All this was not completely clear in Luther's day because the theology of indulgences had not completely matured. Nevertheless, in 1505 Pope Julius II (1503-1513) established an indulgence for gifts to the Vatican for the building of the new St. Peter's (the present one).

Pope Julius's successor, Leo X (1513-1521), renewed this indulgence. To most people, it seemed that by giving alms and gaining the indulgence, they were buying grace, especially since the gift of money was to the Church!

It would have been quite a different case, let's say, if the Church had attached an indulgence to those who bought food and gave it to the poor. In this fanciful case, the Church would not have benefited from the gift of money. As it was, the Church received the money and then granted the indulgence. It seemed that the Church was selling indulgences, especially since those who preached the indulgence did not stress that only those in the state of grace could gain it.

In addition, since the express purpose of the indulgence of Pope Julius was to raise money, the nobles in various parts of Christendom wanted a share of those funds as a reward for allowing the indulgence to be preached in their regions. The nobles wanted a commission. Even bishops and archbishops wanted some share in the money raised by the indulgence in return for allowing it to be preached.

Albrecht, the archbishop of Magdeburg, was also the administrator of Halberstadt and was elected as archbishop of Mainz. But in return for his appointment to Mainz, he owed a tax to Rome and another fee for permission to retain Magdeburg and Halberstadt while serving as archbishop of Mainz.

The archbishop borrowed the money he owed to Rome from the Fugger banking house, but the debt was to be repaid through the indulgence money. The archbishop was to allow the indulgence to be preached in the lands under his jurisdiction for eight years, and during those eight years he could retain half the monies. The archbishop planned to use the indulgence money to repay the loan. It is impossible to defend such trafficking in money given by the people as alms to the Church for the building of one of the great churches of Christendom.

To make matters even more unseemly, those who preached the indulgence misrepresented it to the people as absolutely certain. Particularly, one Dominican, Johannes Tetzel, made it seem that as soon as the alms were given, the indulgence was gained. If the alms-giver intended to gain the indulgence for a soul in purgatory, the soul was immediately released from purgatory and welcomed into the glory of heaven. It seemed to the people that they were buying heaven for their beloved relatives who had died. Who would not contribute with such a promise?

In 1517, Luther began to oppose Tetzel's preaching of the indulgence. He began this controversy in part because he was a parish priest at Wittenberg and some of his parishioners were obtaining the indulgence, even though the indulgence was not offered in Wittenberg.

Frederick the Wise, Duke of Saxony, had not given permission for the indulgence to be preached in his lands — which included Wittenberg — because he did not want to decrease the attention paid to the long-established indulgences available from pilgrimage to the church of All Saints in Wittenberg and because he did not want money from his people enriching Archbishop Albrecht, a member of a rival house to Frederick's.

But Wittenberg was close enough to the border with Albrecht's territories so that Luther's parishioners could easily cross the border to give alms to obtain the indulgence. Therefore, Luther's involvement in the controversy resulted from his responsibility as a pastor who was concerned for the souls of his flock. Luther's emphasis on the awesome majesty of God, who is offended through sin, certainly gave him enough of a reason to question the indulgence, which seemed to trivialize sin and its consequences. By preaching the indulgence to his flock, Tetzel and others were giving Luther's parishioners the idea that the effects of sin could easily be eliminated and that the mercy of God could be purchased. The truth, as Luther saw it, was that growth in holiness demanded constant vigilance and effort. It should be noted that in Luther's initial response to the indulgences, he did not insist on his notion of justification through faith.

Luther's first response to the indulgence question came in April 1517. By October, he had developed a more detailed criticism, and on October 31, 1517, he sent this criticism to the bishops, including Albrecht, who had authorized the preaching of the indulgence.

The criticism Luther authored is the famous ninety-five theses which were supposedly posted on the door of the parish church in Wittenberg. However, they were probably not posted, but rather sent to the bishops. Only after the bishops failed to respond did Luther send these ninety-five theses to theologians and others both in and outside Wittenberg.

Against Tetzel and others, Luther insisted that an indulgence can only remove canonical penalties, not the temporal punishment due to sin. In other words, the Church in granting an indulgence can remit any penalty imposed by the Church, but not anything directly connected with the sin. Anything which pertains directly to sin belongs to God, and the Church does not have power or authority in this area. This assertion, of course, questions the power of the keys — the power of the Church to bind and loose.

With this statement, Luther implicitly questioned the authority and power of the Church with regard to grace and sin. Still, Luther maintained at the time that he was not questioning any authoritative teaching of the Church, nor contradicting Scripture. The ninety-five theses were an invitation to a discussion by scholars and bishops on certain theological issues raised by the preaching of the indulgence.

But the ninety-five theses did not remain solely among scholars for very long. They were rather quickly translated into German and circulated widely. They became very popular because they touched a smoldering resentment felt by many against Rome. The taxes owed to Rome for appointments such as those Albrecht paid caused anger towards the Church and specifically towards Rome. Certainly, the financial maneuverings with banking houses did not long remain secret and caused further consternation.

If the money offered as an alms to St. Peter was the condition for the indulgence, how could that money be diverted? It is a very old maxim that when money is donated, it must be used according to the donor's wishes. Clearly, those who offered alms for the new St. Peter's did not intend their money to be used to pay Archbishop Albrecht's taxes and fees, and even less to be used to pay interest to bankers. Pluralism and absenteeism were still rampant, as is obvious from the case of Archbishop Albrecht, who simultaneously held three bishoprics. He was permitted this breach of the law of the Church in return for paying a fee. The impression left was that one could violate the law if one had sufficient funds to pay for it.

Further, how could the Church preach the horror of sin while at the same time granting indulgences that easily removed at least some of the effects of sin? The message given through the preaching of the indulgence was that one could escape sin and its consequences simply by paying a fee. Many saw this message as directly contradicting the Gospel truth of the horror of sin.

In addition, the implication was that those with means could buy salvation for themselves and their loved ones, whereas those without means could do nothing to aid their loved ones suffering in Purgatory. The apparent favoring of the rich caused considerable anger. The attitude towards the Church in the sixteenth century in northern Europe had not appreciably improved since the time of Wyclif and Hus. If anything, attitudes had hardened and become more critical. With the translation of the ninety-five theses from Latin into German and their widespread circulation, Luther touched an ocean of feelings that had not yet found expression. He gave expression to those feelings.

Clearly, Luther's ninety-five theses, these points of discussion, threatened the success of the indulgence. If people followed Luther's opinions, the indulgence would not be the financial windfall it was expected to be. Touching not just doctrinal and moral issues but finances as well, Luther quickly became a target for those supporting the indulgence.

Since Luther was reacting to the preaching of the indulgence in the lands of Archbishop Albrecht, the archbishop was the one most directly involved. Albrecht asked the opinion of the University of Mainz. This request made sense because Luther posed his opinions as that of a professor of theology at the University of Wittenberg. Albrecht wanted the opinion of other scholars. The faculty at Mainz gave an evasive answer but suggested that the entire matter be submitted to the Pope.

Appeal to Rome

Albrecht sent the theses to the Pope, and the archbishop also asked his own advisors to begin proceedings to have Luther summoned and told not to spread his opinions further. Archbishop Albrecht's advisors dropped the matter, and nothing came of the attempt to censure Luther on Albrecht's own authority.

In addition to Archbishop Albrecht, Tetzel was also directly involved. He and his order, the Dominicans, disputed Luther's opinions at a meeting of the Saxon province of the order in January 1518. Tetzel had used a rather ridiculous ditty in preaching the indulgence: *Sobald der Pfennig im Kasten klingt, die Seele aus dem Fegfeuer springt!* Translation: "As soon as the coin in the coffer rings, the soul from purgatory springs." (This rhyme referred to the obtaining of an indulgence for a soul in purgatory.)

In January 1518, Tetzel maintained that the soul actually was released from purgatory the moment the alms were offered, even before the coin rang in the coffer because it took a second or two for the coin to drop. Further, he argued that an indulgence could be obtained even if one was not in the state of grace. These opinions, of course, demonstrate the lack of theological seriousness or understanding on the part of many who were preaching the indulgence and opposing Luther. Luther had some important and completely orthodox points.

In March 1518, the Dominicans, having decided to denounce Luther at their meeting in January, also brought the matter before the Pope. On the other side, the Augustinians, Luther's own order, backed him at a meeting in April-May 1518. Looking at the matter from the outside, the whole argument seemed to be a dispute between rival religious orders!

Luther was summoned to Rome to give an account of his teachings. However, he requested through Frederick the Wise, the duke of Saxony and the ruler of Wittenberg, where Luther lived, to answer the charges against him not in Rome, but in Germany. However, in making this request he also responded in writing to the objections raised in the summons.

Among other things, Luther wrote that it is possible for both the Pope and a council to err, but that Scripture is without error. He admitted that the Roman Church had not deviated from the truth as proclaimed in Scripture, but he clearly acknowledged that possibility.

In this statement, there is the beginning of the famous teaching of Luther that Scripture is the sole norm for the faith — that the Church is subject to Scripture and not its interpreter. At any rate, the Pope granted Luther's request, and Cardinal Cajetan was asked to meet with Luther.

(Cajetan was in Germany seeking support from the German nobles for the war against the Turks.)

Cajetan and Luther met in October 1518. Cajetan had already published a tract on indulgences in 1517, and so he was very familiar with the divergent opinions on indulgences among both canonists and theologians. Cajetan had a moderate opinion on indulgences which did not reflect the extreme position of Tetzel and some others. Further, the Cardinal took the trouble to read Luther's writings.

Cardinal Cajetan was probably one of the better men available to the Church in the sixteenth century to be chosen to have a discussion with Martin Luther. Unfortunately, the monk and the Cardinal were not able to reach an understanding.

Since indulgences had to do with the forgiveness of sin granted in the sacrament of Reconciliation, Luther's discussion with Cajetan involved an exchange on the sacrament of Reconciliation. Luther insisted that the validity of the sacrament of Reconciliation depended on the faith of the penitent. Cajetan argued that the faith of the penitent was not essential for validity. For Cajetan, the penitent need only believe that the sacraments, including the sacrament of Reconciliation, give grace.

Of course, if a particular person did not believe that the sacrament of Reconciliation gives the grace of forgiveness, why would he or she make use of the sacrament in the first place? At first glance, this distinction may seem insignificant, but it is actually very important. Cajetan is insisting that it is a matter of the Catholic faith that the sacraments give grace. Luther, on the other hand, is trying to create a new condition for the validity of the sacrament — namely, faith.

Cajetan maintained that it is Catholic teaching that the sacraments give grace as long as the penitent does not obstruct it. Luther's position was that grace can only be given if the one receiving the sacrament actually believes he or she is receiving grace. Luther was arguing that there is a requirement of faith in the one receiving the sacrament if the sacrament is to be effective. No longer do the sacraments depend chiefly on the action of Christ, but rather they depend for their effectiveness as much on the faith of the one receiving them as on Christ. In Luther's position, we see his emphasis on faith gleaned from his insight into the meaning of the justice of God. Cajetan remarks that this is a new and dangerous position to take.

The other point of contention was on the question of the treasury of merit. Cajetan held that the merits of Christ and the saints comprised the treasury of merit and that this treasury of merit is identical with the treasury which the Church legitimately dispenses. Luther held that the treasury of the Church is not the same as the merits of Christ and the saints.

If Luther accepted that the merits of Christ and the saints were not separate from the treasury of the Church, there would be no way for him to deny the Church's practice of granting indulgences and allowing them to be gained for the souls in purgatory. But Luther had difficulty with the idea that the Church could in any way ameliorate the consequences of sin.

Cajetan reminded Luther of a papal decree which in effect said that the treasury of Christ and the saints are entrusted to the Church. Luther retorted that the Pope is not above Scripture and that Scripture authorized Luther's interpretation. At that point the discussion ended.

Cajetan had asked Luther to recant on the two points: the requirement of a particular act of faith to receive the grace of the sacraments; and the lack of identity between the treasury of Christ and the saints and the treasury of the Church. Luther refused. Cajetan asked him to think further on the matter and come back when he could recant on these points.

Luther's Fundamental Beliefs

In the interview with Cajetan, Luther invokes all three of the central theological insights which were the foundation stones of his teaching and from which he would never move: (1) the awesomeness and majesty of God; (2) the requirement of faith as the means of achieving holiness; and (3) the superiority of Scripture over the Pope and the Church.

The Church could not grant indulgences which touched the consequences of sin because such indulgences trivialized the effects of sin. If the consequences of sin could so easily be eliminated, then they could not be very serious. And if sin and its consequences were not important, then God, who is offended by sin, could not be important. In Luther's understanding, indulgences diminished the awesomeness of God and the constant effort people should make to remain devoted to Him. Luther's insistence on a particular act of faith as a requirement for receiving the sacraments clearly diverged from Church teaching and represents a non-orthodox understanding of justification by faith. And, of course, the insistence on the superiority of Scripture is the classic Lutheran teaching of *sola Scriptura,* or Scripture alone — that the authority of Scripture is above the Church and the Church is not the authoritative interpreter of the meaning and import of Scripture.

Further, we see in the interview with Cajetan, based on the three central theological tenets, the beginnings of Luther's denial of the Church. Clearly, however, Luther's questioning of the Church and its constitution was a result of his other points. When shown a papal document denying what he held about the treasury of Christ and the saints, Luther either could have accepted it, denied it, or tried to interpret it. He tried a nuanced interpretation, but this failed — even in his own mind. The alternative was to accept it and then accept the more traditional view on indulgences. This he would not do. Therefore, he was forced (by the logic of his own position) to deny the Church. It is at this point that a faithful Catholic would have revised his or her own opinions, rather than stubbornly maintain them. Unfortunately, Luther did not recant. He appealed to Pope Leo X.

As a clarification of the issues Luther raised regarding indulgences and as a definitive statement of the Catholic faith, Pope Leo X issued a doctrinal statement on indulgences dated November 9, 1518. In this constitution, *Cum Postquam,* the Pope declared that the Pope can remit the punishment due to sin through an indulgence from the treasury of merit of Christ and the saints. Although Cardinal Cajetan, still in German lands, published this constitution in December, it remained without much effect on most people's minds because they were too annoyed and irritated by the Vatican's policy of using indulgences to raise money for Roman projects.

Luther meanwhile continued to maintain his own positions, arguing that he would only change them if they were contradicted by Scripture as he understood Scripture. In fact, before the publication of the papal constitution, Luther had appealed to a general council of the Church. In making this appeal, Luther held that a council was superior to the Pope in matters of faith.

While always maintaining that the text of his appeal to a council was not to be published except in the case of his excommunication, the printers published it almost immediately. It is hard not to believe that Luther wanted the appeal made public. In making the appeal to a council, Luther obviously feared the worst from Rome (as shown by his acknowledgment that

Rome might excommunicate him) and was trying to counter any Roman move before it was made. It is also hard to imagine that Luther, who had declared the superiority of Scripture as he understood it and who had refused to change his opinions unless he could be convinced they contradicted Scripture, actually would submit to any decree of a council which contradicted his teaching.

In seems that by appealing to a council, Luther was giving the impression that he would accept its decisions. But what he had already said proved that he would not accept even a decision of a council if it opposed him. Of course, he was convinced he was correct and he may have thought that a council would uphold him. But if one appeals to a council, there is an implicit agreement to accept any decision it gives as binding. Luther clearly did not intend this concession, and therefore his appeal to a council was mostly intended to deflect any attack on him from Rome.

Martin Luther had raised theological issues which needed clarification. At the same time, these issues challenged the teaching of the Church, and even the Church itself. In the early years of the Reformation, then, the Church's teaching authority was challenged and the Church responded through Cajetan and then through the constitution of the Pope, *Cum Postquam*.

Theological Reaction to Luther

Meanwhile, theologians disputed with Luther on the points he raised. A theologian at the University of Ingolstadt, John Eck, had composed a treatise against Luther's ninety-five theses. A colleague of Luther's at Wittenberg, Karlstadt, had answered Eck. In an amicable conversation with Luther in October 1518, Eck proposed that there be a debate among Luther, Eck, and Karlstadt. This disputation was held June-July 1519 in Leipzig and was a very public affair attended by abbots, counts, princes, and students.

Eck and Karlstadt began the debate, but soon Eck and Luther traded arguments on the nature and structure of the Church. If the Church taught authoritatively and interpreted Scripture authoritatively, then Luther was bound to acknowledge the papal constitution *Cum Postquam*. However, if Scripture was superior to the Church, then Luther just might be correct in his view on indulgences.

Eck defended the primacy of the Pope as the successor of St. Peter and the vicar of Christ on earth. He asserted that this primacy was given to Peter by Christ Himself. Luther disputed these points, and Eck responded that Luther was embracing the positions of Wyclif and Hus. Luther began to defend some of the positions of Hus. Eck responded by quoting the Council of Constance. Answering this argument of Eck, Luther said that a council could err and in fact the Council of Constance had erred in condemning Hus. The only criterion for the faith was Scripture. Neither a Pope nor a council is authoritative if the teaching proclaimed contradicts Scripture.

Of course, this position is the only one Luther could take to defend his teaching if it was contradicted by a Pope or a council. But with these statements, Luther had formally and publicly decreed the famous *sola Scriptura*, Scripture alone, as one of the major themes in his teaching. This principle was to become one of the cornerstones of the Reformation. It involves, as Eck clearly saw and Luther confirmed, a totally different view of the Church than what was taught by Catholicism.

Luther's Popularity

Still, Luther had touched a chord deep within the people. People could see his intensity and his determination to hold to the truth as he understood it, even at incredible personal cost. Further, they realized, even if they could not put it into words, that the Church needed reform. Many thought that Martin Luther would be the one to spearhead that reform.

Part of his success was certainly his marketing skills. He published many of his writings not just in scholarly Latin, but also in vernacular German. At one point during the Leipzig disputation, he insisted that he be allowed to speak in German so that those attending could understand him better. Certainly, the invention of the printing press in the previous century facilitated the rapid and widespread publication of Luther's writings. In addition, Luther's initial objections touched a money-raising project. Clearly, everyone had an interest in such an endeavor.

Luther's intense personality, his devotion to religious truth as he saw it, the unfortunate situation of the Church in his time, his folksy German style, the availability of the printing press, as well as the initial object of Luther's criticisms: an indulgence promulgated to raise money — all contributed to Luther's success and popularity.

1520: Decisive Break With the Church

After the Leipzig disputation, Luther authored three tracts which marked a further development of his thought: *The Address to the German Nobility, The Babylonian Captivity,* and *The Freedom of the Christian Man.* The first appeared in the summer of 1520, the second in October of the same year, and the third in November 1520. Erasmus saw in the second work, *The Babylonian Captivity,* the definitive break with the Catholic Church. In *The Address to the German Nobility,* Luther argues that the authority of the Church is not superior to the secular power, that the Pope and the bishops are not the only ones who have the right to interpret Scripture authoritatively, and that the Pope is not the only one who can legitimately call a council. Further, in this treatise, Luther expands his criticism of the sacraments. He denies the hierarchical priesthood and holds that all are deacons, priests, and bishops through Baptism.

In *The Address to the German Nobility,* Luther is concerned with denying the priesthood in order to deprive Rome of any and all authority. But he affirms the common priesthood of all believers. Still, he must replace the authority of Rome in the Church with some kind of guiding hand, and so he turns to the secular powers.

Arguing that all share the common priesthood, he states that since Rome, the Pope, and the bishops have failed to hold to the obvious meaning of Scripture, the secular powers must intervene and take up their duty as Christians — i.e., as priests — and save the Church from its misguided priests, its bishops, and the Pope. Luther suggests a reform movement which includes the elimination of the payments to Rome, of penalties reserved to Rome, of celibacy for priests (because there are no differences among Christians founded on the hierarchical priesthood), and of the numerous feast days. He also advocates a reform of the universities and some social measures which he thinks should be taken. *The Address to the German Nobility* testifies to Luther's popularity: it sold 4,000 copies in the first week.

The second work, *The Babylonian Captivity,* presented Luther's ideas on the sacraments. Earlier in 1520, he had already preached sermons on Baptism, Eucharist, and Reconciliation. In these sermons, Luther denied the existence of the Sacraments of Confirmation, Matrimony, Holy Orders, and the Anointing of the Sick.

This denial followed from his assertion of the primacy of Scripture.

Since he did not find Confirmation, Matrimony, Holy Orders, and the Anointing of the Sick in Scripture, he claimed that they were not true sacraments. Further, as we have seen, with his understanding of faith, he made the sacrament of Reconciliation dependent on the faith of the penitent. As long as the penitent believed that forgiveness was received, it was. In addition, the penitent did not have to confess sins to a priest because the sacrament did not depend on the action of the priest, but rather on the faith of the penitent.

Luther came to these conclusions by applying his principles of the primacy of Scripture and justification by faith to the sacraments. The *Babylonian Captivity* repeated Luther's denial of all the sacraments, except Baptism, the Eucharist, and Reconciliation. He repeated his insistence on the requirement of faith for Reconciliation, eliminating the role of the priest.

While he did not depart as radically from the teaching of the Church regarding the Eucharist, his emphasis has indications of his basic premises. He holds that the Eucharist is not a work — not something we offer to God — but rather a gift of God to us. We are needy and desperate people who cannot offer anything to God. The Eucharist is the Father reaching down to us and offering us His love and mercy. It is not, above all, a sacrifice we offer to the Father.

Although Baptism fared better than the other sacraments in this work, the re-interpretation of Reconciliation, the denial of the aspect of sacrifice in the Eucharist, and the refusal to acknowledge the other four sacraments were definitive breaks with the Church. Again in this document we see Luther's three basic principles applied: the awesome majesty of God, as opposed to our own sinful condition (thus, we cannot offer a sacrifice); granting of holiness through faith (justification by faith); and the primacy of Scripture.

The third significant treatise of the momentous year 1520 was *The Freedom of the Christian Man*. In this work Luther paints the life of a Christian, emphasizing faith that results in works. We are not saved by observing the commandments or doing works (because we are incapable of offering anything to the awesome majesty of God), but faith leads us to observe the commandments and do pious works. Further, the Christian is entirely free and autonomous, subject to no one as long as the Christian accepts the

Gospel. (Clearly, Luther has the Pope and the bishops in mind when he argues that the Christian is subject to no one.)

Luther and the Papacy

On June 15, 1520, Pope Leo issued the Bull *Exsurge Domine*, which condemned forty-one of Luther's propositions. Unfortunately, this document was not well drafted. In censuring Luther's statements, the Bull did not distinguish between heretical statements and those which were merely misleading. Even scholars could not understand why some of the statements had been included in the censure.

However, until the Council of Trent (1545-1547, 1551-1552, 1562-1563), *Exsurge Domine* was the only papal document concerning Lutheran teachings. The Bull did not excommunicate Luther, but rather gave him sixty days to recant. John Eck was asked to publicize the Bull in Germany, but had difficulty because of Luther's popularity and the animosity towards Rome. At the urging of an advisor, Luther addressed the Pope in a letter in October 1520.

In this document, Luther tries to draw a distinction between Pope Leo and the Vatican bureaucracy. Still, there is an absolute refusal to recant or change his opinions. At the same time, Luther was authoring works vilifying the Bull *Exsurge Domine* and calling the Pope the Antichrist for issuing it. Luther argues that the Bull should be withdrawn, and if not withdrawn, then no Christian should heed Rome, the enemy of God!

With Luther's refusal to recant, the Pope issued another document, *Decet Romanum Pontificem*, on January 3, 1521, which excommunicated Luther. At this point, according to traditional medieval practices, Luther should have been outlawed by the state. In other words, the secular arm should have carried out the effects of the sentence of excommunication. However, Luther was far too popular with the people for the Emperor simply to execute the sentence.

The new Emperor, Charles V (1519-1556), had promised at his election not to outlaw anyone without a hearing. In addition, Charles V had promised Luther's ruler, Frederick the Wise, that he, the Emperor, would interrogate Luther. The representatives of the Church objected to this procedure because it appeared that the civil authority was claiming the right to judge Luther on matters of faith. Further, it was unseemly for the Emperor and his nobles, the defenders of the Church, to be negotiating with an excommunicated priest.

Despite these objections, Luther was granted a safe-conduct to the Diet of Worms. Martin was summoned so that he might identify his writings and then recant. Conceding the inevitability of an interview with Luther by the Diet and the Emperor, the representatives of the Church wanted Luther to recant before he was granted an appearance before the Diet. In this way, the Diet would not be setting the dangerous precedent of negotiating with an excommunicated heretic. The Diet rejected this proposal, but only summoned Luther for the purpose of hearing his recantation. They did not foresee a mutual exchange of ideas with Martin Luther.

On April 17, 1521, Luther stood before the Emperor and the nobles at the Diet of Worms. He identified his writings and was then asked to recant. Luther asked for time to reflect and was sent home for the day. At first glance, it does seem strange that Luther would have asked for time to study since he had steadfastly defended his writings for some years already. However, the solemn assembly was unlike any meeting Luther had yet addressed.

The Emperor himself was present. Charles V represented the vast power of the civil authority. Almost anyone would have been a little awed by the power represented by the Diet. Further, Luther was out of his element. He was accustomed to dealing with priests, bishops, and cardinals, not Emperors and nobles.

Recalling Luther's temperament, it is not surprising that in this context he would have been a little bit hesitant and so requested a day to think about his position. So, on the next day, April 18, Luther was again asked if he would recant and he refused, claiming that he could not repudiate Scripture as he understood it. Still, the matter was not definitively settled.

Charles V asked Luther to consider his position for three days. During those days, there was a special committee appointed to try to persuade Luther to abjure his previous writings. When those efforts failed, others approached Luther privately. Still he refused. Therefore, on April 25, Charles V sent Luther his decision: the Emperor would enforce the effects of the excommunication.

On May 26, 1521, Charles V signed the Edict of Worms banning Luther, his followers, and his writings. Further, all books about the faith were only to be printed with the permission of the local bishop. Luther left Worms at the end of April and was "kidnapped" by pre-arrangement and taken to Wartburg castle. Frederick the Wise, Luther's ruler, had arranged this "kidnapping." He gave Luther sanctuary in Wartburg to protect him from the effects of the Edict of Worms.

Luther at the Wartburg

At the Wartburg, Luther was alone. The change was almost overwhelming. He had been at the center of an exciting and sometimes exhilarating debate for almost four years and all of a sudden he was cut off from the mainstream, living alone. He was physically afflicted with insomnia as well as constipation. But even worse than the loneliness and physical distress were the doubts. He asked himself if he alone were wise, if all the people of the past centuries were totally wrong. These particular doubts passed, but then he reproached himself for not standing strong and firm at the Diet of Worms. He thought he should not have wavered and asked for a day to reflect. In short, Luther's personality, with all the mood swings and the possibilities it possessed for self-doubt, survived the first years of the Reformation!

One might even suggest that between October 1517 and November-December 1521 Luther's emotions were at a high and at the Wartburg, they swung the opposite way and as a result he became depressed. But he cured himself of most if not all of these afflictions with work. Cut off and alone as he was, he could still write, and that he did.

Luther's most important work during the Wartburg "exile" was the translation of the Bible into German. His was not the first translation of the Scriptures into German, but Luther's German had a power of expression not found in the earlier German translations.

In Luther's Bible, the German language became inextricably bound to the message of the Scriptures. This gave Luther's Bible a unique form. Its words were easily grasped and remembered. Luther's translation is uniformly acknowledged as a literary work of great importance, not only because it represented and was itself a force in the development of High German (from a number of different dialects), but also because Luther brought his understanding of the Scriptures, the fruit of years of study and prayer, to his work.

For Luther, Scripture was actually the Word of God: God speaking directly to him. The events recorded in the two Testaments did not belong to history, rather they were current events: stories and accounts of powerful encounters with God which revealed God — Father, Son and Holy Spirit. The Scriptures were almost like newspaper accounts of events which were central in his life. The intense interest he brought to the Scriptures might be compared to that of generals waiting to hear news of how their soldiers have done in the most important battle of the war, or that of parents waiting to hear if their son will live or die after surgery.

For most of us, it is hard to imagine reading the Scriptures in this fashion, but for Luther, he never approached the Word of God in any other way. Therefore, his translation had a power and a form which were absent from earlier translations of the Bible into German.

Theological Difficulties

While crediting Luther for his monumental work in translating the Bible into German, it is necessary to acknowledge certain tendencies in the translation. First, the intensity he brought to his work is partly the result of his own personal encounter with the Scriptures. He had a tendency to view all of Scripture from the point of view of his own personal experience with it. So, for example, the phrase "the justice of God" was not always translated in a way totally faithful to the original meaning. Luther gave such phrases an interpretation which was consistent with his own experiences. Second and more serious, he decided what was Scripture and what was not.

In the Old Testament, he abandoned the use of the Greek Old Testament, that is, the translation of the Hebrew Scriptures into Greek (with some additional books for the most part written in Greek—the deutero-canonicals), which the Church had always used, in favor of the Hebrew Old Testament.

Thus, the Reformation Bible did not include about seven books that the Catholic Bible always had included. Further, he had serious questions about James and the Apocalypse (Revelation) in the New Testament and decided that these books were not of the same importance as the other books of the New Testament. But, of course, there is a paradox with this position. For Luther, Scripture was authoritative, so how could he decide that some books were less important? In effect, Luther established himself as the authoritative teacher of Scripture.

But how can Luther argue that his interpretation of Scripture was authoritative and at the same time hold that everyone could interpret Scripture for himself or herself? Why could Scripture not mean something else to another whose experience of Scripture was different from Luther's? Thus, even in translating the Scriptures, Luther confronted one of the most difficult questions of the Reformation: Who authoritatively decides what Christ revealed in the Scriptures or anywhere?

Luther never truly solved this problem. In effect, he became the interpreter of Scripture for his followers— that is, he put himself in the place of the Church. But, given his principle of personal faith, this solution in itself was contradictory and not completely satisfactory.

In addition to the problems in teaching his personal interpretation of Scripture without allowing others to interpret Scripture for themselves — either those more radical than him or, even less, the Catholics — Luther's theology had other difficulties. While rejecting transubstantiation as an imposition on the scriptural texts, Luther never truly solved the difficulty of how the bread and wine were also the body and blood of Christ. He suggests that it is something like the presence of the divinity hidden by the humanity of Christ.

Of course, this point of view can be reconciled with the Catholic faith: Catholics often speak of the body and blood of Christ as veiled or hidden under the appearances of bread and wine. But if Luther meant that the bread and wine are still present as the humanity of Christ is always present together with the divinity in the mystery of the Incarnation, then his position is not consistent with the Catholic faith. But Luther is not clear.

Much of what he does say can be interpreted in a Catholic sense. Tied to the Scriptures as he was, he could not very well deny, as others did, lines like "This is my body" or "This is my blood." (See Matthew 26:26-28.)

Luther's substitution of the authority of secular rulers for the authority of the Church undid centuries of struggle, at least in the West, between the Church and the Empire. Constantly fighting for its own independence especially from the German Emperor, the Church had achieved a certain independence from the secular powers. Luther's rejection of the papacy and his appeal to the civil rulers tied the Reformed Church to the secular powers. This alliance was to have very serious consequences in the wars of religion of the sixteenth and seventeenth centuries.

Luther's Influences

While Luther was at the Wartburg, others were drawing practical conclusions from his teachings. As a university professor and a troubled soul, Martin Luther proposed theological ideas as part of his profession and out of his personal need. Even though he had the care of a parish in Wittenberg, the origin of his ideas seems to have come from his research and his personal insights. He brought to the flock the results of his research and of his prayer life.

In this sense, Luther was focused on himself. With this narrow perspective, he was probably surprised at the public reaction to his initial teachings. He was equally surprised by some of the practical applications of his teachings made by his followers while he was at the Wartburg.

Melancthon, professor of Greek at the University of Wittenberg, Karlstadt (the same Karlstadt who had debated with Luther and Eck in 1519), professor at the University and archdeacon at the Castle church in Wittenberg, and Gabriel Zwilling, a monk of the same order as Luther who was also from Wittenberg, began to implement and apply Luther's teachings. None of Luther's teachings, except those against indulgences, had changed the lives of ordinary people.

Melancthon, Karlstadt, and Zwilling implemented reforms which did change the lives of ordinary people. The first change was the marriage of priests. In *The Babylonian Captivity* Luther had advocated the marriage of priests partly because God had established marriage (and human laws cannot contravene God's will). Luther also argued that priests should be allowed to marry because all Christians were priests by their Baptism and therefore there should be no special privileges or obligations of the clergy. Further, Luther argued for married priests because many priests were not living according to their promises of celibacy. Since some were not following the discipline, Luther argues not that the discipline should be enforced, but that it should be changed. In Wittenberg in 1521, priests married, including Karlstadt.

Further, since there was no special vocation to the priesthood and since everyone was brought to salvation by faith, what was the purpose of a monk? In 1521, Zwilling preached to the monks in Wittenberg against the monastic life. Fifteen left. But Luther had some questions about the status of monks. Initially, Luther believed that there could be a distinction between the promises of a priest and the vows of a monk, because a monk entered into his life willingly whereas a priest candidate had no choice but to embrace celibacy if he wanted to be ordained. The priest was therefore more or less compelled whereas the monk made a free promise.

Eventually, Luther held that even a monastic vow did not bind forever. The virtues must be observed, he said, and if the vows helped someone to be virtuous, then they should be kept. However, as soon as the vows interfered with the practice of virtue, one should abandon them. For example, if one found it difficult to be chaste under the vow of virginity, then the vow should be abandoned and marriage should be embraced, because marriage can make it possible to practice chastity. On the practical level, this position was a *carte blanche* permission to the monks to leave the orders.

The most obvious changes came in the celebration of the Mass. It has been said that it is the Sunday Liturgy that touches most of the faithful most directly. If the liturgy is changed, people are affected and the Church eventually changes. In denying that the Mass was a sacrifice, Luther opened up the possibility of changes in how the Mass was celebrated.

While he was at the Wartburg, his followers in Wittenberg began to change the liturgy. It was translated from Latin to German. All references to the Mass as a sacrifice were deleted. Communion was distributed under both species; that is, people received both the host and the cup. Some celebrated Mass without vestments. Private Masses and the adoration of Christ present under the appearances of bread and wine were abandoned at Wittenberg.

These reforms of the liturgy went beyond anything Luther had foreseen or even wanted. Frederick the Wise was concerned and asked Luther's help. He returned to Wittenberg and preached against those who in his judgment had gone too far. Luther did not want to offend those with weak consciences — those who might be scandalized by the changes. They needed time to adjust. Second, he was much more concerned with spiritual attitudes than with external forms. Finally, he genuinely valued and treasured the traditions of Christianity.

At Wittenberg, then, after Luther's intervention, the Mass was again celebrated with vestments and in Latin. In fact, little had changed except that the references to the Mass as a sacrifice were left out. However, it was too late. The German Mass had spread far and wide and would eventually replace the traditional Latin liturgy in the Churches of the Reform (Lutheran Churches). But what was also clearly occurring was a split among the Reformers, with Luther taking the conservative role and Karlstadt, among others, taking a radical role.

Luther and Society

It is hard for most of us to imagine the ferment Luther had begun. He had challenged the authority of the Church, and his attitude gave permission to others to do the same thing. This attitude found fertile soil in those who were already dissatisfied with society.

In the late fifteenth and early sixteenth centuries in Germany, there was a growing movement by "peasants" against the "lords." These "peasants" were farmers who were doing very well and demanded rights and privileges commensurate with their new economic status. Although successful in economic terms, they were for the most part legally serfs with hardly any rights. They wanted serfdom eliminated. They resented the traditional payments to their lords and their lack of rights, particular the rights of hunting and fishing which were restricted to the nobility. Often they were particularly hostile to clerical domination and to monasteries.

Simultaneously, in the cities, the lower classes fought against the government officials. Journeymen and craftsmen railed against the masters and patricians. There was widespread social conflict in Germany even before Martin Luther began publishing his theological ideas. However, Luther's insistence on individual freedom before God and his example of resisting authority combined with the pre-existing causes of social conflict. Luther's teachings and his example were not the sole cause of the so-called Peasants War (which broke out in 1524), but Luther certainly provided an impetus which was a contributing factor in the upheaval.

The rising of the "peasants" began in the Black Forest region in May-June 1524. The movement soon spread to Swabia, Alsace, Franconia, Thuringia, Saxony, Tirol, and Carinthia. In their demands, which included the free election of pastors, elimination of certain dues owed to the Church, the use of other dues owed to the Church as salaries for pastors, the rights of hunting and fishing, and an end of serfdom, the "peasants" quoted the Gospel.

The "peasants" looked to Luther as one who would support them. However, he was appalled by what he saw. Luther regarded the "peasants" as lawless rebels. In accord with his substitution of the authority of the state for the Church, he asked that the civil authority ruthlessly and mercilessly destroy the rebellious movement, and it was done.

By siding with the "lords," Luther lost much of his earlier popularity. His actions were consistent with his theology, but they also show that he had failed to grasp the impact his thoughts and ideas had on society. He was truly shocked that people could use his intellectual work as an excuse to rebel against lawful authority — even though he had done the same thing in opposing the Church. His support of the nobility cemented even further his alliance with the princes.

Luther's alliance with the nobility was a source of support for him. On their part, some nobles were more than willing to follow the Reform and support it because it enriched their coffers. Since monasteries had no place in Luther's theology — Luther himself not only abandoned the monastery but married in 1525 — monks and nuns who were persuaded by the teachings of Luther left their monasteries and convents.

The institutions died; there was no one left to manage and staff them. Abandoned, the princes saw an opportunity to alienate the lands belonging to the monasteries and convents and take them for themselves. These religious institutions were, for the most part, fabulously wealthy because they had existed for centuries and received gifts and bequests from almost every generation. Since the monastery never ceased to exist, the holdings remained with the institution. As the generations passed, more and more lands came under the control of the monks and nuns.

The lords were naturally pleased to acquire these substantial holdings as part of the Reform movement. Of course, in some cases, the monks and nuns were forced to leave by a prince who had become Lutheran. In these cases, the prince confiscated the monastic lands.

With the possibility of acquiring vast wealth, there was a vested interest on the part of many princes to abandon the ancient faith and embrace the Reform. Even some Catholic principalities administered by bishops and heads of orders embraced the Reform; for example, the Teutonic order which controlled East Prussia went over to the Reform.

The Lutheran princes were threatened by the Catholic Emperor, who had the duty to defend the Church. They banded together in an alliance called the Schmalkaldic League. The King of France, Francis I, allied himself with the Schmalkaldic League, beginning a long tradition of the French kings forming alliances with non-Catholics in order to oppose the Habsburg Holy Roman Emperors and the Spanish Habsburg kings. (France felt threatened by the Habsburgs on the east from Germany and on the south from Spain.)

Charles V tried in vain to find a formula for peace that would prevent the religious division of Germany. He also asked the Pope to call a council. He was not successful in either endeavor. Neither France nor England wanted a council and the Popes were not sanguine about one because the councils of the previous century had caused a considerable amount of trouble for the papacy. (The fifteenth-century councils had tried to establish the Church council as a permanent body — much like the Parliament in England. This movement is called Conciliarism.)

Charles V was also unsuccessful in seeking a peaceful solution. In 1546, the Schmalkaldic League began a civil war in Germany. This religious war continued for nine years until the Peace of Augsburg in 1555. At that time, the famous formula of *cuius regio, eius religio* (literally, "whose region, his religion") was one of the foundations of the peace.

With this principle, the religion of the local prince was to be the religion of the people living in that area. If the ruler was Catholic, then all the people were Catholic or they had to leave that principality. If the ruler was Lutheran, then all the people were Lutheran or they had to leave the territory of that prince. Clearly, the alliance of Church and state initially taught by Luther reached a high point with the Peace of Augsburg, but it did assure peace, at least for a time.

There is no question that Martin Luther is one of the characters in history most difficult to grasp. Nevertheless, he is a pivotal figure. Without him, it is hardly possible to believe the Reformation would have occurred. It certainly would not have developed in the same way. But there were other major figures who colored the whole period, including Ulrich Zwingli, John Calvin, and John Knox.

Martin Luther

This founder of the Lutheran Church taught that human beings were saved by belief in Christ alone (not works). He taught that only Scripture contained the Revelation of Christ, not Tradition, and that the Church was not the sole interpreter of the authentic Revelation found in Scripture. He held to the awesome holiness of God and the horrific nature of sin.

22

Zwingli

Zwingli: Beginnings

As mentioned in the previous discussion on Luther, there was a climate of opposition to the Church, particularly to Rome and the papacy, in the German-speaking lands in the fifteenth and sixteenth centuries. Further, as already discussed, there were some legitimate reasons for this attitude.

When Luther objected to some Church practices, eventually breaking with the Church and resisting imperial authority that defended the Church, he metaphorically threw the lit match into the waiting pool of gas and oil. In the situation in the German-speaking lands at the time of Luther, all that was needed for a revolution was the catalyst, someone to sound the voice of protest against the traditional authorities. Luther was that catalyst. But he could not control what he had started. Almost immediately, other voices were heard which went far beyond what Luther ever intended — for instance, Karlstadt (already discussed). But there were others. In Zurich, Switzerland, Ulrich Zwingli, independently of Luther, was critical of the abuses in the Church.

Ulrich Zwingli was born on January 1, 1484. He received his first education from his uncle, the pastor at Walensee. At ten, he was at the Latin school at Basel and he completed his early studies in Berne in 1497 when he was only thirteen years old. The next year he was at Vienna, then back in Basel in 1502.

In 1506, he received the Master of Arts degree, was ordained a Catholic priest, and was appointed a pastor. Assisted by others, his duties were not burdensome, and he devoted himself to the study of Scripture (using the Latin Vulgate), the ancient authors, and the Fathers. He even learned Greek on his own in 1513. It was in these years that Zwingli also became very interested in politics, particularly in the relationships between the relatively independent Swiss cantons on the one hand and the papacy and French on the other. In 1516 he moved to the Benedictine Monastery at Einsiedeln in Switzerland, began to study Erasmus's Greek New Testament, and had a particular interest in St. Paul's letters.

After becoming rector of the cathedral in 1518, he began a series of sermons on the New Testament which continued to 1525. At first, Zwingli's preaching could be interpreted in an orthodox sense, much like Luther's earlier texts. However, in 1519, Zwingli encountered some of Luther's writings and saw in them some of the same ideas he had already embraced independently. While generally approving of Luther's ideas, Zwingli had difficulty with Luther's attitude when the German Reformer was threatened with excommunication. Zwingli remained cautious in his promotion of Luther and Luther's ideas.

Zwingli's Break With Rome

Zwingli himself dates his break with the papacy to 1520 when, preaching a series of sermons on the Psalms, he embraced the notion of salvation by faith alone. From certain glosses Zwingli made earlier on St. Augustine's writings, it does seem that he came to this conclusion without the aid of Luther's writings, but on the other hand, he was familiar with them and it is hard to believe that he did not at least see in them a confirmation of what he was thinking.

In 1520, Zwingli lost his pension because he opposed the Cardinal of Zurich's policy of raising a levy of fifteen hundred men from the city in support of the Pope. Despite Zwingli's opposition, the city council approved of the Cardinal's levy of men. But when the men's wages were delayed, many in Zurich were more than a little annoyed at the Cardinal and the Pope. Of course, this attitude (in addition to all the other grievances against the Church) fostered a hostility towards the official Church.

Zwingli's definitive break with the Church came in the spring of 1522 in a minor incident. Some friends of Zwingli's decided to have a dinner of sausages in Lent, contrary to the Church's law of abstinence. Zwingli was present but did not eat the sausages. Still, it was clear that direct disobedience of fasting laws were partly the result of Zwingli's preaching.

In fact, in April 1522, Zwingli defended the freedom of every Christian to fast (or abstain) or not according to his or her own understandings.

Further, about the same time, Zwingli entered into a secret marriage with a widow living in his neighborhood. The link between the encouragement to disobey the fast-and-abstinence laws of the Church and the disobedience of the celibacy requirement was the principle that the Christian is only bound by the Scriptures. Zwingli, through his own study of Scripture and his encounter with Luther, had come to the principle that the only norm for Christian behavior was the Scriptures.

The Reform in Zurich

A complaint by the bishop of Constance that, despite the condemnation of Luther by the Pope and Emperor, similar ideas were promoted by many priests in Switzerland was the catalyst for the next development. The response from Zurich to Constance soon came. The chapter of the Cathedral (a chapter was the name given to the priests serving at Cathedrals who assisted the Bishop in administrative duties) approved the principle that Scripture was to be the sole guide for all that was preached.

In September 1522, Zwingli published a sermon arguing against using tradition or the authority of the Church in interpreting Scripture. Almost immediately, on October 10, 1522, Zwingli resigned his position, but the city council established a preaching position for him. He broke with the Church, and the secular authority constituted itself as the governing body of the Church and appointed Zwingli to be the first pastor of the Reform in Zurich.

Zwingli had always been interested in politics. In the break with Rome, he did not hesitate to replace Church authority with secular authority. Luther had done the same thing, but in a theoretical way (at least at first) through his writings. In his protest, Luther broke with Rome but did not receive a position from the secular authority (although, clearly, Frederick the Wise did protect him).

Zwingli, however, simultaneously broke with the Church and received his position from the city council. The city council was certainly able to make this highly political move because of the resentment of the people towards the Church, aroused partly by the Cardinal's policy and the failure to pay the wages of the soldiers.

Zwingli needed to solidify his new position. At his urging, the city council met on January 29, 1523. At this meeting, Zwingli presented sixty-seven theses. He rejected the papacy, the Mass, the intercession of the saints, fast and abstinence laws, religious orders, celibacy, and the misuse of excommunication. Scripture was to be the sole authority.

While all this is mostly consistent with Luther's teaching, there were some differences. First, Zwingli clearly questioned the use of the penalty of excommunication. (Luther had not.) Second, Zwingli did not accept Luther's specific teaching on indulgences. The meeting concluded with the resolution that nothing was to be preached which could not be justified by the Scriptures. But just as in Wittenberg, some were reluctant to put into practice all the consequences of the decisions. Others wanted to implement everything immediately. Of particular importance was the practice of the Mass — the Sunday liturgy — because it touched the people most directly in their spiritual lives.

While tolerating the Mass in Latin, Zwingli changed only the Eucharistic prayer of the Mass and references to it as a sacrifice. However, two years later, by April 1525, Zwingli believed the time had come. At a meeting of the city council, Zwingli proposed his new understanding of the Mass, and the city council approved his teaching and abolished the old Mass. This act was not in response to demands from the people. Even less was it a recognition of an existing situation. The city council simply abolished the old liturgy because Zwingli asked that it be done.

Differences Between Zwingli and Luther on the Eucharist

While there were some differences between Zwingli and Luther in the relationship with the secular authority, on indulgences and on the matter of the use of excommunication, the major point of contention between the two Reformers was the real presence of Christ in the Eucharist. This matter was discussed at a meeting called by Philip of Hesse which convened in Marburg on September 30, 1529.

Luther wanted to discuss other points first, but Zwingli and the Swiss delegates protested that the meeting had been called on the matter of the Eucharist. Insisting on the obvious meaning of the words of Scripture, "This is my body," Luther held that Christ's body and blood were present in the bread and wine. Zwingli said that these famous words of the Gospel were meant metaphorically. He argued that there was no possibility for any material thing to be the means of a spiritual blessing or grace. So for Zwingli it is impossible that even Christ's own flesh and blood could be the means of the gift of grace, because the body and blood of Christ are physical and material. (This point, of course, calls into question the entire sacramental system, because with this principle no sacrament can confer grace since all the sacraments are material signs.) Zwingli further argued that the Eucharist did not make Christ's death present. Rather, for Zwingli, the Mass was simply a memorial, a reminder of what Christ had done for us.

This point is consistent with the idea that the Mass is not a sacrifice. In acknowledging the Real Presence of Christ in the Eucharist, Luther still denied that it was a sacrifice. But it is difficult to argue both of these positions. If Christ's body and blood are present, how can it not be a re-presentation of His sacrifice? However, such an inference would contradict Luther's fundamental stance about faith. And yet, he was too faithful to the Scriptures to deny the Real Presence. Luther held both that Christ's body and blood were present and that the Mass was not a sacrifice.

Zwingli agreed that it was not a sacrifice, but also (more consistently) held that Christ's body and blood were not truly present. Nevertheless, he still had to account for the words "This is my body." Zwingli argued that the "is" in this phrase meant "signifies." He said that there were other passages where "is" had the meaning of "signifies." It is impossible that Christ could have meant that people should consume His body and blood because it would be cannibalistic and repulsive as well as useless (since Christ's body and blood, as material elements, could not be the means of grace or any other spiritual blessing).

For Zwingli, the Eucharist was a memorial — a reminder of what Christ had done for us — nothing more. The meeting broke up with a common statement, but Luther and his companions interpreted it one way and Zwingli and his followers interpreted it in another way. (One might suggest: so much for the clarity of written texts — even those of Scripture! In other words, the problem of the authoritative interpretation of Scripture had no more been recognized, let alone settled, by Zwingli than it had been by Luther!)

A Religious War in Switzerland

Although Zurich had been guided by Zwingli in its embrace of the Reformation, five cantons of the Swiss confederation remained Catholic.

In the loose Swiss confederation, the religious differences among the cantons caused problems. Zurich imposed a blockade on the Catholic cantons, and they declared war. Two thousand five hundred men from Zurich, including Zwingli, faced the twelve thousand from the five Catholic cantons.

On October 11, 1531, Zwingli died defending his principles against the Catholics. As a result of the peace treaty, Zurich renounced its previous policy of forming alliances with reformed principalities and kingdoms outside of the Swiss confederation, a repudiation of Zwingli's policies. As a result, the Reform in Switzerland slowed. Eventually, in 1549, the Reform party in Zurich came to an agreement with Calvin. The Swiss German-speaking Reform merged with the Swiss French-speaking Reform.

Zwingli's Reform

Zwingli embraced everything Luther taught except Luther's teaching on indulgences, excommunication, and the Real Presence. Zwingli, as opposed to Luther, taught that the Eucharist was only a symbol of Christ's body and blood and that it was a memorial of Christ's sacrifice enabling us to remember what Christ did for us.

23

The Anabaptists

Beginnings of Anabaptism

WHEN THE ZURICH CITY COUNCIL INSTITUTED THE REFORM IN ZURICH IN 1523, the Latin Mass was retained except for references to the Mass as a sacrifice and certain wording in the Eucharistic prayer. It should not surprise us that this "bow" to the "old" liturgy offended those who demanded more rapid changes.

A few radicals broke with Zwingli and established their own congregations independent of any authority, civil or ecclesiastical. The leaders of this movement were Konrad Grebel, son of a member of the Zurich city council, and Felix Mantz, son of a canon of the cathedral. Tied to both religious and civil authority through their fathers, these young men (they were twenty-five and twenty-three years old in 1523) rejected their heritage and, to a certain extent, the careers of their fathers, and set off on their own. They were the founders of the Anabaptists.

The Anabaptists believed that the Church Christ founded was never intended to be the Church of the masses, but only of a select few who believed properly and could embrace a strict Christian life. Since membership was totally voluntary and was the result of a serious faith commitment, which in turn led to a virtuous Christian life, authority was unnecessary.

Baptism was the sacramental sign that signified that the members had come to embrace the Christian life and joined the Church because of their conversion. Baptism was the sign of the conversion and the means of becoming a member of the Church. Baptism was the result of conversion of heart and not the cause. The only obvious effect of Baptism was to incorporate the person into the Church. Since the Anabaptists viewed Baptism as the result of conversion, not the cause, they objected to infant Baptism and regarded it not only as useless but as not even a true Baptism.

Rejecting both ecclesiastical and civil authority as well as infant Baptism, the Anabaptists quickly came into conflict with the civil government in Zurich. The dispute began in late 1524 when Grebel did not allow his infant son to be baptized. After a public disputation in January 1525, all those who did not allow their children to be baptized within eight days of birth were to be expelled from the city. Further, Grebel and Mantz were forbidden to speak.

As a result, the Anabaptists left Zurich and settled in the small town of Zollikon. But the Anabaptist withdrawal from Zurich did not satisfy the city council. Since Zollikon was subject to the Zurich city council, the council was able to establish the death penalty (by drowning) for all those who accepted re-Baptism — that is, for all those who were re-baptized as adults and thereby joined the new Church.

Growth of Anabaptism

Subject to the severe sanctions of the Zurich city council, Anabaptism was almost eliminated in the canton of Zurich, but those who had embraced the Anabaptist creed spread to other parts of Europe. Jörg Blaurock, severely whipped by order of the Zurich council, left Zurich and preached in Tirol, where in 1527 he was burned. Anabaptism had some success in southern Germany through the preaching of Michael Sattler. Anabaptism reached Moravia through Jakob Hutter.

Melchior Hoffman, originally a Lutheran lay preacher in the Baltic area (northern Germany), learned of the Anabaptist movement and joined it. He brought Anabaptism to northern Germany and Holland. Hoffman believed that he perceived signs of the end of the world — of the second coming of Christ. This apocalyptic vision was unique to Hoffman and the Anabaptism of north Germany and Holland.

Although Anabaptism spread, it was severely persecuted. We have already mentioned the sanctions used against it by the Zurich city council. The Tirol did not tolerate Anabaptism and burned Blaurock. Ferdinand I of Austria, the prince who governed Moravia, took decisive steps to prevent the growth and spread of Anabaptism. In the Holy Roman Empire, the Anabaptists were persecuted as heretics, but even the princes embracing or leaning towards Reform could not tolerate the Anabaptists.

Hoffman and his followers were persecuted in Holland. Hoffman's deputy and eight of his followers were beheaded in Holland in 1531. Hoffman went to Strasbourg, where he died after ten years' imprisonment. Many of the remaining Dutch Anabaptists fled to Münster, where the Anabaptists and other religious extremists were able to take over the city council. After holding the city for more than a year, the religious extremists were defeated. The leaders suffered torture and death. It must be said that the Anabaptists were persecuted by both Reformers and Catholics. They seemed to have an incredible stamina in the face of persecution.

After the debacle at Münster, Menno Simons, a Catholic priest who had left the Church, assumed a leadership role in the Anabaptist circles of northern Germany. While rejecting some of the extreme ideas of those previously active in Münster, he tried to form a community out of the peaceful Anabaptists (as opposed to those who had participated in the movement at Münster). He was successful and even gave his name to this group of Anabaptists: the Mennonites.

Anabaptist Beliefs

In addition to their rejection of infant Baptism and their acceptance of adult Baptism, the Anabaptists wanted to reestablish the primitive community of the Jerusalem Church in the decade after Christ's Ascension. The life of the individual member of the Anabaptist congregation was to be characterized by a fidelity to Scripture, particularly the New Testament.

The real presence was denied as was the sacrificial nature of the Eucharist. However, the Lord's Supper as a love feast, as an event binding the community together, was emphasized. Penalties like excommunication were accepted for those who had committed themselves to the Anabaptist creed but did not live it. (This acceptance of ecclesiastical penalties was an acceptance of authority, and it contradicted the initial emphasis of the Anabaptists.)

The Anabaptists stressed missionary activity, and some expected the second coming of Christ almost imminently. Military service, oaths, and the death penalty were rejected. (Of course, these positions challenged contemporary society rather drastically.) In addition, the Anabaptists believed that all property belonging to a member should be able to be used by other members if necessary.

There is no question that the Anabaptists represented the extreme left wing of the Reform. By contrast, even Zwingli looks conservative. However, while severely persecuted, they managed to survive. The Mennonites and several break-away groups such as the Amish continue to exist today throughout the world.

The Anabaptists

The fundamental belief of the Anabaptists, as opposed to the other Reform Churches, was that infant Baptism was wrong and that only adult Baptism — as a sign, not a cause, of conversion — was appropriate.

24

Calvin

Calvin's Early Life

JEAN CALVIN WAS BORN IN NOYON IN THE NORTH OF FRANCE (PICARDY) ON July 10, 1509. Today, his father would have been called the business manager of the cathedral because Jean's father managed the properties of the cathedral chapter. From a young age, Calvin was well acquainted with the Church and its operations. His earliest education was with the sons of a friendly noble family, and he even journeyed to Paris with them in 1523 when he was fourteen.

Calvin entered the University of Paris in that same year. He took the Licentiate degree in Arts (the step before the Master's) in 1528, but even though the cathedral chapter in Noyon had given the young Calvin an ecclesiastical appointment or benefice, he did not take up theology. In fact, he never had a formal course in theology. Instead, he began a study of law at Orléans, and in the next year, 1529, he continued his legal studies in Bourges. He earned the Licentiate in Law in 1532. Calvin's father may have influenced him to avoid theology and take up the law.

In 1528, the elder Calvin was excommunicated because of a law suit against the Noyon cathedral chapter. Clearly, in that year in which Jean Calvin began his legal studies, his father would probably not have been well disposed towards the Church and would also have had an interest in legal matters!

Having completed his legal studies and with his Father's influence removed by the elder Calvin's death in 1531, Calvin went to Paris and began to study the classics. (This relatively quick abandonment of a legal career after his father's death adds credence to the suggestion that Calvin's study of law was undertaken under fatherly influence.)

Calvin probably encountered Luther's writings in the 1520s, but it was not until the early 1530s, perhaps 1533, that he experienced a religious conversion. Calvin's turn towards religion was not the result of a personal struggle with the teachings of the Church, as Luther's was. Still less was it a dramatic new understanding of the Gospel. Calvin's conversion was a personal realization that he was called to reform the Church — to restore the Church to what he thought was true piety.

After his conversion, Calvin wandered throughout France for several years. He stayed at Angoulême for a while. Then, in quick succession, he was at Poitiers, Orléans, Strasbourg, and in 1535 he was in Basel (which in religious matters followed Zwingli). In May 1534, during his travels, the ecclesiastical appointments he had received as a young man from the Noyon cathedral chapter were given to others. This separation from his ecclesiastical office is usually cited as Calvin's definitive break with the Church.

During these years of wandering, he began the *Institutes of the Christian Religion*. He probably wrote the first words of the *Institutes* in Angoulême, but he was continually revising this work until the definitive edition was published in 1559-1560. Further work on the *Institutes* was done at Basel in 1535. Since some of the Reformers in France were suffering persecution at the hands of the French king, Calvin believed that a defense of the Reform was necessary.

The first edition of the *Institutes*, published in 1536, was designed to fulfill that purpose. Calvin defended the reformed churches by arguing that the Church exists in order to foster the glory of God, to proclaim the truth of the Gospel which God revealed in a glorious way, and to establish God's glorious kingdom on earth. However, the Church in his view is not confined to any simple, visible structure and certainly not on one involving a Pope and bishops. Rather, the Church is characterized by the preaching of the Gospel and the dispensing of the sacraments. (Of course, Calvin did not mean the same thing as the Church does when he used the phrase "dispensing of the sacraments.")

The Roman Church was a caricature of the Church of Christ because it had wandered from its mission of fidelity to the glory of God, to the Word of God, and to the work of establishing the true kingdom of God on earth. In this early form, the *Institutes* might have been taken as another statement of the general principles of the Reform begun by Luther. Calvin's distinctive emphasis on the glory and authority of God points to the future, but it is not featured as clearly as it is in later editions of the *Institutes*. It is interesting to note that even though he was working on the *Institutes* at Basel in Switzerland, he was not much influenced by Zwingli's ideas. Further, he demonstrates an impressive familiarity with the Scriptures and with some of Martin Luther's writings.

Geneva: First Act

After the publication of the *Institutes* in 1536, Calvin went to Geneva. The Reform had already taken hold. The Reform was established in Geneva in 1536 (before Calvin's arrival) by a decree of the city council. For a few months, Calvin only preached occasionally, but at the end of 1536 he was appointed by the city council as the preacher and pastor of the Geneva church.

In this capacity, Calvin wrote a proposal for the organization of the Church. Such a plan was much needed because, in embracing the Reformation, the citizens of Geneva were much more interested in achieving political freedom from the authority of the bishop, who was a tool of the Duke of Savoy, than they were in the doctrines of the Reformation. Thus, when the bishop left Geneva, there was a spirit of freedom which in some cases meant a spirit of license.

The city council adopted Calvin's proposal. Calvin also wrote a catechism in French as well as a creed. Church officials were to make sure that everyone lived according to the religious rules and that everyone accepted the creed. The city council was to punish those who broke the religious laws or who did not embrace the creed. Unlike Luther, who was much more interested in theology and in the personal relationship of each Christian with Christ than in church organization and structure, Calvin demonstrates from his earliest activity in Geneva a skill and interest in organization. His legal background shows in these endeavors, as well as in his insistence on strict enforcement of church laws with penalties of excommunication and even death (in the case of those who teach doctrines unacceptable to the religious authorities).

However, while Calvin's proposals regarding the organization of the Church were enacted by the city council, opposition soon surfaced. This opposition could hardly have been unexpected since the citizens of Geneva had not ousted the bishop only to accept a similar authority under a different guise! Opponents of the new Church organization, the catechism, and the creed were elected to the city council, and Calvin was ordered to leave Geneva. He left, spending the spring and summer months in Basel and then going to Strasbourg.

In Strasbourg, Calvin became a preacher in the French community living there as well as a lecturer in Scripture at the secondary school. During his stay in Strasbourg, he enlarged his *Institutes*. Living on the German border (in Strasbourg), Calvin was able to participate in religious discussions with leaders of the Reformation in Germany. These discussions were held at Frankfurt, Hagenau, Worms, and Regensburg. Although Calvin never met Luther, he was in contact with Melancthon.

Meanwhile in Geneva, there was a movement to return to the old Church. This movement was given impetus by a very friendly and gentle letter from the bishop of Carpentras (a town in France, northeast of Avignon) inviting the citizens of Geneva to return to the ancient faith. The Reformers in Geneva did not know how to reply, and so they requested that Calvin formulate an answer to the bishop.

Calvin's answer to the bishop's letter convinced the populace of Geneva to continue along the path of the Reform. But it was clear that the pastors in Geneva were not up to the task. An invitation went to Calvin as early as 1539 to return to Geneva, but he declined. Again in 1540 a petition was sent to Calvin to return, but he did not. Finally, in September 1541, Calvin returned to Geneva.

Geneva: Second Act

Calvin almost immediately proposed an organization for the church in Geneva which was accepted by the council. This structure differed somewhat from what he had proposed in his previous stay in Geneva because it was modeled on the organization of the church in Strasbourg. He also issued a catechism and an order of the liturgy.

The organization of the church included pastors, doctors, elders, and deacons. The pastors were the pastors of the churches. Doctors were teachers of theology. The elders numbered twelve and were members of the city council. Deacons managed the goods of the church and took care of the poor and the sick. The elders were charged with the enforcement of religious laws. They were to visit the homes of the people, in part to insure conformity with the laws. Those who were guilty of any immorality or crime were brought before a religious council composed of the pastors and elders. In the case of crime, the city council had jurisdiction.

In Calvin's Geneva, the secular authority had considerable jurisdiction over the church. While Luther had defended the principle that the state should substitute itself for the authority of the Church — i.e., Rome and the bishops — Calvin actually implemented the principle in a practical way in Geneva. However, the degree of jurisdiction of the civil authority over the church went further than Calvin wished. But having accepted the secular power as a means of governing the church (as a substitute for the old structure), it was difficult, not to say impossible, to prevent the secular authority from extending its powers and jurisdiction over the church.

While Calvin had some difficulty with the extent of civil authority over the church, others opposed the imposition of such rigid rules, especially those pertaining to the moral life. The mayor objected to the strict moral rule when his father-in-law was refused communion because of immoral conduct, his brother-in-law was jailed for eight days for unacceptable behavior at a wedding, and his wife was criticized for dancing. The mayor and others did not enjoy the strict laws. (They had, after all, embraced the Reform in order to escape the authority of the bishop and the Catholic Church.) However, in the 1555 election, those opposed to Calvin suffered a severe defeat. When those opposed to the new regime demonstrated and rioted, they were either banished or executed.

Calvin's Theology

Needless to say, between Calvin's return to Geneva in 1541 and his death on May 27, 1564, his theological views continued to develop. Calvin accepted the principle of justification by faith. He also held Scripture, the Word of God, to be the sole norm of the faith. He shared these views in common with all the Reformers.

However, the guiding theme of Calvin's theology is the glory of God — an idea already present in the first edition of the *Institutes* in 1536. Every characteristic and power of God shares in His glory, and these characteristics and powers are infinite. Every act of God is a manifestation of this glory, including the Creation of the world and of human beings.

All of Creation and most especially human beings exist to give glory to God. Since human beings are persons with minds and wills, they acknowledge God's glory and praise Him by accepting His will. Unfortunately, human beings are incapable of accepting God's will and acting in conformity with that will because they are wounded by original sin. It is now impossible for them to see the good, the glory of God, let alone accept it. God in His great mercy rescues some of them from this fallen state through the cross of Christ, but Christ's work must be accepted and made a part of all those who are saved. This acceptance of the work of Christ occurs through the grace of faith which allows each to be united with Christ. This union occurs, not through any effort on the part of each, but only through the gift of the Spirit.

For Calvin, faith is a gratuitous gift of God — that is, the gift of the Spirit. Faith leads to repentance and to a Christian life. The Christian life is a constant struggle to follow the law. (Here, we see the influence of Calvin's legal education.) Faith is justification. While we always remain sinners, we put on Christ's holiness and are saved through faith. However, sanctification — the effort to live more and more like Christ — occurs gradually through the Christian effort to live according to the law.

Unlike Luther, Calvin makes a distinction between justification and sanctification. Sanctification does not lead to justification. Rather, sanctification (holiness) is the result of the effort stimulated by justification (i.e., by the gift of faith) to live according to the law. After justification, we are covered with the holiness of Christ, but it is only gradually that we acquire the freedom to act like Christ. (Calvin's insistence on gradual sanctification results in a very strict moral code which demands a genuine Christian heroism.)

The effort Calvin expects of Christians is at least as much as what the Catholic Church expects of its members. However, the difference between Calvin's view and that of Rome is that for Calvin justification (or salvation) can never be lost unless there is a loss of faith.

Catholic teaching, however, holds that grace — justification — can be lost through a serious offense against God, a mortal sin, although faith remains. Further, for Catholics, works merit greater rewards. For Calvin, the reward, salvation, is granted through justification. Sanctification, the increase in our ability to act as Christ did, is simply the manifestation and result of justification. The Christian's works of holiness increases his or her sanctification, his or her likeness to Christ, but they do not merit anything greater than what was already granted by justification.)

Needless to say, if we are justified by the gratuitous gift of faith and not everyone is given this gift, then it is obvious that God gives this gift to some and not to others. In choosing to justify some, God chooses to bring them to heaven. In choosing not to justify others, God chooses to send them to hell. Both destinies, heaven and hell, have nothing to do with what human beings do or do not do. Rather, both the call of some to heaven and the condemnation of others to hell are acts of God's providence, and since divine providence is an aspect of the glory of God, human beings are bound to accept God's will and glorify Him in His mysterious decisions, even in His decision not to justify some.

Calvin argues that if there is no reason that can be found for the free and gratuitous mercy of God in giving the gift of faith, then there is no reason to be found for the divine refusal of this gift. Both the decision to justify and the decision not to condemn particular human beings belong to the inscrutable mystery of God, which must be simply accepted.

Such is the Calvinist concept of predestination. In preaching these conclusions from his fundamental theological principles, Calvin, in his rigorous logic, took the point further than Luther and his followers did. However, although later the doctrine of predestination came to be the central tenet of those following Calvin, for him it was not the centerpiece of his theology, but rather a conclusion from the central principles.

Calvin's mature view of the Church did not differ substantially from the first edition of the *Institutes* (1536). For Calvin, the Church comprised all those who worship one God and Christ, who profess unity in doctrine and charity through partaking in the Lord's Supper, who are baptized into the faith and who hold and preach the Word of God.

For Calvin, the heart of the Church is not its visible form. Rather, the essential element of the Church is the praise and glory returned to God through worship by acceptance of the gift of faith and by holding as well as preaching the Word of God. Calvin acknowledged that the Roman Church has certain vestiges of the true Church, but Calvin argued that the Catholic Church is not the true Church of Christ because lying and falsehood are so prevalent and widespread in it. Of all the Reformers, Calvin's Geneva had the most rigorous organization and discipline.

Calvin and the Secular Power

As briefly noted above, Calvin always fought for the independence of the church, but it was necessary, as with Luther, to substitute some authority for that of the Pope and the bishops. The only authority available was the secular power. Therefore, in Calvin's Geneva, the city council had considerable power over the church. In a certain sense, although defending the principle of independence of the church more than Luther did, Calvin actually created a structure where the church yielded considerable powers to the secular authority. Thus, in theory, Calvin wanted more independence for the church than Luther, but in fact Calvin created a structure where the civil power had more authority than Luther would have granted to it in theory.

The difference between Luther and Calvin on the practical level was that Calvin was giving structure and organization to a church whereas Luther did not tackle this problem. In the practical order, Calvin was much closer to Luther's theory of the relationship between church and state because it was the only way to solve the problems Calvin faced in the practical order. The organization and discipline of the church in Geneva, as established by Calvin, rivaled and even superseded anything the Roman Church had ever attempted to institute. In the structure and organization, discipline and penalties of the Geneva church, we also see evidence of Calvin's legal training coming into play.

Calvin's Theology

Calvin rejected all the sacraments except for Baptism and Eucharist. (For Calvin, justification comes through faith, the gratuitous gift of God. However, Baptism was a sign that God had given faith to a particular person.)

Baptism for Calvin does not change a person or confer anything new, as the Catholics teach. Rather, Baptism is a sign of something that has already occurred. Through Baptism, God assures the baptized that they have been justified, i.e., that they have received from Him the gift of faith. Baptism does not cause faith, but it is a sign that God has given the gift of faith to the one who is baptized.

Calvin's doctrine on the Holy Eucharist offered a third way between Luther and Zwingli. Luther held to the real presence of Christ in the Eucharist, but also that the Eucharist was not a sacrifice. (This position was not that of the Catholics, who repeatedly said that the body and blood of Christ were present under the appearances of bread and wine and that the Eucharst made Christ's sacrifice on the cross present. Nevertheless, Luther's position was the closest to Catholic teaching among the Reformers. Both the Catholics and Luther accepted a physical presence of Christ.) Zwingli taught that the bread and wine were symbolically the body and blood of Christ and merely a memorial, a reminder, of Christ's passion and death.

Calvin took a position midway between Luther and Zwingli. Calvin agreed with Zwingli that it was impossible for Christ to be present in (or, for that matter, under the appearances of) the bread and wine. Christ's body was physically in heaven and it was impossible that it be physically in other places (i.e., in the bread and wine) at the same time. Since Christ's body and blood are not physically present in the bread and wine, it is senseless to offer these elements adoration. Further, Calvin agreed with Luther and Zwingli that the Eucharist was not a sacrifice.

In spite of his agreement with Zwingli, however, Calvin had difficulty with Christ's command to "eat his flesh" and "drink his blood." In reducing the Eucharist to a mere remembrance of something which had already occurred, Zwingli, argued Calvin, ignored Christ's own words. But there could be no question of actually physically eating Christ's body and blood because Christ was not present in the bread and wine.

Rather, Calvin taught that the bread and wine were symbols of what occurred in the souls of believers through faith. The believer, the one who is justified, actually does share in the flesh of Christ through the gift of faith which he or she has already received. In other words, the sharing in Christ's flesh and blood occurs through the faith of each believer. The bread and wine are symbols of what occurs independently of them through God's gracious gift.

The sacrament of the Eucharist is a sign of something which has occurred or which is occurring, i.e., the gift of faith through the spirit of Christ, but there is absolutely no question of the "sacrament" — the bread and wine — actually giving grace. Calvin's understanding of Baptism and Eucharist are that they are signs of realities which occur independent of the sacraments. However, the two sacraments are important because they remind us and teach us not just of what Christ did on the cross centuries ago, but about what God is doing in our lives today through the gift of faith.

They should elicit from us praise for God and His work in us through the gift of faith. As we have mentioned, Calvin and the successor to Zwingli in Zurich reached an agreement on the Eucharist in 1549.

Calvin's Contribution

Calvin's contribution to the Reform was significant. Through his own natural talents and gifts as well as his legal background, Calvin was able to systematize and organize. His theology was more consistent and logical than anything the other Reformers of the sixteenth century had written before him. Of course, younger than Luther by twenty-six years, he benefited from the experience and writings of the earlier Reformers. Calvin was able to bring the theology of the Reformation clearly and consistently to the French-speaking world.

Calvin was unable to solve adequately the problem of the authoritative interpretation of the Scriptures. Nor did he find a way for the Reformed church to remain independent of the civil authority. His view of the sacraments eviscerates them of their power, but not to the same extent that Zwingli's views of them do. His famous teaching on predestination troubles many, as does his belief that original sin hopelessly weakened human nature to the point that no human being is able to do anything good without justification — that is, without the gift of faith.

Despite all that, the *Institutes* represents the definitive appeal of the Reformation to the mind. In systemizing and organizing, Calvin made the arguments of the Reformation cogent and consistent. That some of them do not convince does not take away from his achievement.

Calvinism in France

Calvin had a wide sphere of influence. Calvinist preachers were sent from Geneva into France. They found in France some who had embraced the Reformation. From this group and other converts, the Calvinist preachers formed congregations on the Geneva model.

Calvinists in France came to be called Huguenots, a word possibly derived from the German *Eidgenossen* (allies or confederates). By 1558, there were sufficient numbers of French Calvinists to hold a meeting in Paris. Many nobles, perhaps as many as half the nobles in France, were Huguenot by the 1560s. They were attracted by the possibilities of governing the Church in their territories and of determining the religion of the people under their authority.

The French nobility embraced the Reformation for some of the same reasons that the German nobility did. When the noble of a territory became Huguenot, so did most of the people under his authority. Nevertheless, in some instances, peasants converted while their lord remained faithful to Rome. Towns also converted to the Calvinist teaching, but this meant that those in the government of the town led it into embracing the Reform. More often than not, when the town leaders and skilled artisans became Huguenots, the journeymen and lower working classes remained Catholic (because of their opposition to the leader and artisan class).

King Francis I (1515-1547) of France and his son, King Henry II (1547-1559), opposed the Huguenots, but Henry II died suddenly in 1559, leaving a widow and three sons. The widow, Catherine de Medici, tried to govern in the name of her sons. However, France fell into religious civil war between 1562 and 1598.

The war was fought between Catholic and Huguenot nobles with Admiral de Coligny and Henry of Navarre leading the Huguenot party and the Guise family representing the Catholics. Catherine at first tried to balance one party against the other, but in 1572 she decided that the Huguenot party had too great an influence over her son, King Charles IX (1560-1574).

Since a large number of Huguenots were in Paris for the wedding of Henry of Navarre, she decided to take advantage of the situation. She had most of the Huguenots in Paris slaughtered during the night of August 23-24, 1572. This event is known as the St. Bartholomew's Day Massacre. As might have been expected, the Huguenots redoubled their efforts and the war intensified with roving bands of armed men, some of them mercenaries, devastating France. However, neither side could win.

In 1589, with the death of King Henry III (1574-1589), the last surviving son of Catherine, the crown was inherited by Henry of Navarre, who reigned as Henry IV, but the Catholics would not accept him. Finally in 1593, Henry renounced the Calvinist faith and embraced Catholicism. With this step, Henry was accepted by most of the Catholics. He ended the religious wars with the Edict of Nantes in 1598 allowing the Huguenots to practice their faith in freedom.

But in 1627 the Huguenots revolted against the crown. Cardinal Richelieu, the minister of Marie de Medici (the wife of Henry IV, not to be confused with Catherine, the wife of Henry II), and her son, Louis XIII (1610-1643), put down the rebellion and amended the Edict of Nantes. The Huguenots lost their political powers. They could no longer maintain standing armies, hold fortified cities, or enjoy their former military and territorial rights. However, they were still allowed freedom of religion and their civil rights.

Only in 1685, over eighty years after its issuance, did Louis XIV (1643-1714) revoke the Edict of Nantes and officially end the religious freedom of the Huguenots. After the revocation of the Edict, some Huguenots emigrated and others remained in France, secretly practicing their religion.

Calvinist Influences Outside of France

Calvin also influenced present-day Belgium and Holland. In part, this influence was the result of French Huguenots fleeing France during the French religious wars and crossing the border into Belgium and Holland. In any case, Calvinism was sufficiently strong in the Netherlands to play a role in the revolt of the Netherlands against Spain in 1566. Philip II of Spain (1556-1598) responded to this religious threat by establishing the Spanish Inquisition in the Netherlands, which of course increased the opposition to Spain in the Netherlands. Eventually, the northern provinces (present-day Holland) became Calvinist and succeeded (in 1609) in establishing the Dutch Republic. The southern provinces, present-day Belgium, declared their loyalty to Spain and to Catholicism.

Emigration of Calvinists also led to the growth of Calvinist communities in the lower Rhine (northwest Germany). There were emigrations of Protestants from England in 1553 when Mary Tudor (1553-1558), the Catholic daughter of Henry VIII (1509-1547), became Queen. Calvinists also came to the lower Rhine from the Netherlands, fleeing the Inquisition instituted against them by Philip II of Spain. The presence of both Lutherans and Calvinists in Germany caused some friction among the Reformed churches. Of course, there were always troubles between the Reformed churches and the Catholics.

Not only did Calvinism penetrate the French- and German-speaking lands, but it also influenced the English-speaking world. In Scotland, in

1542, Mary Queen of Scots became Queen of Scotland when she was only a week old. The regency for the young Queen was exercised by the Earl of Arran, who was favorably disposed to the Reformation.

The Earl of Arran, like many nobles across Europe, saw the possibilities of acquiring Church lands and of governing the Church through the Reformation. The Church in Scotland had suffered some of the same ills as the Church throughout Europe in the fifteenth and sixteenth centuries. Ecclesiastical monies were often spent on the illegitimate children of the clergy. Priests and bishops did not often preach. When they did preach, they were often woefully unprepared, sometimes even unable to explain the most fundamental passages of Scripture.

Given this situation, the Reform appealed to many. George Wishart (1513-1546) had spent some time in Switzerland and Germany where he became acquainted with the ideas of the Reform. He brought these ideas to Scotland and associated a man named John Knox with him. Wishart died as a heretic in 1546, but Knox was to become the leader of the Reform in Scotland. (Even though the Earl of Arran was Protestant, the mother of the young Queen Mary was Catholic. As in many other places, representatives of the Reform and the Catholics struggled for influence and power. At the time Wishart died, the Catholic influence was the strongest.) Knox's work did not began immediately because he was imprisoned by the French between 1547 and 1549. With the death of Wishart, the absence of Knox, and the influence of the Queen mother, Catholics were able to force those sympathetic to the Reform into the background. With Knox's return to Scotland in 1549, he was able to reinvigorate the Reform.

At a church synod in 1552, it was decided to publish a catechism. This work accepted the ideas of the Reform, particularly the teaching on predestination. In the years between 1554 and 1555, Knox was in Geneva and learned more about the teachings of Calvin. From that visit to Geneva until his death in 1572, Knox fought without reserve against the Catholics and for a rigorous Calvinism. As in France, a civil war broke out in Scotland in 1559 between the Catholic party and the Reform. But in 1560, after the death of the Queen Mother (which, of course, weakened the Catholic party), the so-called Reformation Parliament, a meeting of the nobility, was held in Edinburgh. As is suggested by its name, the Reformation Parliament adopted the Reform, accepting John Knox's positions. The authority and jurisdiction of the Pope were abolished. The Mass and all else opposed to the Reform were forbidden, and the Scottish confession was adopted.

In 1561 Mary Queen of Scots took the reins of government, but guaranteed toleration of the Calvinists. Nevertheless, she remained Catholic. Of course, there was tension between the crown and the nobles, who were for the most part Calvinist. In 1567, when Mary's second husband was murdered, she was accused of complicity in the act and was forced to flee for her life.

Her son James became King of Scotland and is known as James VI of Scotland (1567-1625). Later, while retaining his kingship in Scotland, he also became King of England. As King of England, his title was James I (1603-1625). Since James had been raised as a Calvinist, there was less of a conflict with the Calvinist Reform, but there was no persecution of the Catholics. However, the priests and bishops of the Catholic Church were gradually replaced by Calvinist preachers. As in the case of France and Germany, the Reform quickly became a matter of politics as well as religion. In Scotland, it triumphed, but it did so partially as a result of the political struggle between the nobility and the crown.

Andrew Melville succeeded Knox and advocated a new church organization. Instead of state control of the church, councils of laymen and ministers were to insure church discipline and govern the church. According to Melville, no power on earth should govern the church because the only head of the church is Christ. This proposal was the beginning of Presbyterianism. However, Melville's ideas conflicted with the crown.

King James saw clearly that Melville's proposals for the organization of the church would threaten secular control over the church and could even mean that the church would dictate to the crown what should be done. James opposed Melville. But he also opposed the Catholics who were active in trying to win Scotland back.

In 1581, James issued the Negative Confession, which rejected everything not in conformity with the Scottish Confession of 1560. All the people of Scotland were asked to give their assent to the Negative Confession. With this act, Scotland became officially Calvinist. But James had angered Melville in rejecting his proposed church organization.

In the ensuing conflict, the King was imprisoned in 1582, but he escaped to England. King James was able to reestablish himself and he moved against Melville, asserting the authority of the crown over the church. King James won, but the struggle between the Calvinist crown (which wanted state control over the church) and the Presbyterian organization (which Melville had advocated) continued.

John Knox was not a theologian as Luther, Zwingli, and Calvin were. He was *par excellence* a church leader who was relentless in his rejection of Catholics and in his promotion of Calvinist ideas. He is important in the Reformation period primarily as the chief architect of the Calvinist Reform in the English-speaking lands.

Calvinists in England never were able to establish themselves effectively. They were either Huguenot refugees from France or Englishmen who became familiar with Knox's ideas in Scotland. They came to be called Puritans around 1566 because they demanded a church which was absolutely in accord with Scripture — "purely" scriptural. (While there were those who had embraced some or all the ideas of the Reformation in England earlier, they had generally not taken these ideas from Calvin, but rather from the German Reformation — from Luther and his followers.) When the Calvinists separated from the Anglican Church in 1567 and tried to found their own congregations (on a Presbyterian model — i.e., without bishops — lay men and ministers governed the church), they were persecuted. Many went to prison and some left England. One group colonized Massachusetts, sailing to the new world on the now-famous *Mayflower*.

John Calvin

This reformer accepted most of the ideas of Luther and brought organization and structure to the Reformed Churches. He did not accept the Real Presence in the Eucharist, as Luther did, and he taught that God inscrutably predestined us to heaven or hell.

25

Anglicanism

Henry VIII

HAVING ALREADY CONSIDERED LUTHER, ZWINGLI, CALVIN, AND JOHN KNOX, a brief word should be said about the Reformation in England. All the details of Henry VIII's break with the Church need not be discussed because the story has been told in many places and in many ways.

Henry VIII (1509-1547) had been given the title Defender of the Faith by the Pope for a book he wrote against some of the ideas of the Reformation. Henry's *Defense of the Seven Sacraments* appeared about 1520. However, lacking male heirs to his throne, Henry VIII wanted to divorce his wife, Catherine of Aragon, and marry Anne Boleyn.

Henry asked the Pope to annul his marriage with Catherine, but since Henry lacked sufficient grounds, the Pope refused. Henry arranged to be declared Head of the Church and then appointed Thomas Cranmer archbishop of Canterbury in 1533. Cranmer obligingly declared the marriage of Henry and Catherine to be null and void. Henry's marriage to Anne was therefore legitimate and, most importantly, the children born to the union of Henry and Anne would be legitimate.

As is well known, Henry put Anne to death three years after the marriage and married four others before he died in 1547. But in 1534, while he was married to Anne, Henry tried to secure the succession by requiring all his subjects to swear to the Oath of Succession.

St. Thomas More and St. John Fisher refused to take this oath and died accused of treason. Henry VIII had made himself Head of the Church in order to secure an annulment of his marriage with Catherine. But like the nobles of other European countries, he did not ignore the economic advantages. While he was Head of the Church in England, he suppressed the monasteries in England, taking their lands and distributing them to his followers.

However, in spite of his break with the Church, Henry VIII never intended to change or alter Catholic teaching. He wanted to be Head of the Church for the annulment and for the lands, but he never accepted or instituted the teachings of the Reformation. His break with Rome was a schism, not a heresy, even though there were some Protestant influences already in England during Henry VIII's reign.

Edward VI

However, at Henry's death, his ten-year-old son, Edward VI (1547-1553), inherited the throne. A regency was established, but it was dominated by those who had accepted Protestant ideas.

A follower of Martin Luther, Martin Bucer, came to England, taught at Cambridge, and was influential among the regents and the higher clergy, especially, Archbishop Cranmer. He even was received by the King. Bucer's influence can be traced in Cranmer's *Book of Common Prayer* published in 1549. For the six years of Edward's reign the German Reformation reached England, but it failed because Edward's reign was too short.

Mary I

With Edward's death, his half sister, Mary, the daughter of Catherine and Henry, succeeded. Mary Tudor (1553-1558) attempted a Catholic restoration, but it failed. She instituted a persecution of the Protestants which stirred up opposition. Some also resented her alliance with Spain and especially her marriage to Philip II of Spain (1556-1598). Most of all, Mary's attempt at a Catholic restoration failed, just as the attempt to establish the Reformation under Edward VI had failed. Both reigns were too short for such efforts to succeed.

Elizabeth I

Elizabeth I (1558-1603) succeeded Mary and in 1559 established the Anglican Church (called the Episcopalian Church in the U.S. and some other parts of the world). All subjects of the English crown were required to be members of the Anglican Church.

Doctrinally, the Anglican Church was founded on the thirty-nine articles accepted at a meeting in 1563. These articles were a revision of forty-two articles Cranmer had drafted in 1552. Rejecting Catholic teaching and embracing the Reform, many of these articles allowed for more than one interpretation, but they had Calvinist tendencies.

The Anglican liturgy followed Cranmer's *Book of Common Prayer.* As in other areas where the Reformation took hold, the first changes made in the Liturgy were somewhat restrained. So also in England. By adopting the *Book of Common Prayer* and allowing the ambiguity to exist in the thirty-nine articles, Elizabeth I was trying to create what we might call today a "big tent."

She wanted her subjects to be able to embrace the officially sanctioned state religion with the least difficulty possible. She tried to have "something for everyone." For those who yearned for Rome, there was the *Book of Common Prayer* (clearly, this book did not enshrine the Latin Liturgy, but many elements of the tradition were present). For those who embraced the Calvinist teachings, there were the thirty-nine articles. For those who accepted Lutheran teachings, the thirty-nine articles allowed for that interpretation as well.

This created within Anglicanism a tension between a "high Church" element (those wishing to be closer in liturgy, style, and even doctrine to Rome) and a "low Church" faction (those wishing to be more Protestant, more "pure," more simple). Still, the Catholics could not accept the Anglican "solution" and, as we have seen, neither could the pure Calvinists.

By 1600, Europe was divided religiously. There were Catholics, Lutherans, Calvinists, Anglicans, Presbyterians, and Anabaptists. Luther had touched off a firestorm. That firestorm had powerful ideas at its center, and some of those ideas would give rise to other thoughts in the next centuries. Jansenism, Quietism, and Deism are movements rooted in the Reformation.

Anglicanism

This Reformed Church was instituted in England as a compromise between Catholicism and the Reform. The *Book of Common Prayer* is liturgically more traditional than the worship services of most of the Reformed Churches, whereas the thirty-nine articles have a definite Calvinist tendency.

26

❧

Jansenism

Grace and Free Will

LUTHER, CALVIN, AND ZWINGLI HAD RAISED THE QUESTION OF THE RELA-
tionship between grace and free will. Of course, this issue had been discussed before, most notably by St. Augustine in his disputes over Pelagianism.
It also was involved in the Semi-Pelagian controversy.

Within the Catholic world during the Counter-Reformation in the
late sixteenth and early seventeenth centuries, there were discussions on
the relationship between grace and free will. These discussions turned on
some very technical theological issues and involved disputes between the
Jesuits and the Dominicans.

The Jesuit associated with these discussions was Luis de Molina and
his followers were named Molinists. The most important advocate of the
Dominican position (which fundamentally adhered to the thinking of St.
Thomas Aquinas) was Domingo Báñez.

The question turned on two principles, both of which had to be maintained and which seem, on the surface, to be contradictory: (1) the absolute
and unquestioned effectiveness of God-given divine grace; and (2) the equal
and unquestioned principle of human freedom.

If one denies the second principle — i.e., denies human freedom and
makes everything dependent on grace —then human beings cannot be held
responsible for their own acts because the cause of their acts is something
beyond their control, the presence or absence of divine grace. Further, grace
would be essential for all human acting, and therefore God would have
been required to give it to all human beings. Divine grace would no longer
be gratuitous, but something owed to human beings. On the other hand, if
one affirms the second principle — i..e., human freedom — implicitly claiming that men and women are able to make good moral choices without the
help or influence of grace, the conclusion is that salvation is earned without

grace and is not dependent on grace. Of course, the tension between these two principles touches at the heart of the mystery of the relationship between God and human beings.

Since the precise relationship between God's grace and human free will is at heart a mystery, the tension between these cannot be fully resolved this side of heaven. In the dispute between the Molinists and the Dominicans, the Church finally asked both sides not to publish any materials without the approval of the Vatican.

Cornelius Jansen

Into this controversy of the relationship between human freedom and divine grace, Cornelius Jansen (1585-1638) stepped with the posthumous publication of his work *Augustinus* in 1640.

Jansen studied at Louvain and became a professor there and eventually (in 1636) was appointed bishop of Ypres. The thirteen-hundred-page book *Augustinus* represented Jansen's life work. In it, Jansen used St. Augustine, but unfortunately Jansen took the most extreme interpretation possible of St. Augustine's work. Further, he relied heavily on St. Augustine's responses to the Pelagians (who had overemphasized the human will as opposed to God's grace) without sufficiently considering that these works of Augustine had to be read in the context of the saint's polemic against the Pelagians.

Although Jansen was more in tune with the ideas of those who followed St. Thomas on the issue of man's freedom in its relationship with grace, he specifically rejected the medieval theological approach of St. Thomas and others as overly rationalistic. Instead, Jansen preferred to rely on St. Augustine. In this respect, he followed some of the Reformers.

Jansen accepted St. Augustine's pessimism about human nature after original sin. After the first sin, human beings are incapable of performing a good act. Concupiscence and self-love have totally taken over human nature. For Jansen, freedom is the seeking of pleasure. It continues in fallen human nature, but pleasure is sought through self-love. In seeking pleasure through selfishness, fallen human nature turns away from God and from selfless love.

Grace is given to fallen human beings through Christ, but far from destroying freedom, grace elevates freedom (the power by which men and women seek pleasure) to the pursuit of true pleasure and happiness through the love of God.

Although Jansen was attempting to answer a most vexing and perplexing question — the relationship between freedom and grace — his thought only arrives at a solution by eliminating freedom!

To argue that freedom consists in the natural tendency in human nature to seek pleasure and that human beings are incapable of resisting this inherent movement within them is, in effect, to make all human beings slaves to their nature. Fallen human nature — the nature of all human beings living after original sin (except, of course, the Lord Himself and Mary, His mother) — is in Jansen's understanding incapable of doing anything except acts of self-love.

Similarly, blessed with God's grace, human beings are incapable of doing anything but seeking spiritual pleasure, which is found exclusively in the love of God and neighbor. In neither instance are human persons responsible for their acts. They are determined either by their fallen nature towards the pleasures of self-love or by grace toward the more spiritual pleasures of selfless love. By giving or not giving grace, God, and God alone, determines who will be saved and not saved. Free will in the classic sense has no part to play in human relationships with God or, for that matter, in any human act.

The ideas of Jansen were taken up in France by Jean Duvergier de Hauranne, whom Jansen had met while in France from 1609 to 1616. The two had even shared a residence for a time. While working on the *Augustinus*, Jansen corresponded with Jean Duvergier, who became abbot of Saint-Cyran and was a close friend of Robert Arnauld d'Andilly, a diplomat at the French court.

Duvergier's friendship with Robert Arnauld d'Andilly would be a footnote in the Jansenist movement if it were not the case that Robert's sister was Mother Angelique, the abbess of the Cisterican abbey of Port-Royal in Paris. Through Saint-Cyran, Jansenism reached France, the Arnauld family, and most importantly the abbey of Port Royal.

In 1641, the year after the publication of Jansen's *Augustinus*, there was a lecture series at Louvain against Jansen's ideas. Jansen was accused of resurrecting the errors of Calvin, of eliminating human freedom, and of granting salvation only to a chosen few. But there quickly formed, both at Louvain and in France, two parties: an anti-Jansenist group led by Jesuits and a pro-Jansenist group.

The anti-Jansenist group appealed to Rome, and in 1643 a document from Rome hostile to the Jansenist positions, *In eminenti,* was issued. *In eminenti* was promulgated by the Holy Office (now called the Congregation for the Doctrine of the Faith) on the grounds that Jansen had made statements which had been previously condemned.

However, there were difficulties with *In eminenti.* First of all, there were doctrinal and legal problems in the text of the document. Second, there were several versions of the text. Third, responsible officials of the Church in France and Holland were not provided copies of the document in timely fashion, and as a result, the Jesuits printed it before it was officially published.

In eminenti did not succeed in ending the controversy. Antoine Arnauld, the youngest brother of the abbess of Port-Royal, published a work questioning *In eminenti.* He also published a work on Communion defending some ideas of Saint-Cyran which occasioned opposition from the anti-Jansenists. With Saint-Cyran and Arnauld as well as the members of the Port-Royal convent supporting Jansenist ideas, France became the hotbed of the Jansenist movement.

Jansenism in France

Still, with the opposition of both the papacy and the French court to the Jansenists, the anti-Jansenists, sensing their strength and the growing weakness of the Jansenists, called a meeting in Paris in 1649. Several propositions were proposed for study. The first five were very important and are worth quoting:

1. Some of God's commandments cannot be followed by the righteous with the help of those powers available to them in the present state even if they want to follow them. Neither do they have the grace which makes it possible for them to be followed.

2. In the state of fallen human nature, no one ever resists interior grace.

3. In the state of fallen nature, merit or demerit does not require man's freedom from inner compulsion; freedom from outer constraint is sufficient.

4, The Semi-Pelagians admitted the necessity of antecedent inner grace for the individual acts, also for the beginning of faith. Their error was to maintain that human will could resist or obey this grace.

5. It is Semi-Pelagian to assert that Christ has died or shed His blood for all men.

These and the other propositions occasioned a very stormy discussion. In the end, after several intermediate steps, they were referred to the Holy See.

These propositions certainly can be taken as heretical. Four of the them rest on the second one. If it is true that no one can resist interior grace (2), then obviously anyone who disobeys a commandment does so because he or she does not have the interior grace to observe it (1). But if interior grace is responsible for good actions and the absence of it is responsible for evil actions, then merit or demerit cannot depend on the absence of internal compulsion. Grace interiorly compels one to spiritual pleasure — i.e., selfless love — while the absence of grace compels one to the pleasures of self-love. Merit or demerit thus cannot depend on the absence of interior compulsion, but only on the absence of external constraint (3). Since grace cannot be resisted, the error of the Semi-Pelagians was that men and women could resist grace (4). Christ could not have died for all people because some men and women are and remain sinners. They would not be sinners if God gave His graces, but He does not always do this. Therefore, Christ could not have died to merit grace for everyone (5).

There is no question that these propositions could be interpreted in a heretical sense. Nevertheless, both the Jansenists and the anti-Jansenists tried to present their arguments to Rome. In May 1653 Rome issued the document *Cum occasione,* which condemned the five Jansenist propositions.

Decisions of Right vs. Decisions of Fact

Unfortunately, as with so many other heresies in the history of the Church, the decision of Rome rendered clearly and unequivocally in *Cum occasione* did not end the controversy. Arnauld presented an argument that while every Catholic had to agree with the condemnation of the five propositions as heretical, they did not have to agree with Rome that these five propositions were actually proposed by Jansen.

In this argument, Arnauld made the distinction between decisions of right and decisions of fact. In other words, Arnauld held that Rome had an obligation and duty to decide on doctrine and morals and all Catholics were to assent to what Rome taught. However, on matters of fact — whether or not a particular author actually said a particular thing — Catholics were under no obligation to assent to Rome's decisions.

These decisions, argued Arnauld, were matters of fact. If Rome erred on fact, all that was due to Rome from Catholics was a respectful silence. Of course, this argument cannot stand because all that the Church can judge are texts — the Scriptures, canons of the Church and councils, etc. Part and parcel of the decision on doctrine is the interpretation of texts. Nevertheless, Arnauld's arguments did serve to support certain Jansenists by a claim that *Cum occasione* did not apply to them! In a decision at the University of Paris in 1655, Arnauld's arguments were rejected and he was expelled.

With the anti-Jansenists winning more and more support in official circles, the Jansenists launched an attempt to influence popular opinion. Blaise Pascal, whose sister was a member of the Port-Royal convent, collaborated with other pro-Jansenists in a series of publications called *Provinçales*. Purporting to be letters to a friend in the country, these letters were sarcastic and polemical attacks on the Jesuits, who were a significant force in the anti-Jansenist party.

With Pascal's genius behind them, the *Provinçales* were very influential especially on the general public and severely tarnished the reputation of the Jesuits. The French court was more than a little irritated by the *Provinçales* and renewed its attempt to eliminate Jansenism once and for all.

A meeting of the French bishops in 1656 requested a definitive decision from the new Pope, Alexander VII (1655-1667), an anti-Jansenist, on Arnauld's distinction between questions of right and fact. In October 1656, Rome issued another document, *Ad sacram*, which repeated the condemnation of the five propositions and also stated explicitly that these five were found in the writings of Jansen.

Louis XIV

On the basis of this Roman document, the French bishops drew up a formula of faith which all the clergy and nuns were to sign. Although officially the French court was anti-Jansenist, there was not much insistence by the secular authorities on the formula of faith until Louis XIV (1643-1715) began his personal rule in 1661. One of Louis's goals was the unification of his kingdom and the elimination of as many divisive factors as possible, including those of religion. Influenced by his Jesuit confessors, Louis took a strong anti-Jansenist stance and insisted on the signing of the formula of faith which the bishops had drafted in 1657.

There was much resistance to the formula. Jansenists tried to make Arnauld's argument of decisions of fact as opposed to decisions of doctrine and to insist that this distinction be added to the formula, but this argument was not accepted. The Port-Royal nuns were asked to sign and initially refused. In an attempted move to conciliate the Jansenist nuns at Port-Royal, the archbishop of Paris suggested that questions of fact taught by the Church only required "human faith" while questions of doctrine required divine faith.

This suggestion failed to satisfy the Jansenists. The archbishop then took rather draconian measures. Twelve of the nuns were taken to other convents. The nuns remaining were refused the sacraments and even placed under police guard. Finally, a few nuns did sign, but only a few. The small number embarrassed the archbishop.

Meanwhile, four bishops joined the opposition, including the bishop of Angers, the younger brother of Arnauld. A claim was made that only the Pope could demand Catholics to sign such a formula. As a result, Pope Alexander VII issued the document *Regimini apostolici*, in 1665.

The decree was published in France by the four Jansenist bishops, but the publication included the Jansenist distinction between decisions of fact and decisions of doctrine. In other words, *Regimini apostolici* confused matters even further, not because of its contents but because of its publication together with the Jansenist distinction between fact and doctrine.

Pope Alexander VII was more than a bit annoyed at the four bishops who were responsible for the confusing publication of the new papal document. He condemned their use of the Jansenist distinction between fact and doctrine and was about to put them on trial, having appointed a group of judges. However, the Pope died before this trial could take place.

The Clementine Peace

The next Pope, Clement IX (1667-1669), wanted to settle the issue. He agreed to allow the Jansenists to sign *Regimini apostolici* with supposedly secret stipulations which included the distinction between fact and doctrine. In the end, even the nuns signed, and the so-called Clementine peace was initiated in 1669. This peace lasted until 1701.

At first glance, it may seem surprising that Jansenism could maintain itself over thirty years after the Clementine settlement. But it had been popularized through the *Provinçales*. Further, following the policy of Saint-Cyran, it had been planted in abbeys and religious houses which taught it to each new generation of novices.

Jansenism had taken on several characteristics other than the teachings of Jansen. It had an anti-Jesuit element which made it very popular in certain circles. Some Jansenists also became ardent defenders of the liberties of the French Church (as opposed to the Vatican) which also appealed to certain elements of the French clergy. A moral rigorism, a legacy of Saint-Cyran, was associated with Jansenism, and this stance was attractive to many. An additional characteristic of the Jansenists, and one that came to dominate the whole movement, was the distinction between fact and doctrine.

This distinction (originally introduced only as a means to defend the teachings of Jansen) became the major contested point between the Jansenists and Rome. This position also appealed to many because it questioned the authority of Rome as did the emphasis on the liberties of the French Church. If the survival of Jansenism had depended on the teachings of Jansen, it is doubtful it would have persisted. But these other and somewhat secondary elements attracted many.

It should also be noted that the various characteristics associated with Jansenism were diverse enough to entice people of different viewpoints. Not all Jansenists embraced all these various characteristics, but each tendency had its own followers. Naturally, there was also some splintering of the Jansenists into different groups supporting one or more of these characteristics, but the Jansenists were never so divided as to threaten the movement's existence.

Jansenism Resurfaces

In 1701, the struggle was renewed when a priest asked the professors of Paris whether or not a penitent could be forgiven if he said that he could only maintain a respectful silence to decisions of the Church regarding fact.

A Jansenist drafted an answer saying the penitent could be forgiven, and forty professors approved of the answer.

In 1702, the whole case was published, but in the next year the Vatican issued a statement condemning the Jansenist opinion. In other words, the Church ruled that the penitent could not be forgiven.

With this controversy and the Jansenist public defense of their position, the strength of the Jansenist party was revealed. It had existed underground, even though almost everyone, including King Louis XIV, thought it had died. In fact, it was very much alive.

Louis XIV determined to eliminate the Jansenists. He urged the Pope to issue another document condemning the notion that Catholics could maintain a respectful silence on matters of fact if they disagreed with Rome.

Pope Clement XI (1700-1721) complied with the request with the document *Vineam Domini Sabaoth*. Perhaps because Clement did not believe his document would have much greater effect than previous ones, *Vineam Domini Sabaoth* was not as strong or as clear as the anti-Jansenists wanted. There was no hope that this document from Rome would settle the problem.

King Louis XIV wanted the nuns of Port-Royal to sign the papal document, but they insisted on the reservations they had been allowed in 1669. In response, King Louis XIV suppressed the convent, dispersed the nuns to other convents, and even destroyed the building to insure that it did not become a place of pilgrimage.

King Louis also had a conflict with Quesnel, who had succeeded Arnauld as the leading Jansenist after Arnauld's death in 1694. Quesnel published a work called *Reflexions morales*. In this work, Quesnel resurrected the Jansenist position on grace. Although initially receiving the support of the archbishop of Paris, Quesnel's writings were attacked by other bishops. With this conflict, King Louis XIV wanted a papal condemnation of Quesnel's work so that the issue would be definitively settled. Reluctantly (because he questioned whether it would have any positive results) Pope Clement XI in 1713 issued the papal document *Unigenitus Dei Filius*, which condemned over one hundred propositions from Quesnel's work.

Appellants and Acceptants

Just as with previous documents from Rome, *Unigenitus* did not succeed in putting an end to the Jansenist movement. The Jansenists rejected

Unigenitus and appealed to a general council of the Church, hoping that a council would overrule a Pope (as though in the constitution of the Church a council was above the Pope). Since there were large numbers of clergy, bishops, and laity on both sides of the issue, the Church in France was badly divided.

In each diocese, there were appellants (those who agreed with an appeal to a council) and the acceptants (those who had acknowledged *Unigenitus*). In 1718, there was a document from Rome condemning the appeal to a general council. In the same year, Pope Clement XI also issued another papal document excommunicating all those who did not accept *Unigenitus*.

The archbishop of Paris, Noailles, supported Quesnel and was also involved in the appeal to a general council. However, in 1728, six months before Noailles died, he abandoned his previous positions and submitted to Rome. Since Quesnel had died in 1719, with Noailles's change of heart and his death, the Jansenists lost their leading figure.

There was no one who could take up the leadership role for the Jansenists. There were four French bishops who continued to insist on their right to appeal to a council, but none of these had the position or the qualities necessary to carry the Jansenist banner. Further, the court and the king became active against the Jansenists, as Louis XIV had been, and many Jansenists were exiled or imprisoned.

Some Jansenists had found refuge in Holland. The Church in Holland was governed by apostolic vicars since about 1700. One of these, Pierre Codde, was a Jansenist and firmly held to his position, even enduring exile. After him other anti-Jansenist apostolic vicars were appointed by the Church, but Utrecht refused to recognize these anti-Jansenist appointees.

The cathedral chapter acted as administrator of the diocese, recommended men to be ordained priests, and even chose a bishop for themselves, Cornelius Steenhoven. A bishop was found who ordained Steenhoven, and he ordained three others. Further, Utrecht divided itself into three dioceses, with Utrecht as the archdiocese. Even though there were about ten thousand in Utrecht, as opposed to two hundred thousand Catholics in all of Holland, the schismatic Church in Utrecht was able to maintain itself even into the nineteenth century! Jansenism, a heresy, became, at least in Holland, a schism as well.

The Convulsionaries

Lacking a forceful leader, having failed to advance their cause with the distinction between fact and doctrine and by the appeal to a general council, and having spent all the energy generated by the movement, the Jansenists in the 1720s and 1730s claimed the favor of God by pointing to miracles.

In 1725, a woman was cured of uterine bleeding during a Eucharistic procession in which the priest carrying the Blessed Sacrament was an appellant. The Jansenists concluded that this miracle was an intervention by God which showed God's favor for their positions. Two years later, miracles began to occur at the grave of an appellant in the diocese of Rheims.

In the cemetery of Saint-Medard in Paris, at the grave of an appellant, there were many alleged miracles in the late 1720s and early 1730s. At this site, after some were cured of illnesses, they were afflicted with seizures. More and more people flocked to the Parisian cemetery, and more and more were afflicted with convulsions. When the cemetery was closed because of the mass hysteria, the "convulsionaries," as history knows these Jansenists, held meetings in homes, and instead of experiencing miracle cures, they uttered prophecies.

In late 1732, some experienced trance-like states and then asked to be "relieved" with beatings. Supposedly the pain from the beatings would "relieve" them of the trance. Some of these beatings were particularly severe, and people were wounded with swords, nails, whips, etc. While the historical records are extensive, it is difficult to understand this phenomenon. Of course, the Jansenists interpreted all of these events as proof of God's approval of their position.

By the 1730s, Jansenism was one hundred years old. While there have been heresies within the Church that lasted longer, Jansenism had considerable staying power. However, unlike Arianism, Jansenism did not survive by maintaining the focus on one aspect of the faith.

Certainly, Cornelius Jansen began the discussion on the question of the relationship between grace and free will. He was most assuredly simply trying to contribute to the ongoing discussion about the way to understand the operation of God's grace in union with human freedom. But Jansenism soon took on a spiritual rigorism which was promoted by Saint-Cyran. It also became associated with an anti-Jesuit spirit.

Further, Jansenism embraced the movement to achieve and maintain certain liberties for the Church in France. Most of all, the major focus changed very early from grace and free will to what Rome could expect all Catholics to accept: the distinction between fact and doctrine.

The issue of fact and doctrine came to dominate the dispute. After the Clementine peace, when the whole issue was resurrected in the 1700s, it quickly moved from theological opinion and dispute to the right for the bishops, clergy, and faithful to appeal to a council over the decision of a Pope. When all these approaches failed, Jansenism sought to justify its positions by an appeal to miracles, demonstrating the approval of God. This appeal also failed in the end.

By the middle of the eighteenth century, Jansenism was all but dead. However, certain Jansenist viewpoints, especially a certain rigorism in spiritual matters, continued to have some impact. Jansenist influence was especially strong in certain religious orders, and of course many members of orders were the teachers and professors in clerical schools.

A spiritual austerity which was not heretical, but certainly was on one end of the spiritual spectrum, was taught in many schools. French clerical schools had a significant influence on English-speaking Catholics (because the Church could not legally function in England until the nineteenth century). Many of the Irish clergy were educated in France and many Irish were sent abroad as missionaries to various countries, including the United States.

It is possible to trace a certain spiritual tradition in the United States and other English-speaking countries to Jansenist circles. Of course, this Jansenist spiritual tradition is not the only one present among Catholics in the English-speaking world.

Jansenism
This heresy taught that human beings after original sin were not capable of acting freely. They either acted under the compulsion of their fallen nature or under grace. As a result, salvation depended solely on God, and His gift of grace.

27

Quietism

Michael de Molinos

WHILE JANSENISM GREW OUT OF THE REFORMATION AND COUNTER-Reformation discussions of grace and free will, Quietism had different roots within the thought of the Reformers. It also arose in a time when discussions of spirituality and prayer, especially with the growth of religious orders, was almost commonplace. One thinks of the discussions of mystical theology that were written particularly in Spain during the Counter-Reformation, for example, the writings of St. Teresa and St. John of the Cross.

Quietism is a name given to the body of teachings by the Spaniard Michael de Molinos, who lived in Rome during the last half of the seventeenth century. Molinos was first and foremost a spiritual director. Some twelve thousand of his letters to various people were part of the evidence used in the condemnation of his ideas and his work in 1687. However, most of his key ideas are found in a work published in Rome in 1675.

Molinos taught that the path to union with God, even on earth, was to "quiet" or abandon all use of any human faculties. In other words, the interior powers of mind, will, imagination, and memory were to be entirely emptied and those who wanted to approach God were to remain almost lifeless within their bodies.

In doing absolutely nothing, either outwardly or inwardly, the individual becomes pleasing to God. Those who would approach the highest union with God were not to think of themselves, of eternal damnation or of eternal happiness, of heaven or of hell, of their own state, or even of temptations. In fact, in this quieted state, if the body was to suffer temptations nothing was to be done about them (because this would involve an act and would be the use of human faculties.)

Molinos even permitted stirrings of nature which were not to be resisted because resistance involved human acts which, he taught, were displeasing to God. Molinos also taught that any delights arising from prayer were unclean and to be avoided.

For Molinos, no external acts were necessary to salvation, including works of charity and penance. Molinos also de-emphasized the sacraments.

Molinos taught that sometimes the devil is allowed to take control of certain advanced or even perfect souls and to force them to perform sinful acts. According to him, such things are not to be mentioned in the sacrament of Penance or Reconciliation because the interior life abandoned to God has nothing to do with outward acts like the sacrament of Reconciliation. Further, by not confessing such occurrences, the soul overcomes the devil and attains a closer union with God. Allegiance to spiritual superiors — the bishop or superior of an order — extends only to outward acts. Interiorly, only God and the spiritual director are to be the guides.

Difficulties With Molinos's Teaching

There are a multitude of problems with Molinos's teaching, which is the reason it was condemned by Pope Innocent XI (1676-1689) in 1687 and Molinos was imprisoned for life and died in 1696. God would not have given us our minds, wills, imaginations, and memories and then asked us not to use them. Further, all temptations need to be resisted. Also, obviously, the greater the love for God, the greater the hatred of sin and the greater the desire to do charitable works for others.

Intense love for God leads to intense love of neighbor (hence, charitable works) and to intense dislike of the devil. It should also be obvious that the greater the love for God, the more important the Church, the mystical Christ, becomes. The sacraments, including the sacrament of Reconciliation, would also grow in importance. All this, of course, is the testimony of the saints of the Church over centuries.

Molinos's teachings conflict with the experience of the saints, the teachings of the Gospel, and the conclusions of theology. Nevertheless, Molinos wrote in order to help those interested in prayer. Although he erred badly, interest in these matters was part and parcel of the era of the Counter-Reformation.

It is also clear that many of Molinos's ideas are related to the ideas of the Reformers. His de-emphasis of the visible Church and of the sacraments clearly echoes some of the teachings of the Reformers. Further, his denial of the importance of good works, i.e., external acts, accords well with Luther's teaching that we are saved by faith and not by works.

Molinos's insistence that the relationship between the individual and the Church — the bishop or religious superior — is relatively unimportant compared to the individual's direct relationship with God not only echoes the ideas of some Reformers, but it also has almost a modern, evangelical ring to it.

Fortunately, Quietism never had the same impact as Jansenism, although Fénelon, a French bishop (of Cambrai) was accused of promoting some similar ideas. A few of his ideas were condemned by Pope Innocent XII (1691-1700) in 1699 and go under the name Semi-Quietism.

In the case of Molinos and Fénelon, the papal intervention seems to have accomplished its purpose and Quietism, at least in the Catholic world, did not have any significant impact after 1699.

Quietism
This heresy taught that the path to God was to abandon the use of all human faculties. All external acts, including the celebration of the sacraments, were unnecessary to holiness. What was necessary was the quieting of all human faculties.

28

Deism

Sources of Deism

DEISM WAS A SCHOOL OF RELIGIOUS THOUGHT WHICH EXALTED NATURAL reason at the expense of Revelation and the Church. While all religions have had members who doubted truths taught as revealed (and therefore exalted reason at the expense of Revelation), Deism is the name specifically applied to a constellation of ideas which were proposed first in England and then in France in the seventeenth century and throughout most of the eighteenth.

The recourse to natural reason, as opposed to Revelation, had two sources. One was the work of men such as Newton, Locke, Spinoza, Bacon, and Descartes. All these had turned to reason to discover truths. Newton with his scientific observations and Locke with his emphasis on natural law and natural right had especially impressed people with what natural reason could accomplish. The other source was the idea of the Reformers that the Scriptures were subject to individual interpretation — that is, subject to the judgment of the individual. (Of course, the Reformers insisted that the Holy Spirit inspired individuals, but this principle became very difficult to maintain when individuals disagreed on interpretations of the same scriptural passage!)

The emphasis on individual interpretation together with the newfound discovery of the possibilities of human reason led directly to Deism — the application of rational principles as discerned by individual philosophers, scientists, and men of letters to matters of the faith.

Stages of Deism

Deism had several stages. At first, the promoters of what came to be called Deism insisted that everyone had a natural right (shades of natural law theory as propounded by Locke) to determine religious truth for himself or herself. Accompanying this principle was a demand for toleration of all points of view. Clearly, such a principle calls into question the teaching authority of the Church.

Some Deists moved beyond this first stage to a second one when they began to cast doubts on the moral teachings of the Church and on the principle that God rewards good acts and punishes evil acts.

A third stage was reached when some Deists attempted to reduce Revelation to the conclusions of natural reason unaided by Revelation. These Deists denied those truths contained in Revelation which reason could not affirm without Revelation, such as the Trinity.

In effect, Deism reduced Christianity to truths known to natural reason. Clearly, in its mature form, Deism denied the Trinity, the divinity of Christ, the activity of the Holy Spirit, the Church and especially the role of the Holy Spirit in guiding it, the mystery of grace, and the inspiration of the Scriptures (because these are not truths unaided reason can affirm).

For the Deists, the one non-triune God was the Creator, the first cause of the universe. He was a personal God, although He did not involve Himself in the world. Rather, like the child who throws a top on the tile floor and watches it spin, so God creates the world and observes its function without any further involvement.

Another image used for the Deist Creator-God is that of a watch-maker. While the watch is an intricate piece of equipment constructed by the watchmaker, once the watch is made and sold, the watchmaker has nothing more to do with the watch. So God created the complicated and intricate universe, but has nothing more to do with it.

The men identified with Deism in England include Lord Herbert of Cherbury (d. 1648), Charles Blount (d. 1693), John Toland (d. 1722) and Thomas Morgan (d. 1743). However, very similar ideas were prevalent in France in the Enlightenment, i.e., in the eighteenth century before the French Revolution beginning in 1789. Men such as Voltaire (d. 1778) and Rousseau (d. 1778) promoted Deistic ideas.

Voltaire

Voltaire insisted repeatedly on religious toleration. He detested the clergy as the source of intolerance, bigotry, and superstition. Together with the English Deists, Voltaire preached a natural religion claiming that there was not only no need of any supernatural Revelation but that the claim to such Revelation, such special knowledge, led to intolerance and cruelty. He insisted that unaided human reason could develop a natural religion with a belief in God and an acceptable moral code.

In Voltaire's history, he insisted that Christianity and all other religions be understood as mere human institutions which developed from human needs. In other words, all belief systems, all faiths, were simply a human response to human needs. In his history of the world, he ignored the usual format: beginning with Creation and following the Bible to Christ and the Christian era. Such a format presumes a belief in divine providence — in the belief that God has gradually revealed Himself through history and that God exerts a certain fatherly care over His children. Voltaire did not accept a God who was active in human history.

Rousseau

Rousseau had some things in common with Voltaire, but he also disagreed with his contemporary on some issues. With Voltaire, Rousseau rejected the Church, the clergy, and any claim of supernatural Revelation. However, Rousseau had great respect for the Scriptures and for the beauty of the cosmos. He also accepted God, not only as the first cause but also as a God of love and beauty.

Since Rousseau emphasized the love and beauty of God and accepted the Scriptures, he was considered more of a threat to the Church than Voltaire. After all, Voltaire was a clear enemy of the Church, rejecting almost everything. Rousseau appeared to be more religious and yet rejected essential teachings of the Church. The appearances made him more of a threat. Further, his novels were widely popular and emphasized feeling and sentiment as well as mystical insights over reason. To some, the appeal to a certain mysticism, or even emotion and feeling, made him seem more attuned to religion, which also appealed to something beyond reason. Rousseau was condemned both in France by the Catholic Church and in Geneva by the Calvinists.

The Deism of the seventeenth and eighteenth centuries died in the upheaval of the French Revolution, but in its broad principles it is still very much a part of the world of the twenty-first century. Many in our own century accept the concept that reason determines truth, even supernatural truth. Further, many in our own era, even though they might not realize it, live their spiritual lives as though God were truly not involved in the world. It is not so much that Deism has directly influenced the twenty-first century world as that the Deists proclaimed certain ideas that repeatedly surface in human thought, even though they are in error when applied to the faith.

> ### Deism
> This heresy taught that all truth was accessible through reason. Therefore, Deists rejected revealed truths of the faith such as the Trinity. Deists also believed that the Creator-God had created the universe, but once the act of Creation was completed God had no more involvement with the world.

Conclusion to Part III

THIS PART HAS COVERED OVER ONE THOUSAND YEARS OF CHURCH HISTORY. It has discussed thirteen different heretical ideas: those of Berengar, the Cathars, the Waldensians, Joachim di Fiore, Wyclif and Hus, Luther, Zwingli, those of the Anabaptists, of Calvin, of the Anglicans, of Jansen, of Molinos, and of the Deists. All of these heresies, with the exceptions of the Cathars and the Deists, had to do with the activity of the Holy Spirit. It is the Holy Spirit who gives the divine life, grace, to all of us through the sacraments. (Of course, it is true that the sacraments are also the work of the Father and the Son. However, sanctification, the gift of God's holiness to us in divine grace, is attributed to the Holy Spirit.)

Certainly, Berengar's erroneous teaching on the Eucharist qualifies as a heresy against the Holy Spirit. The Waldensians attacked the sacraments, including the Eucharist. Wyclif, Hus, Luther, Zwingli, the Anabaptists, Calvin, and those promoting Anglicanism also questioned the Church's teaching on the Eucharist. The Waldensians, all of the Reformers of the sixteenth century, and even the Anglicans questioned the Holy Spirit's guidance of the Church in interpreting the sacred texts. Joachim and his followers also had some very odd ideas regarding the Holy Spirit. The Jansenists and the Quietists emphasized the role of grace at the expense of the role of the human faculties. These ideas also represent a questioning of the work of the Holy Spirit. The Reformers, Luther, Zwingli, the Anabaptists, Calvin, and those promoting Anglicanism also insisted on false notions about grace, which is the gift of the Holy Spirit. There is no question that the preponderance of heresies in this period were attacks on the work of sanctification, the work of the Holy Spirit.

What is also clear in this long period is that increasingly, especially with Jansenism, the attacks against doctrine and the teachings of the Church became very quickly attacks against the Church. Eventually, every heresy which is publicly taught and has followers is addressed by the Church. When the Church condemns the heresy, those holding it either abandon their position (which does happen) or they attack the Church. In the next period, the mystery of the Church, itself, is the target of heretical ideas. Whereas in other periods, the Church was the secondary target — attacked only after it defended a true teaching of the faith — in the last period, it is the mystery of the Church which is the primary target. In the seventeenth and eighteenth centuries, the Deists foreshadowed this trend because they also had the Church as their primary target.

PART IV

The Church: Heresies from 1789 to 2000

We believe in one holy catholic and apostolic Church.
We acknowledge one baptism for the forgiveness of sins.
We look for the resurrection of the dead,
and the life of the world to come.

AFTER THE CREED CONFESSES THE CHRISTIAN FAITH IN THE TRINITY, IN THE Incarnation, and in the work of the Holy Spirit, it acknowledges that the Church is also an object of faith. In other words, just like the Trinity or the Incarnation, the Church itself is a mystery of the faith. Therefore, the Church as a revealed mystery of the faith cannot be totally or completely understood in human terms.

This reality — the Church as a revealed mystery — is not today generally acknowledged even by Catholics. Most think of the Church as a large bureaucracy or perhaps, when thinking of the Vatican, as a kind of worldwide government for Catholics. They see the trappings of office — the papal entourage, the offices of the chanceries, or of the Vatican, as well as the administrative procedures — and think of the Church as merely a human institution. Of course, the Church is a human institution; it has all the marks as well as the problems of a large organization. However, it is still an object of faith — a revealed mystery.

The Church is a revealed mystery of the faith because behind all that is visible, it is the mystical Christ continued through space and time. The Church carries on the work of Christ by continuing to teach and interpret what Christ revealed and by continuing to sanctify people through the power of Christ's cross. The Church carries on Christ's twin missions of Revelation and Redemption. If the Church did not exist, then the work of Christ would not have been extended to succeeding generations. But He promised, "I am with you always to the close of the age." (See Matthew 28:20.) He gave us the Church to continue His presence and his missions of Revelation and Redemption.

The Church, then, has a very visible human appearance which we all recognize, but it also has a hidden, veiled inner life, the life of grace. Just as Christ's humanity veiled His divinity, so the Church's visible structure veils its divine life. The divinity of Christ was revealed in and through His humanity. So also with the Church. Through the eyes of faith, the visible Church reveals its hidden life. Just as the hidden divinity of Christ made His twin missions of Redemption and Revelation efficacious, so the hidden divine life of the Church is the more important aspect of the Church; this life is what makes the Church be the mystical Christ and it is what makes it possible for it to carry out the missions of Revelation and Redemption.

The true reality of the Church as the mystical Christ can only be seen through the eyes of faith. Just as those without faith saw in Jesus only a Jewish carpenter who (in their eyes at least) had pretensions of grandeur as a religious figure, so without the eyes of faith, the Church is only and merely human. Without faith, the Church can even look exploitative. But to those who see with the eyes of faith, the Church is Christ continued through space and time.

After the controversies on the Trinity, on the Incarnation, on the Holy Spirit, there are those who question the Church as a divine revealed mystery of the faith. It is not surprising that the attacks on the Church have come after those on the Trinity, the Incarnation, and the Holy Spirit. The reality of the Church as the mystical Christ clearly depends on these other truths of the faith. The hidden life of the Church is the Holy Spirit, who was sent by the incarnate Son, who could only be God made man if there truly is a Trinity of Persons in God. In other words, these other truths of the faith had to be fixed and settled before questions regarding the Church could be addressed. But, in this most recent period of the Church's history, 1789-2000, it is the Church itself as a mystery of the faith which has been called into question.

Of course, if the guiding idea of this volume is correct — that the various heresies proposed against the teachings of the Church have generally chronologically followed the order of the creed, it is predictable that the last mystery of the faith to be addressed would be the Church.

29

Old Catholics

Infallibility and the First Vatican Council

THE OLD CATHOLICS IS THE NAME GIVEN TO A GROUP OF PEOPLE WHO RE-
jected the definition of papal infallibility by the First Vatican Council (1869-
1870). Both before and during the First Vatican Council there were long
discussions about the teaching on papal infallibility to be promulgated by
the council.

Opposition to the proposed teaching was particularly strong among
some theologians in Germany. In the preliminary balloting on the constitution *Pastor Aeternus,* which contained the teaching on infallibility, eighty-
eight of the bishops present voted *non placet* — i.e., that they did not accept
the document. Another sixty-two bishops cast votes of *placet juxta modum*
— that they accepted the document, but with reservations. With some further negotiations and alterations of the text, all but about sixty bishops
accepted the document.

Rather than vote against *Pastor Aeternus* in the presence of the Pope
whose teaching authority was affirmed in the document, these sixty bishops decided to leave Rome before the final vote was taken. As a result, there
was almost a unanimous approval of the teaching on infallibility by the
First Vatican Council. However, despite the vote, everyone realized that
there was a significant minority of the bishops of the Church who had
difficulties with the teaching on infallibility.

Nevertheless, all the bishops soon accepted the teaching of the council, even those who had chosen to leave Rome before the final vote. Still, a
number of theologians in Germany were strongly opposed. Some non-aca-
demic Catholics also voiced their unwillingness to accept the new teaching.

In August 1870, some 1,300 Catholics in the Rhineland protested
the teaching of the council. Claiming to represent traditional Catholic

thought and teaching, some three hundred delegates from Germany, Switzerland, and Austria met in Munich in September 1870.

The schismatic Church of Utrecht (Jansenist) had representatives in Munich, as did the Anglicans and the Orthodox. One of the key leaders of the movement, Doellinger, argued vehemently against the establishment of a Church organization separate and distinct from Rome, but he was overruled. A majority of the delegates wanted to establish a new Church.

A New Church Organization

At another congress two years later (1872) in Cologne, the name Old Catholic, emphasizing the traditional point of view these people believed they were accepting, was adopted. Further, a committee was established to prepare for the election of a bishop. In 1873, Joseph Hubert Reinkens was elected by the Old Catholics and ordained by a bishop of the Utrecht Church. Of course, since the bishops of Utrecht were validly (but not lawfully) ordained, Reinkens was as well.

Later, Reinkens provided for his successors by ordaining two of his priests as bishops of the Old Catholics. Reinkens was placed under interdict by Pope Pius IX, but established his Church administration in Bonn.

Some German bishops responded to the movement by denying the sacraments and imposing the penalties of canon law on the dissenters including suspension (for priests) and excommunication. In turn, the Old Catholics complained to the civil authorities about the harsh treatment they were receiving from the Pope and the bishops. Some of the German governments (Germany was not united under one government and there were many separate states within Germany) responded to these complaints by recognizing the Old Catholics as Catholics; i.e., some German governments officially regarded the Old Catholics as a "branch" of the Catholic Church. With this recognition, it was possible for the Old Catholics to use some Catholic property.

Kulturkampf

The Catholic bishops opposed the governments that recognized the Old Catholics. This opposition by the Roman Catholic bishops (and other factors as well) led the state to pass laws against the Roman Catholics — i.e., to institute a persecution which was called the *Kulturkampf.* Catholic bishops were arrested or went into exile. Restrictions were placed on Catholic worship and education. The Jesuits were expelled. The state was trying to enlist the Old Catholics as an ally against the Catholic Church.

But it soon became clear that the Old Catholics were not truly Catholic! The Old Catholics established synods as governing bodies. The synods were to elect bishops and initiate reforms as needed.

The Old Catholics abolished celibacy for the clergy in 1879 (against the strong opposition of Bishop Reinkens and others) and introduced German into the liturgy in 1880. With these innovations, it became harder and harder to maintain the fiction that the Old Catholics were indeed Catholic or even traditional, and so support from the civil authorities dwindled.

Further, the *Kulturkampf* against the Catholics had strengthened Catholics in their own beliefs. In facing opposition to the Church, most of the faithful reacted by re-affirming their Catholic faith. The strength of the Catholic Church led the authorities to see that the *Kulturkampf* campaign was a failure and that the Old Catholics were too weak to help the state in its campaign against the Catholics and Rome. Without the support of the state, with a strengthened Catholicism, and with a liberalized Old Catholic Church (which caused one to question the "traditional" nature of Old Catholicism), the Old Catholics lost much of their influence and strength.

As an indication of the weakness of Old Catholicism in Germany, the Old Catholic professorships on the theological faculty at Bonn were lost after 1901, except for one. Since Old Catholicism had originally been a movement of theologians, the loss of these positions was significant.

Old Catholics In Austria and Switzerland

In Switzerland, Old Catholicism gained a foothold in 1875 when the first synod met. Eduard Herzog was ordained as bishop for Switzerland in 1876 and established Old Catholicism on the basis of the Bible and Eucharist. A theological university was founded at Berne and became important, especially after the academic positions at Bonn were lost at the beginning of the twentieth century.

In Austria, Old Catholicism developed very gradually. The state officially recognized a few Old Catholic communities in 1877. Old Catholicism in Austria was guided by an episcopal administrator, and there was a bit of growth in the 1890s, but Old Catholicism was never as important in Austria as it was in Germany or Switzerland.

In 1889, the Old Catholics and the Utrecht Church united, and this union produced a certain ecumenical movement. Anglicans and Orthodox were invited by the Old Catholics to meet and discuss theological topics, but except as a distant foreshadowing of the ecumenical efforts of the twentieth century, these small efforts had little effect. The Old Catholics still exist, but are a relatively small denomination separate from Rome.

Without a doubt, the Old Catholic movement was a rejection of the teaching authority of the Church and of the position of the Pope. Old Catholicism was originally a movement of theologians who could not accept the teaching of the Church. In a rather disturbing way, this nineteenth-century break with the Church foreshadowed the reaction of many theologians to the teaching of Pope Paul VI in the famous encyclical, *Humanae Vitae* (On Human Life).

Old Catholicism
This heresy denied the teaching on papal infallibility taught by the First Vatican Council.

30

Modernism

Sources of Modernist Thought

THROUGHOUT THE NINETEENTH CENTURY, THERE WAS A RENEWAL OF HIS-
torical studies. The massive editing and publications of sources, in part
symbolized by the *Monumenta Germaniae Historica* (MGH) and Migne's
patrology, betrays the interest of historians in the sources.

Leopold van Ranke's famous dictum, *Wie es eigentlich gewesen war*
("As it actually was"), also is a testimony to the "scientific" history of the
nineteenth century. Historians wanted to found everything they said or
wrote on a critical examination of the sources. The editing and publishing
of the sources, of course, is absolutely fundamental to historians working
today, even though most historians today would doubt the ability of any
historian to approach his or her subject without any bias.

This new "scientific" history combined with movements in philosophy to influence the work of some theologians. Kant had carried Descartes's
questioning of human knowledge to a new high (or low, depending on
one's point of view). Unable to establish any moral truth, Kant had resort to
a vague obligation of duty. The radical questioning of the ability of the
human intellect to know truth, moral or otherwise, led to an effort to replace absolute and unchanging truths (dogma) with statements that would
correspond more with the lived experience of individuals, especially the
emotional and sentimental experiences.

Since it was doubtful how much absolute truth one could ever know,
why not turn to lived experiences of individuals — which, because they
were actually lived, were objectively verifiable? This trend was reinforced
by new trends in evolutionism. Why could dogmatic truths not develop
and even evolve to meet the new and ever-changing experiences of each
generation?

These intellectual trends in history and philosophy influenced theologians in France, England, and Italy. While not all those who described themselves as modernists adhered to all of the concepts usually identified as modernist, still the broad outlines of the modernist movement are discernible.

Jesus of History vs. Christ of Faith

Applying the methods of historical criticism (i.e., the critical assessment of sources) to the Scriptures, modernists called into question many of the teachings of the Church. They also made the now famous distinction between the Jesus of history and the Christ of faith, arguing that the historical Jesus was in many ways fundamentally different from the Christ people have come to accept through faith.

Modernists suggested that Jesus never intended to found a Church or to institute the sacraments. They argued that the Jewish Jesus taught about His own religious experiences, which later were interpreted by the community in certain ways. This process of interpretation led to intellectual statements of the Lord's experiences, and these statements are the formulations of the faith, i.e., dogmas. However, the dogmas are simply formulations, statements that stand for the religious experience of Jesus' experiences. The Christ of faith is constantly changing according to the community's experience of Jesus' original experiences.

Implicit in these ideas is the possibility that subsequent generations can reformulate their experiences of Jesus into different statements which might be more understandable to them than the earlier formulations. Unlike the principles of the development of dogma, which allow different ways of repeating the same truth or of seeing more clearly what was already implicit in earlier statements, the modernists claimed that the dogmas, no matter how or when they were formulated, did not contain unshakeable truths. Rather, dogmas were the understanding of the faith community of their religious experiences of Jesus' experiences, but these might not bear much resemblance at all to the Jesus of history.

One century might formulate these experiences one way, and the next might formulate them a different way. The Christ of faith, the experiences of the community of believers of Jesus' experiences, was constantly changing. It was not important to retain or acknowledge previous dogmatic statements. The only essential element was that people living at a particular time needed to understand the statements in terms of their experience of Jesus. When people no longer could make sense out of previous formulations of Jesus' experiences, new statements were to be constructed and the old ones abandoned. What mattered was the experience of Jesus' experiences. The particular formulations of that experience were not only changeable, but they had to be changed for each succeeding generation. Dogmas were therefore changeable and did not contain eternal truths.

This view of Christ's teachings coincided with a theory of the origin of all religious belief and practice. Each one of us experiences the world around us. At some point, we begin to ask questions about that world, especially about its origins. In experiencing the world, we also experience ourselves and begin to ask fundamental questions about our own existence.

This questioning leads to an intuition of a Being greater than ourselves. Obscure at first and present only in the subconscious, each of us gradually becomes aware of (i.e., we perceive in our minds) the existence of this greater Being, God. Knowing of God, each of us seeks God. (This theory is not much different than St. Augustine's famous thought, "Thou hast created us for thyself, and our heart cannot be quieted till it may find repose in thee.") In seeking God, we all begin to have religious experiences. From these experiences, some people are able to construct entire religious systems with beliefs, moral codes, and worship.

In this view, Jesus' religious experience was unique. He was the one who was able to communicate His religious experiences *par excellence*. Therefore, Christianity has a pride of place because of the genius of Jesus in communicating His religious experiences. Nevertheless, the origin of the Church in its beliefs, its moral code, its sacraments as well as its worship, lies in the religious experience of Jesus as formulated repeatedly over and over again through the centuries. The standard by which all dogmas, morality, sacraments, and worship are measured is the lived religious experiences of those alive on earth at a particular moment in history. Everything evolves and changes according to the lived experiences of the present generation.

The precise difficulty with the theory is the divorce between the Jesus of history and the Christ of faith. Once one suggests and accepts that the historical Jesus is different from the Christ of faith, the Christ of faith is then seen (and believed) through the lived experience of each generation. In effect, the Jesus of history disappears in favor of a Christ of faith who constantly changes according to the faith experience of each generation.

The modernist emphasis on the lived experiences of people was an attempt to connect the faith with the actual lives of people. Further, it was a reaction to the dominant role the intellect had held in Catholic thought since the development of Scholasticism in the Middle Ages. Rather than focusing on eternal truths — on knowing truth through the mind — the modernists emphasized the role of freedom, of the will. In fact, one of the projects of the modernists was to free science, history, the government, and private consciences from ecclesiastical dominance.

The modernist principles weakened the authority of the Church because in the modernist system the Church could not claim the authority of Christ! If science, history (in fact, all scholarly disciplines), government, and individual consciences were not subject to the Church's authoritative teaching on matters of faith, and if dogmas were to evolve, there was nothing standing in the way of insuring that Christianity would always be wedded to the spirit of each new age. In the end, the goal of the modernists was not to transform society and culture, but to accommodate Christianity to the culture so that it would ever be modern!

Clearly, the modernist ideas represent a radically different understanding of religious truth, morality, the sacraments, and the Church than that traditionally held by Catholics. The modernist ideas threatened all of theology— dogmatic, moral, and sacramental. Most of all, Modernism called into question the very constitution of the Church. No longer resting on Christ, the Church was constructed from the religious experiences of the faith community in every age. It is no wonder that Pope Pius X (1903-1914) called Modernism the "synthesis of all errors."

Arguably, the most famous representatives of modernist thought were Loisy in France and Tyrell in England.

Alfred Loisy

Alfred Loisy is probably the name most often associated with Modernism. He was born in 1857 and lived a long life, dying in 1940. In his twenties, he devoted himself to a study of the Old Testament and the Gospels, applying the methods of textual criticism to the Scriptures. In publishing his results, Loisy called into question many of the traditional doctrines of the Church.

Moving from his scriptural investigations to the area of dogma, Loisy published a work in 1902 entitled *L'Evangile et l'Eglise* ("The Gospel and the Church"). In this work, Loisy argued that Jesus had not intended to create a Church or to institute sacraments, but rather to proclaim the kingdom of heaven. The Church grew from the understanding of the early Christian community of Jesus' teaching about the kingdom of heaven. In turn, the Church taught dogmas, established sacraments, and developed a hierarchy. But since the heart of Christianity was the truth of the kingdom of heaven taught by Christ, this truth could be expressed in the future in different ways than it is at present. In other words, neither Catholic dogmas, the hierarchy, nor the sacraments are necessarily permanent.

In a later work, Loisy wanted to free historians from any subservience to Church teaching. He argued that the virgin birth, Christ's divinity, His Resurrection or any other direct intervention by God stands outside of history. History should only concern itself with the belief of the early Christians in Christ and the events of His life, including the Resurrection. What Jesus said and did were outside of the competence of history, but what early Christians believed about Christ was part of history. This distinction, of course, is the separation of the Jesus of history from the Christ of faith.

In the modernist project, this distinction is part and parcel of freeing history from the authority of the Church. Loisy then turned to a work on the Gospels of Matthew, Mark, and Luke. However, in 1903, before the work on the Gospels was published, Rome condemned Loisy's works.

George Tyrell

George Tyrell, a Jesuit, was one of the leading figures in the modernist movement in England. Born in 1861, he died in 1909 of Bright's disease. Irritated by the constraints put on his work by the hierarchy, he began to doubt and question the authority of the Church. He was encouraged in this attitude by the works of the modernists on the continent. He also wondered about the frequent use of medieval expressions for the Catholic faith. He was interested in the contrast between the conception of dogma as an expression of truth and the historical development of doctrine. Further, he was interested in the unique approach to the truth which characterized every individual.

Tyrell tried to show that Jesus never intended to be a teacher of an eternal body of truth. Dogma, said Tyrell, was simply an attempt to express the divine within man in rational ways. He opposed the idea of the Church as a guardian of truth and specifically the claim to authority by the Roman curia. For Tyrell, the Church was to be the place to learn of divine love on earth.

The individual's religious experience was the important element in any religious system, not structures like the Church. He was expelled from the Jesuits for his views, and before he died he did try to find an acceptable path between those who espoused traditional theology and those who defended the new trends in philosophy. This attempt ended when he strongly protested the encyclical letter *Pascendi*, in which Pope Pius X severely criticized the modernist viewpoints. Tyrell was excommunicated for these views and after publishing a small book criticizing papal authority and traditional Catholicism, he died a premature death.

Modernism in Italy

Tyrell and Loisy both influenced the Italian Catholic intellectual world, but Tyrell had the greater impact. Still Italy developed a distinct modernist movement. Some of the characteristics of Italian Modernism can be traced to the movement for Italian reunification, the *Risorgimento,* which sought, among other goals, the elimination of Church authority over secular matters. Italian Modernism adopted this attitude against Church authority and applied it not to secular affairs, but to ecclesiastical matters. In other words, the individual should be free from papal and episcopal authority even in religious matters. In addition, in emphasizing the common political heritage of all Italians, the *Risorgimento* was the source for the Italian Modernist emphasis on the community of all the members of the Church.

This view of the Church contrasted with the received tradition of the Church as constituted by the hierarchy. These characteristics of Italian Modernism were supplemented by a desire among the Italian modernists to share the new insights with the ordinary lay people of the Church.

While French and English Modernism were primarily promoted among the clergy and academicians, Italian Modernism had a distinctly populist flavor. As an indication of this tendency, several Italian modernists were striving to improve the religious education of the Catholic lay people. More and more, Italian modernists wanted reforms in the Church including the suspension of clerical celibacy, a reduction in the number of dioceses, reform of seminaries and of the traditional pastoral initiatives, and a modification of the procedures of the *Index of Forbidden Books*.

Many younger clergy were drawn toward the modernist and reformist concepts. In contrast to Tyrell and Loisy, most Italian modernists hoped to work within the Church. Still, the movement was doomed after the issuance of Pius X's encyclical against Modernism, *Pascendi*, in 1907.

Church Reaction

Preceding the encyclical *Pascendi* was the decree of the Holy Office (now called the Congregation for the Doctrine of the Faith) entitled *Lamentabili sane exitu* which condemned sixty-five modernist statements. *Lamentabili* was issued in July 1907, and in September *Pascendi* was released. Taken together these documents constituted a fatal blow to the modernists.

Most of the proponents of Modernism submitted to the Roman decrees. Of course, there were some who, realizing that their attempt to work within the Church had failed, broke with the Church completely, including Tyrell and Loisy.

Pius X instituted seminary visitations in Italy, and both the Biblical Commission and the Index Commission were employed in assuring that the judgments of *Pascendi* would be implemented.

In 1910, Pius X instituted the famous oath against Modernism which all the clergy were to take. Most of the bishops of the world complied with the wishes of the Pope and the Roman Curia. But the backlash against the modernists caught more than the modernists in its ever-widening net.

The conservative anti-modernists called themselves the integralists because they insisted that they stood for integral Catholicism, that is, Roman Catholicism in its integrated wholeness, both doctrine and practice. The integralists saw in every innovation, every new idea and approach, the hint of the Modernist heresy.

Many Catholic intellectuals abandoned speculative theology and concentrated on historical questions or worked on matters which were accepted within the neo-Thomistic theological framework. Clearly, the reaction to *Pascendi* and *Lamentabili* went beyond what was strictly necessary. However, this is the historian's judgment after years have passed. At the time, the threat to the Church's belief system was real and those who enthusiastically accepted the papal condemnation of Modernism wanted to assure themselves that it would not rise again.

Relationship Between Truth and Freedom

Modernism was first and foremost an attack on the Church. It questioned the Church's very existence, its sacramental system, and its teachings. Its insistence on the individual and the freedom of the individual was a challenge to the claim the Church makes to teach the truth and to bind people, not with arbitrary laws or power, but with the truth. As with the Deists, Modernism wanted to free society from the authority of the Church. But more than the Deists and certainly more than the Old Catholics (who at first only attacked one particular way the Church teaches — that is, with infallibility), the modernists posed *the* question that would plague the twentieth century: the relationship between truth and freedom.

This same issue was the driving force behind the crisis in the Church which followed the Second Vatican Council. Could the Church, in preaching the truth, insist on its acceptance, at least by Catholics, or was this insistence a violation of the freedom of the baptized? The issue of freedom and truth is at the heart of the life of the Church since the1960s.

Modernism

This heresy held that the individual lived experiences of Jesus' experiences were to be the norms of belief and acting. Modernists questioned dogmas, the interpretation of Scripture, the practice of the sacraments, and the moral teachings of the Church.

31

No Salvation Outside of the Church: The Feeneyites

Priest, Editor, and Teacher

LEONARD FEENEY WAS BORN IN LYNN, MASSACHUSETTS, ON FEBRUARY 15, 1897. At the age of eighteen, in 1914, he entered the Jesuit novitiate in New York, and after fourteen years of education and formation, he was ordained as a Jesuit priest on June 20, 1928. In the 1930s, only a few years after his ordination, Father Feeney became literary editor of the Jesuit journal *America* and also authored several books. He continued publishing books throughout the 1940s. Father Feeney was a recognized literary figure and lecturer.

In 1942, Father Feeney was transferred to the St. Benedict Center in Cambridge, Massachusetts. This center had been founded by Mrs. Catherine Clarke in 1940 as a Catholic educational center for students attending Harvard and other nearby universities. Father Feeney was very successful in attracting students to the center and in conveying the faith. He won praise from the young and very gifted Avery Dulles, who was connected with the Center. In fact, Dulles was responsible for beginning the publication of the quarterly journal *From the Housetops*.

Outside the Church There Is No Salvation

In 1947, an article published in *From the Housetops* taught that there was no salvation for those outside the Church. In 1948, an article repudiated interfaith movements because the points of disagreement with other faiths were more important than the points of agreement. In these same years, according to reports of those who came into contact with him, Father Feeney became increasingly hostile to any secular learning and even denounced Cardinal Newman, claiming that Newman had done incalculable damage to the

Church. In the December 1948 issue of *From the Housetops*, an article appeared which clearly and unequivocally argued that there could be no salvation outside the Church. Although Father Feeney had signed none of these articles, it was clear that the Center and its leaders embraced the strict position that no one could be saved who was not a full member of the Roman Catholic Church.

Rev. Philip J. Donnelly, S.J., of the theology department at Boston College responded, but *From the Housetops* answered the Donnelly paper. The next development was initiated by the Center. Three members of the Center who were also faculty members at Boston College (although not members of the theology department) wrote the President of the College that the theology department was not teaching that submission to the Pope and membership in the Catholic Church were necessary for salvation. Another letter claiming that heresy was taught at Boston College was sent to Pope Pius XII by twelve members of the Center. The three members who had sent the first letter to the President of Boston College signed another letter (together with a fourth member of the Center who was also a professor at Boston College) to the Father General of the Jesuits. In April 1949, the President of Boston College invited the three professors (who had authored the first letter addressed to him) to a meeting and at the meeting asked them to retract their letter. They refused and were dismissed, together with the fourth professor who had signed the letter to the Father General of the Jesuits.

Father Feeney wrote a letter to Archbishop Cushing of Boston in defense of the four professors. In addition, Center members addressed another letter to Pope Pius XII on April 15, 1949. Neither letter had any effect. Archbishop Cushing, appointed as arbiter in the dispute between Feeney and his fellow Jesuits, removed Father Feeney's faculties and interdicted the Center. (Interdiction is a penalty in the Church forbidding the celebration of the sacraments in a certain geographical location — usually a parish or chapel.) By the archbishop's order, Catholics were forbidden to visit the Center. This action by Archbishop Cushing was partly in response to a letter by the Jesuit provincial (Father Feeney's superior in the Jesuits) regarding the practices and teachings at the Center. The archbishop took sanctions against Father Feeney because he failed to obey his religious superiors.

Since Father Feeney continued to hear confessions despite the archbishop's interdiction, he incurred the penalty of suspension; his priestly faculties were removed until he conformed to the requirements of the decree of the Archbishop. Seeing that the Archbishop's letter and interdiction were partly the result of pressure brought by the Jesuits against Father Feeney, Center members and supporters were very optimistic that Pius XII would answer their two letters with a positive statement affirming their belief in the principle that there is no salvation outside the Church.

On the contrary, however, on August 8, 1949, the Holy Office (now known as the Congregation for the Defense of the Faith) issued a Protocol condemning the viewpoint expressed in *From the Housetops*, vol. 3. (This volume included the December 1949 issue with the "no salvation" article.)

Slaves of the Immaculate Heart of Mary

Those remaining devoted to the Center and Father Feeney now organized themselves into a religious community called the Slaves of the Immaculate Heart of Mary. There were about twelve married couples together with unmarried men and unmarried women. The single men and women each formed religious communities. The married couples lived together in a house separate from the single men and single women. The children of the married couples were to be raised in common. Eventually, the incorporation of the married couples and their children in a communal lifestyle caused problems.

Remaining under the sanctions of the Church, the community appealed again to Pope Pius XII in 1952 against Archbishop Cushing and against the Protocol of August 8, 1949. They charged the archbishop with allowing heresy in his archdiocese by permitting the teaching that people could be saved outside the Church. They further claimed on technical canonical grounds — i.e., on a technical point of Church law — that the August 8, 1949, Protocol was defective, i.e., without legal force.

The Vatican responded by summoning Father Feeney to Rome. Father Feeney asked Rome for a formal declaration of the charge against him. The Vatican again ordered Father Feeney to come to Rome. In December 1952, Father Feeney responded by refusing to come to Rome.

The Holy Office summoned Father Feeney for a third time and ordered him to appear by January 31, 1953, or suffer the penalty of excommunication. Father Feeney refused again and accused Rome of making the whole issue public contrary to canon law. The excommunication was applied automatically because of Father Feeney's refusal to appear in Rome.

Doctrinal Difficulties

Both the Protocol of 1949 and the document of excommunication in 1953 make it quite clear that the sanctions imposed on Father Feeney and on St. Benedict's Center are the result of a refusal to accept and obey the authority of the Church. There is no question that membership in the Church is essential for salvation. It is. This teaching was given by Christ. However, the interpretation of this teaching is not in the hands of individual Catholics, even priests and theologians. The Church through the Pope and the bishops have the obligation not only of teaching what Christ taught, but also of interpreting what the Lord taught. Father Feeney and his followers were not mistaken in upholding the principle that outside the Church there is no salvation. However, they were very mistaken in claiming that they could interpret the proper meaning of that principle even in opposition to the Pope and the bishops, who taught that all those who are not full members of the Church but are trying to do the will of God, do in fact belong to the Church but in an imperfect way.

In effect, Father Feeney claimed to know what Christ meant when He taught that membership in the Church was a normal requirement for salvation. Father Feeney made this claim in the face of the full authority of the Church, which interpreted the teaching of Christ differently than he did. The Pope and the bishops were wrong about what Christ meant, and Father Feeney was right!

Father Feeney's claim was an attack on the teaching authority of the Church. He was appropriating to himself the interpretation of doctrine, not unlike the Old Catholics and the Modernists. In so doing, he claimed to himself the Reformed notion of individual interpretation, not of Scripture, but of doctrine. This appropriation of a Reformed principle is a bit peculiar in that the members of the Reformed Churches (who generally embraced this principle of private interpretation) were the very ones Father Feeney would deprive of the chance of salvation!

Reconciliation

In 1958, the Center sold its property in Cambridge and moved to Still River, Mass. Father Feeney, the men, the women, and the married couples continued to live there, but by 1971 there arose a rather serious division. There were those who insisted that the children should be raised to be religious — sisters, brothers, or priests. Others in the three communities insisted that the children needed to be free to decide for themselves in accordance with the guidance given to them individually by God. The single men, single women, and married couples broke into two parts, with the larger group in favor of allowing the children to choose their own vocations and the smaller one insisting that the children embrace religious vocations.

The larger group also wished to explore the possibility of a reconciliation with the Church. In 1972, after a number of meetings, exchanges of letters, and negotiations, Rome lifted the excommunication of Father Feeney. In light of his age and his health, all that was required was that he make a profession of faith. The smaller of the two Still River groups was very much opposed to this reconciliation, and care had to be taken to prevent the smaller group from sabotaging the reconciliation or from influencing Father Feeney to the point that he would refuse Rome's outstretched hand.

Ironically, Father Feeney's own position had led to a development in the Church on the teaching about salvation outside the Church. This development, anticipated in earlier papal teaching, was fully presented in the documents of the Second Vatican Council. That very development, opposed by the thoughts of Father Feeney, led to a much more tolerant attitude to those Christians (and even non-Christians) who were not members of the Church. Some, favoring the reconciliation, pointed out that the new development in Church teaching had led to toleration towards those separated from the Church, but that Father Feeney had not benefited from this new development.

The very idea he opposed — that it was possible for those outside the Church to come to heaven — was the major reason he was reconciled to the Church! By January 1974, the larger group at Still River was also reconciled with the Church. When Father Feeney died on January 30, 1978, he died as a son of the Church.

There is no question that part of the difficulties connected with the case of Father Feeney had to do with disputes within the Jesuit order. Further, there was difficulty between those who supported secular education for Catholics at such institutions as Harvard and those who thought that secular education was so worldly as to endanger the faith. Nevertheless, the position that there can be no salvation outside the Church — that all those outside the Church and not willing to submit themselves to the Pope were condemned to hell — is untenable. It is an exaggeration of a truth of the faith.

As we have seen before in history, some take a truth of the faith and, in exaggerating it or making excessive claims for it to the exclusion of other truths of the faith, result in maintaining a heretical doctrine. Pelagius did this with an upright Christian life as did Montanus, the founder of the Montanists. Father Feeney exaggerated the truth that outside the Church there is no salvation to the point that it was not true. In refusing to accept the interpretation of the Church in 1949 and again in 1953, Father Feeney attacked the teaching authority of the Church. Without a doubt, this stance represented the most serious claim of his position. This position was the one which Rome noticed when imposing sanctions.

Certainly, by 1953, if not in 1949, Father Feeney should have submitted and he certainly can be faulted for not abandoning his position. But, as with so many other heretics, he stimulated the thought of the Church so that the Second Vatican Council was able to enrich the Church with its new insights and understandings about salvation for those not fully joined to the Church. Although guilty of a theological error and a serious opposition to the Church's teaching authority, Father Feeney was certainly steadfast in his beliefs. Perhaps in the reconciliation with the Church in 1972, he found his reward and a modicum of peace.

It should be noted that the document *Dominus Iesus*, issued in 2000, teaching that the fullness of the faith is found in the Roman Catholic Church, affirms the doctrinal point which was behind Father Feeney's (false) interpretation about salvation outside the Church. Even though the Roman Catholic Church has the fullness of what Christ came to reveal, it does not teach that those who do not fully belong to the Church cannot come to heaven.

Father Feeney's "Outside the Church There Is No Salvation"

This heresy taught that all those who are not full members of the Roman Catholic Church are condemned to hell.

32

✦

Crisis in the Church: 1962-2000

Freedom and the Liturgy

BOTH INSIDE AND OUTSIDE THE CHURCH, ALMOST EVERYONE REALIZES THAT Roman Catholicism in the last decades of the twentieth century underwent a radical alteration. In fact, if a Catholic born in the 1920s who was a faithful Catholic for some thirty years was suddenly transported from the 1950s to the 1980s, there is hardly a question that such a person would find the Church quite changed. In fact, our imaginary ecclesiastical time machine would probably result in a religious shock of rather significant proportions.

New forms of liturgy and worship would seem strange to our time traveler. Catechetics and the teaching of the faith at all levels and at many Catholic institutions would be shocking. The absence of an accepted common code of morality among all Catholics would astound our fictitious faithful Catholic from the 1950s. The practice of each of the sacraments would be inexplicable. The architecture of churches and the nature of "sacred art," music, statuary, vestments, and paintings would be incomprehensible. The "Catholic" books and periodicals published would also astonish the fictitious visitor to the 1980s. The Church known in the '50s would seem to have disappeared. At the very least, our time traveler would probably speak of a revolution.

Lincoln talked about a "new birth of freedom" for the U.S. after the Civil War. One interpretation of the vast alterations in the Church in the last decades of the twentieth century is that there was a claim by many individual Catholics and by Catholic institutions for freedom: freedom from the authority of the Church.

In the 1980s, a parish priest ordained in the early 1960s remarked that all he wanted from the Church was "no rules, no more rules." He was reacting to his perception of the Church's administration and policies in the 1950s: everything circumscribed by specific rules. That view may have been a caricature, but his reaction to it was common. There was in the 1960s a cry for freedom. How did this start?

One of the first topics addressed by the Second Vatican Council was the liturgy. The changes in the liturgy launched by the first constitution of the Second Vatican Council had its roots in the liturgical reform movement of the earlier twentieth century. It should also be noted that the reform initiated by the Second Vatican Council had been preceded by the reform of the Holy Week liturgies in the 1950s under Pope Pius XII.

Nevertheless, the reforms initiated in the wake of the Second Vatican Council struck most Catholics of the 1960s as nothing less than a revolution. Of course, the liturgical reforms authorized by the council were in keeping with sound theology and were for the most part rooted in older traditions. Further, they were necessary and inspired by the Holy Spirit. But for most Catholics, the previous liturgical norms had been as sacred and as untouchable as the doctrinal or moral teachings of the Church. (This perception was erroneous, but we are discussing perceptions.) When liturgical changes were introduced, it seemed to many as though the Church was abandoning everything that had gone before!

Not only were the mandated changes surprising, but there were also many different options allowed to the celebrant, so that from parish to parish the way the Eucharist was celebrated differed widely. Further, there was experimentation in various liturgical rites permitted at certain sites. Some of these experiments struck many Catholics as rather odd. Not only were there differences from parish to parish, shrine to shrine, oratory to oratory in the middle years of the 1960s; there were also new changes almost every week as implementing documents from Rome and the bishops began to inaugurate the reforms. Nothing was ever the same from place to place or from week to week. This constant state of flux in the liturgical rites was particularly difficult, since the Catholic liturgy had been substantially the same everywhere for centuries.

What had been rigorously enforced for everyone — the liturgical norms — now seemed to have no fixed rules whatsoever. Each parish or even each priest seemed to be able to do whatever seemed appropriate. Sometimes liturgical committees in parishes were formed to plan the liturgy. With the issuance of the new rite of celebrating Mass, the *novus ordo* of Pope Paul VI, in 1969, some of the liturgical practices of the previous years were incorporated. Particularly noteworthy was the number of options given to the celebrant or to those who planned the liturgy. Almost every prayer and gesture had several options.

The clear message of the liturgical revolution seemed to be that each priest, each parish, each liturgical planning committee was to exercise his or its own best judgment. They seemed to have been given a freedom of choice with regard to the liturgy. Of course, some relaxation of the previous rather specific norms (which were to be observed absolutely) was needed. However, the perception was that the Church had loosened all of its rules. This perception of a loosening, of a new freedom, soon was demanded in other areas as well.

It is well to remember that the Second Vatican Council met from 1962 through 1965. The liturgical reforms were introduced beginning as early as 1963, but were particularly noticed after 1964. This was the same age that the so-called "baby boomers" were maturing. The "baby boomer" generation was the largest group of young people in the history of the world.

Their very numbers overwhelmed schools, sporting facilities, and youth programs of every kind. It has been remarked that the overwhelming numbers meant that individuals could be lost in the crowd if they did not insist on their own individuality. As a result, there was a new emphasis on the individual, on his or her rights and on personal freedom. Whether this theory explains the new emphasis on freedom in the 1960s might be debated, but what is absolutely clear is that there was a new emphasis on the individual and on personal freedom. The loosening of the liturgical norms in the Church certainly paralleled the new emphasis on freedom. In turn, the new emphasis on freedom together with the Church's relaxation of liturgical norms encouraged Catholics to seek more and more freedom from the authority of the Church.

The "Pill"

At the same time, the contraceptive pill was introduced. Perhaps as nothing else in the history of the world, this chemical gave men and women the possibility of seeking sexual pleasure supposedly without any responsibility. (Of course, this attitude toward sexual expression is untrue. The gift of self in the sexual act, whether procreative or non-procreative, is, by its very nature, the language of love; i.e., it is the gift of self and the acceptance of the other. This language of love necessarily creates a responsibility of the two partners to each other.)

It was said that the "pill" "freed" women to be just like men. Both women and men would now be "free" of the responsibility of children and could engage in the sexual act with anyone at any time.

The Church, of course, had always taught that contraception was gravely immoral, as did all Christian churches until 1930. But it was at least conceivable that the new contraceptive pill might work in a way consistent with Catholic moral teaching. Pope John XXIII (1958-1963) appointed a commission to study the matter, and this commission was continued by Pope Paul VI.

When the texts of the Second Vatican Council were published, people read the now famous footnote where the council Fathers mention that Pope Paul VI had withdrawn consideration of the contraceptive pill from the council. The Pope would decide the issue himself. From 1965 onwards, with this footnote in place, many moral theologians suggested that a change in Church teaching was in the offing. As the demand for freedom escalated in society, it also escalated within the Church. (After all, Catholics live in the same society as everyone else.)

It was harder to argue that to be Catholic was to be subject to the norms and traditions as taught by the hierarchy, because the Church had already (it seemed to many) given way on the liturgy. If the Church could change liturgical norms and give people freedom in that area, why could it not change and give people freedom in other areas? In other words, many Catholics believed that the Second Vatican Council had endorsed freedom and this freedom of the people of God (a phrase of the council) was perceived to be in opposition to traditional norms and teachings. (Of course, that is not what the conciliar Fathers meant, but that was the widespread perception.)

Humanae Vitae

On July 25, 1968, Pope Paul VI issued his encyclical *Humanae Vitae*, "On Human Life," the so-called "birth control" encyclical. In this relatively short document, Pope Paul VI reaffirmed the Church's teaching that contraception was a serious violation of the language of love between husband and wife and that it should never be used. In the context of the era, this teaching seemed to be a denial of everything the Church had done since the council. The Church was now perceived as taking away the freedom that it seemed to have granted. Catholics were no longer able to exercise personal freedom in the sexual area as their neighbors were — without, that is, acting in a way contrary to the Church.

The reaction was not long in coming. In fact, even before the text of the encyclical was available in English, a group of priests and theologians in the United States signed a statement opposing the Pope's teaching. Various arguments were offered to justify Catholics using contraception. Some argued that the teaching was not infallible and therefore Catholics were not obligated to follow it. Others argued that every moral decision had to be grounded in one's conscience and so each Catholic was free to follow his or her own conscience. A further argument was that experts in moral theology should be consulted on moral issues. Therefore, if one wanted to know the morality of a particular act, a moral theologian should be consulted and not a Church administrator like the Pope. Since many, but certainly not all, Catholic moralists disagreed with the Pope, Catholics who followed this argument could easily justify contracepting.

One interpretation of all these arguments is that they constituted a demand, almost a shrill shriek, for freedom. Many, many Catholic men and women, having experienced the demands in society for freedom, having experienced the liturgical reform with the new freedom granted in the area of the liturgy, now demanded the same freedom in regard to contraception. But, in effect, the demand for the right to make up one's own mind about contraception was a demand for freedom from any moral teaching of the Church.

Every single argument used against Pope Paul VI's teaching — the infallible argument, the conscience argument, or the argument that one should consult a theologian — can be used to justify opposition to any moral teaching of the Church. The widespread dissent from *Humanae Vitae* can be seen in the light of a demand for freedom from (or opposition to) the teaching authority of the Church.

Freedom to Accept or Reject Church Doctrine

It was not long before the demand for freedom from the moral authority of the Church was expanded to the area of doctrine. If the Church could not legitimately ask Catholics to follow the moral norms it taught, how could the Church ask Catholics to believe the doctrines it taught? In fact, the conclusion was that it could not.

Taking a page from the Modernists, some suggested that all doctrines were stated in culturally bound terms. For example, the Nicene Creed was stated in fourth-century language. It was bound to the cultural and intellectual milieu of its origin. It contained a truth, but the truth was the fruit of the religious experience of the people who drafted it.

The suggestion was that if the Nicene Creed no longer reflected the cultural experience of the twentieth century, it could be discarded in favor of new formulations. Everything was evolving as the religious experience of individuals changed and developed. Further, if the Church has its origin in the people (i.e., if it is founded on the people, not on Christ directly), then the Church has to respond to the insights of the people of God, i.e., to their religious experience. If the people of God no longer wished to hear about sin and forgiveness, or the Trinity, then the Church should realize that these beliefs no longer resonated with the religious experiences of the people. These teachings should be abandoned.

Just as with the Modernists and the Deists, the issue presented by the crisis of the Church in the last four decades of the twentieth century was the relationship of freedom to the teaching authority of the Church. Since the Church claims to teach the truth, the fundamental issue is the relationship between freedom and truth. There is no question that during the last thirty-five years (this volume was drafted in the year 2000), it is the Church as teacher of the truths of the faith which has been under siege.

Crisis in the Church: 1962-2000

This crisis is constituted by the claim that the Church should not expect faithful Catholics to agree with what it teaches. Each Catholic should have the freedom of the baptized to accept or reject Church teaching. Theological dissent against *Humanae Vitae* is an instance of this crisis in practice.

Conclusion to Part IV

THE HERESIES OF THIS FINAL PERIOD IN CHURCH HISTORY HAVE ALL RE-volved around "one, holy, catholic, and apostolic Church." Even the documents of the Second Vatican Council testify to this reality because, inspired by the Holy Spirit, the council addressed the mystery of the Church more than any other topic. The word Church is used more often than any other substantive word in the conciliar decrees!

Since Pope John Paul II, as Bishop Karol Wojtyla, was one of the authors of *Gaudium et Spes*, The Pastoral Constitution on the Church in the Modern World, as well as one of the contributors to the other constitution on the Church of the Second Vatican Council, *Lumen Gentium*, The Dogmatic Constitution on the Church, it is probable that the answer to the question posed by those insisting on freedom in opposition to the truths taught by the Church can be found in a reflection on his thought.

Since the question posed concerns individual freedom, the best way to respond to the challenge is with an analysis of individual freedom and its relationship to the truth. In point of fact, this analysis is contained within John Paul II's so-called new personalism. As *the* answer to the problem posed by those who would oppose the authority of the Church, it deserves to be the final part in this work on the heresies of the Church.

A New Beginning:
John Paul II and the New Millennium

Focus on the Individual

THE NEW PERSONALISM OF POPE JOHN PAUL II IS WITHOUT A DOUBT A BRIL-
liant solution to a problem which has plagued the Church and its theology
since the Renaissance and Reformation period. The Renaissance focused
on human beings in a way that was foreign to the Middle Ages. While it is
something of an oversimplification, there is some truth in the statement
that whereas medieval thought began with God, Renaissance thought began with human beings.

In the medieval period, often human beings were conceived of as frail
and weak, needing God's grace. They were also seen within the total framework of Creation. They were to use their talents and skills according to
their position in society for the good of the whole. Their goal was to reach
the glory of heaven after death.

In contrast, the Renaissance saw in human beings incredible talents
to be used in this world. The Renaissance emphasized the wonderful and
unique powers of all individuals, and more and more the goal of individuals
was to maximize their talents and gifts so that they did everything they
undertook well. The emphasis was put on excelling in this world. Of course,
to use one's talents and skills successfully, one had to be free and unfettered
by constraints, especially the kinds of constraints placed on people by medieval society.

The new humanism of the Renaissance necessarily meant that there
were new questions and new modes of thinking. In the Renaissance, questions were asked about human beings, about human accomplishments
like art, about the world. The Protestant Reformation furthered the emphasis on the individual with its insistence on the private interpretation
of Scripture. In other words, the Renaissance and Reformation period
resulted in an extraordinary turn towards the individual and his or her
freedom.

The same tendency can be seen in the development of science and in
the scientific method which gradually developed from the Renaissance

onward. Science is based on observation of individual phenomena, on experimentation and the recording of the data gleaned from experiments. Theoretically, the most widely held theorem of science might be disproved by one experiment. The individual experiment became the source of scientific knowledge, and as scientific knowledge gradually came to dominate the modern world — that is, the centuries following the Renaissance and Reformation — it was almost an axiom that knowledge came from individual experiments and observation.

Science and the scientific method so dominate society in this first decade of the twenty-first century that it is fair to say that many other disciplines have adopted a pseudo-scientific method in order to validate their conclusions. In other words, many, many people cannot accept conclusions and knowledge that do not come from individual observations and experiments.

In human affairs, people are loathe to accept conclusions from principles, but when an individual's "real" experience is quoted, people tend to accept conclusions based on that event. It is observable and individual. Conclusions can be drawn from it, almost as a scientist draws conclusions from an experiment.

The focus on the individual and personal freedom is also one of the touchstones of democracy. The political expression of this personal freedom for each individual in a democracy is the right to vote. To those who live in a democracy and even to those who do not, the idea of majority rule is a commonplace. If the majority chooses a person to represent them or chooses to adopt a particular policy, then almost everyone would agree that it is only fair to follow the choice of the majority.

Opinion polls are taken on any number of different issues, and the clear implication is that if a majority agrees on a particular point of view, that point of view is not only right and good, but also true. We determine the truth of things not by principle or even observation, but by counting how many people believe it.

The emphasis on the individual and freedom has its roots in the Renaissance, the Reformation, the rise of science, and the development of democracy. It results in a concept of the world that is subjective, inductive, and experiential. This concept of the world contrasts with the medieval one, which can be defined as objective, deductive, and principled.

Objective vs. Subjective

Objective means that something is real — true regardless of whether or not I know it to be true. For example, if a blind man is outside but cannot see the trees, the trees are still there. Even though he does not perceive them, the trees are truly there. The existence of the trees does not depend on whether the blind man perceives them or not. Objective reality exists independent of one's perception.

The subjective view of reality claims that only that which I perceive to be real is actually real. Generally, the subjective view of reality is not applied to trees and physical objects. However, it is applied to non-physical realities — truths about the existence of God, truths about morality. The subjective view of reality is clearly captured by the phrase "That may be true for you, but not for me!" What is true depends on what I believe or accept, or better phrased, on what I perceive.

In the medieval world, such a claim would be utter nonsense. In fact, to most medieval academics, the truths of the faith, both dogmatic and moral truths, were more real than physical objects. The medieval world was objective; we are subjective. The medieval world was also deductive, which is corollary to its objective view of the world. Knowledge was derived from principles by the process of deduction, often illustrated in syllogisms. One started with a "given" that was accepted, like "God is a pure spirit," then added what was called the minor term — e.g., "a pure spirit does not have a body" — and drew a conclusion, "God does not have a body."

We determine what is true by experiments, by our own experience and by counting heads — whatever the majority believes. This method of reaching truth or knowledge is the inductive method and it is a different process from the deductive method.

The medieval world was based on widely accepted truths from which conclusions were drawn, on principles. The modern world derives knowledge from experiments and individual experiences. We can see the influence of the scientific method in the emphasis on experience in our way of thinking as we can see democratic tendencies in the inductive aspect of our view of the world.

St. Augustine and St. Thomas

The challenges to the Church represented by Deism, Modernism, and the crises following the Second Vatican Council have been aimed at the Church's claim to teach the truth. They have invoked freedom in opposition to the truth. The Church has been ill-equipped to answer the objections because the truths of the faith — the truths Christ came to reveal about us and God — have been taught in a theological system developed in the Middle Ages: the Thomistic synthesis. Theologians have always used the vocabulary and tools of philosophy as a way of conveying the content of the faith — that is, Revelation.

In the West, the first systematic use of a philosophical system to aid in conveying the faith was St. Augustine's use of Plato's ideas. This union of Platonic philosophy and the faith yielded the Augustinian synthesis — a theology. This synthesis was the way the faith was taught from Augustine's death in 430 until the thirteenth century. By then, modes of thought and the culture had changed.

Arabic translations of works of Aristotle, unknown to medieval Europe, translated into Latin in Spain, became available to scholars in Europe. Later, direct translations from the Greek to Latin were available through increasing contacts with the East at the time of the Crusades. Not only did these new translations provide more accurate texts of works already known, but previously unknown works, at least to medieval Europeans, became available. Aristotle's works changed the academic world of the twelfth century, as did other factors. No longer did the Augustinian system convey the faith in terms easily understood. It was necessary to develop a new synthesis, a new way of conveying the faith.

St. Thomas did what St. Augustine did, except that instead of Platonic philosophy, St. Thomas used Aristotle. The resulting theological synthesis was the second mode of conveying the faith. However, Aristotle's philosophy was founded on truth and on the intellect. For Aristotle, the best life was the rational, the thinking one. This system was less well-equipped to answer questions beginning with freedom and the will. Further, both the Augustinian and Thomistic theological systems were objective, deductive, and principled. Neither spoke to the modern world in a way it could understand.

An Example: The Catechetical Difficulty

The difficulty can be illustrated by the catechetical crisis following the Second Vatican Council. With the reforms of the council, many believed that it was permissible to dispose of the old texts and ways of teaching. In the United States, Baltimore catechisms were discarded or put on dusty shelves by the hundreds. An effort was made to update the teaching methods. Teachers and the teachers of teachers wanted to be able to convey the faith in a modern way using subjective, inductive, and above all, experiential starting points.

New texts were written and developed. An attempt was made to create a new synthesis. However, this task was daunting. It is not too much to claim that both Augustine and Thomas were geniuses. The result of the attempt to marry the content of the faith to a subjective, inductive, and experiential worldview was not successful.

First of all, there no longer was a coherent intellectual order to the faith. After discarding the Thomistic synthesis (and not choosing to use Augustine's), the outline of the faith was also discarded. Every discipline has a certain order or structure. For example, history uses dates. There has to be a structure to human knowledge because it is impossible to remember the content of the discipline without it. In throwing out the order of the Thomistic system, the structure of theology was abandoned.

As a result, topics were treated independently of one another. In the discussion of Christ, the children would learn that He was the Son of God — which, of course, is absolutely true. In the chapter on Baptism, the children would learn that they were children of God by Baptism. The children would conclude that Jesus was the Child of God and that they are children of God. They then would realize that they are not God and they would conclude that Jesus is not God either. This type of error occurs when there is no structure in place.

A second error results from an educational truism: Never teach an idea until the children are capable of understanding it. For example, decimals are not introduced in the study of mathematics or arithmetic until the children know something of fractions and until they are old enough to grasp the concept of a decimal point.

When applied to the faith, however, this pedagogical truism is a disaster: if one never teaches what the children are incapable of understanding, when is the Trinity to be introduced? Without the Trinity, of course, the Christian faith falls.

A third error results from the emphasis on experience. Almost all the chapters in modern religion textbooks begin with an experience the children have had and then move on to the appropriate faith concept related to that experience. However, this procedure makes the concept of the faith dependent on the human experience when it should be the other way around.

As a result of these errors, many children grow up without having an understanding of the faith. The reaction to this state of affairs has been to reintroduce the older structures, that is, to teach the faith in the synthesis of St. Thomas. But the success of this effort has been marginal at best.

In using Thomistic terms, there is no question that a vocabulary totally foreign to most people is employed. The meaning of terms have to be given before the concepts can be taught. For example, what is the usual meaning of the word "substance" in modern terms? Most often, in any usual conversation, people will think of drugs, as in substance abuse. But for St. Thomas, as for Aristotle, the word "substance" meant "that which exists in itself."

There are those who understand the vocabulary of the Thomistic synthesis, and it is a brilliant achievement of western thought. However, most people today, especially young people, do not want to learn the vocabulary before they can come to understand the faith. As once was said to one teacher by a high school student, "Why don't you use the words that mean what you want to say instead of words that do not mean what you want to say?" The student had a point.

The modern, subjective, inductive, and experiential mode of thinking, with its emphasis on the individual and personal freedom, poses questions that the Thomistic and Augustinian systems were not designed to answer. This difficulty has intensified throughout the centuries since the Renaissance. It reached a peak in the Church with the crisis following the Second Vatican Council, the most serious challenge to the Church since the Reformation.

To answer these questions, to build coherent and consistent catechetical tools that convey the faith, to solve numerous problems in every area of Church life, a new synthesis of the faith is needed. The Church needs to convey the content of the faith — i.e., Revelation — in the mode of thinking and in the vocabulary of the twenty-first century. In other words, there is need for another St. Thomas, another St. Augustine. But the problem has been that the faith is objective, deductive, and principled because it is about God. How do you take objective truths which are first principles, from which other things are to be deduced, and put them into a subjective, inductive, and experiential language. It would seem to be impossible!

New Synthesis of John Paul II

However, John Paul II has offered the Church and the world precisely what it needs: a new way of conveying the faith — a new synthesis that harnesses both worldviews together so that they pull in tandem and not in opposition.

In a speech in Cracow in 1958, the then Karol Wojtyla linked the objective content of the faith with the subjective individual. He noted that each one of us is created in the image and likeness of God as unique and separate individuals. Obviously, this truth is in the first chapter of Genesis and has been part and parcel of Judaeo-Christian culture since it was established.

However, the future Pope used the truth of our Creation in God's image in a new way. Since we are all created to be like God and since we are all unique reflections of God, our own experiences, properly understood, reveal something of God. Since we are images of God, our experiences should reveal something about God. Just as someone looking at an image of us knows something of us, so when we look at ourselves and our experiences, we should know something of God.

Clearly, this insight means that our individual, subjective experiences collected inductively — whether gathered from several individuals or several experiences gathered from one person — can reveal something of God. In this way, theologians can make use of the modern mode of thought in their work. However, they must also do what each of us has to do if we are to know ourselves; that is, to know who we are and how to act as images of God, we need to know who God is and how He acts.

Therefore, there is a tie to the ultimate objective, principled Being of the universe from whom everything is deduced. The marriage of the two mind-sets — the medieval and the modern — occurs in the human person, in the individual mystery that each of us is. For this reason, John Paul II's teaching is called the new personalism.

In catechetics, John Paul II's new personalism solves major problems. It makes it possible to use human experience in the proper way to come to know something of God. It provides a coherent system and structure because the Pope has taught us almost the entire *corpus* of the faith in his new synthesis.

It answers the objection of not teaching the children what they are not capable of understanding because it shows that the objection is not valid. Of course, they can understand something about the Trinity because they are images of the Trinity. (Obviously, no one can understand the Trinity completely, but as images of God, we each reflect the Trinity in some way.)

John Paul II's new synthesis does not do violence to the faith, but it does give it a new approach. For example, many young people today will insist that they are persons and have rights. They will often use this argument against authority figures. Many times a parent or teacher will almost seem to deny the truth of what the young people are saying. Something such as, "So, you think you have rights, do you? Well, as long as you live in this house (or are in this classroom) . . . ." But what the young people are saying is fundamentally true. Therefore, it should not be denied.

John Paul II's new approach allows one to affirm the truth of the modern insight. In the example given, the response would be: "Yes, you are a person; you do have rights. Do you know why you are a person and have rights? You are a person and have rights because you are made in God's image and likeness. Now, *act* like it."

In other words, one affirms the truth of what is said and then builds on it. In the example given, to act as an image of God is to follow the commandments, because the commandments are the way God acts and the way an image of God should act. The same content of the faith is taught, but in a different mode that takes the truth of the modern viewpoints and builds on it. It is much more effective than denying what is true!

St. Augustine used Plato and St. Thomas used Aristotle. John Paul II is using phenomenology, a philosophical movement begun in Germany at the end of the nineteenth century by Edmund Husserl. Literally, phenomenology means the study of phenomena.

A phenomenologist is a philosopher who begins with human experience. The experience is analyzed ,and from many such analyses the philosopher tries to build a picture and understanding of humanity. John Paul studied phenomenology in the 1950s at the University of Cracow when he was earning his doctorate in philosophy. His dissertation examined the work of Max Scheler, a German phenomenologist very interested in romantic and sexual love. In these studies, Wojtyla saw the possibilities phenomenology had when applied to the mysteries of the faith.

Ever since those years, but especially as Pope, he has taught the faith in this new system. His *Theology of the Body* and *Theology of the Family* have both become famous for their new insights and approaches. His concept of the Church as the "expert in humanity" is also a fruit of his new synthesis.

John Paul II's new approach does not change the faith at all. If one thinks of the content of the faith — the Revelation of Christ — as a very large diamond sitting on a pedestal under a skylight in the middle of a room in a museum, it is a bit easier to understand what John Paul II is doing. The diamond can be viewed from any point on the 360-degree circumference. The viewpoint of the onlooker is defined by philosophy. St. Augustine looked at the diamond from one vantage point, using Platonic philosophy. St. Thomas moved to another point on the circumference using Aristotle, and John Paul has defined a third point. Nevertheless, they are all looking at the exact same diamond.

Further, one onlooker can point out a feature to another onlooker. In other words, St. Thomas sees the same thing as St. Augustine or John Paul II, but he describes it differently. But they each describe the same feature of the diamond. Therefore, it is possible to "translate" the description of any feature of the diamond from Augustine to Thomas to John Paul II, from Thomas to Augustine and John Paul II, and from John Paul II to Thomas and Augustine. It is always the same diamond.

Why have a new vantage point? Cultures change and develop. New questions arise. The Church needs to convey the content of Revelation, the diamond, in a way that is understandable to people of every generation. That is what St. Thomas did for the thirteenth century — and make no mistake, there were those who insisted on continuing to use the traditional explanations, that is, the synthesis of St. Augustine—and that is what John Paul II is doing for our generation.

If one understands the Thomistic or Augustinian syntheses, is there any harm in using them? Of course not, and they need to be taught to every generation of theologians. However, as a way of conveying the faith to the people of the twenty-first century, it seems that the new John Paul II synthesis is more effective.

Many will insist that John Paul II is a Thomist. Of course, he is! St. Thomas was an Augustinian. Each new synthesis builds on the previous ones. Before you can build a new one, you must study the diamond! How could you study the diamond without standing at a particular vantage point? And what better vantage point to use but one that was well-studied?

There is no question that John Paul II is a Thomist. But there is also no question that he is building a new theological synthesis that will be one of the building blocks of the Church in the twenty-first century and beyond. The Augustinian synthesis was the way the Church thought about Revelation for about eight hundred years! St. Thomas's synthesis was in place for more than seven hundred years. If the pattern holds, John Paul II's synthesis of phenomenology and Revelation will be with us for centuries. John Paul's pontificate certainly qualifies as "interesting times."

John Paul II's New Personalism and Freedom

There remains the question which ended the last chapter: how does the new personalism of John Paul II solve the problem of the supposed opposition between truth and freedom — that is, between authority and the freedom of the individual?

In a brilliant analysis of the temptation of the devil in the Garden of Eden, John Paul II points out that the third lie of the devil to Adam and Eve — that they would know good and evil — really means that they could actually be God. The devil was suggesting that they could make whatever they wanted to be good and whatever they disliked to be evil. They could establish their own world, and whatever they decreed would be reality.

Moral reality would depend on each of their wills. Further, the status of their own lives, their rights, their dignity would depend on each of their wills. But what if their wills were in conflict? What if one of them did not want to grant freedom and human dignity to the other? (This is not unheard of. Slavery existed in the United States and in many other countries!)

If someone tried to enslave any one of us, we would assert that we have "certain inalienable rights." However, this assertion would not hold because no human rights would exist independent of the will of the person creating the reality. If Adam created one reality and Eve another and these two were in conflict, one would have to change or there would be a struggle and the more powerful person's view would prevail. In other words, might makes right! Absolute freedom to the point where each one can create his or her own reality destroys the very things it is trying to affirm.

If Hitler can create his own world and determine what is good and evil, who has rights and who does not, and there is no reality beyond his will (because he is the most powerful one), the claim to human freedom is only valid for one — Hitler.

The Holy Father points out that freedom and truth are two sides of the same coin. We are made in God's image, therefore we are free. But God is not only freedom, He is also Truth. Freedom and truth are both united in God and are not in opposition. They should not be in conflict in us.

As images of God, we are free and are made for the truth. Freedom guarantees that we can all search for the truth, but truth guarantees that all human beings have certain rights and are free.

The Church teaches the truth which makes us free, and freedom guarantees that we can seek the truth. The Declaration of Independence comes close to saying the same thing: "We hold these *truths* to be self-evident, that all men are created equal, that they are endowed by their Creator with certain unalienable rights, that among these are life, *liberty*, and the pursuit of happiness." Truth and liberty (freedom) are in the same sentence! They are complementary and necessary to each other.

Freedom without truth destroys freedom, and truth must be sought in freedom. As one character in a movie once said, "God save us from the self-righteous; it's the rest of us who get broken in half." Truth cannot be forced or imposed; it must be sought.

John Paul II, then, clearly teaches that each and every individual is free to seek the truth and that the individual has an obligation to accept the truth when presented with it. With regard to the truths of Revelation, Catholics believe that God presents them through the Church and that He also gives each of those who hear them the gift of the virtue of faith so that they can be believed. However, no one must be forced to profess beliefs. (This mistake has been made often in the past, by those acting in the name of the Church and by many others.)

If one cannot accept what the Church teaches, no one will use any kind of force. However, that does not change the nature of what the Church teaches. It is still true. This teaching is found in *Dominus Iesus* ("The Lord

Jesus"), a document released by the Vatican in September 2000. In this document the Church teaches that the fullness of Christ's Revelation is present in the Roman Catholic Church. It agrees that other Christian denominations teach and practice the Christian faith, but only the Catholic Church teaches and practices all that Christ revealed. All religions are not the same. Such a teaching may be hard to hear, but it is still true! Some may reject such teachings as those contained in *Dominus Iesus*, and each one is free to accept or reject the teachings of the Church.

However, in rejecting the Church's teaching, an individual may have rejected God's offer of faith. Those rejecting the truths that the Church presents, most especially the members of the Church, have hampered themselves because they have refused the truth and all of us as images of God were made for the truth. Nevertheless, a Catholic like Loisy, the French modernist, can reject Church teaching, but then that individual is no longer in complete communion with the Church.

In John Paul II's pontificate, this is precisely how the Vatican has handled some dissenting theologians. They can teach whatever they believe, but they cannot teach whatever they believe (if it conflicts with Church teaching) under the label "Catholic." The new element here is the repeated emphasis on the individual's freedom, even if the person chooses to dissent from the content of the faith. But the more important new element in this view is the new way that truth and freedom are seen as complementary in us and not in opposition. As images of God we should always strive to reflect Him who is simultaneously Truth and Freedom.

INDEX

Barbelo-Gnostics, 46

Bartholomew Day Massacre, 253

Basel, ecumenical council of, 201, 233, 244, 245, 246

Basil of Ancyra, 93, 96

Basil of Caesarea, 96

Berengar, 164, 165, 166, 167, 168, 169, 170, 283

Bernard of Clairvaux, St., 171

Beziers, 177, 178, 179

Blaurock, Joerg, 240

Blount, Charles, 280

Boethius, 166

Book of Common Prayer, 260, 261

Bonaventure, St., 187

Boniface II, Pope, 120

Bourges, 243

Brothers of the Common Life, 203

Bucer, Martin, 260

Buddha, 62

Buddhism, 63

C

Caecilian, Bishop of Carthage, 106

Caesaro-papism, 150

Cajetan, Cardinal, 213, 214, 215, 216, 217

Calvin, John, 230, 238, 243, 244, 245, 246, 247, 248, 249, 250, 251, 252, 254, 255, 257, 259, 263, 265, 283

Calvinists, 252, 254, 256, 257, 261, 281

Carcassone, 177, 178, 179

Carthage, 67, 69, 70, 71, 105, 106, 107, 108, 116, 117

Casses, 178

Cassian, John, Abbot, 119, 120

Catharist, 171, 175, 180

Cathars, *see also* Albigensians and *Patarini*, 171, 172, 173, 174, 175, 177, 178, 179, 181, 183, 185, 186, 283

Catherine de Medici, 253

Catholic Church, *see* Church, Catholic

Catholic Poor, 183

Celestine I, Pope, 125

Celestius, 116

Chalcedon, council of, 98, 131, 132, 134, 135, 136, 138, 140, 142, 143

Charlemagne, 150, 158, 163

Charles the Bald, 163

Charles V, Holy Roman Emperor, 221, 222, 230

Charles IX, King of France, 253

Christ, *see also* Jesus, 15, 16, 17, 18, 20, 21, 22, 23, 24, 26, 27, 29, 31, 32, 33, 34, 38, 39, 40, 41, 44, 45, 46, 47, 48, 49, 51, 53, 55, 57, 58, 59, 62, 63, 65, 72, 74, 76, 77, 78, 81, 83, 84, 87, 88, 91, 98, 99, 101, 102, 103, 105, 111, 115, 117, 118, 123, 124, 126, 127, 128, 129, 130, 132, 133, 134, 137, 140, 143, 144, 145, 146, 147, 148, 149, 150, 151, 152, 154, 155, 158, 159, 161, 163, 164, 165, 166, 167, 168, 170, 172, 178, 182, 186, 188, 191, 192, 193, 195, 204, 208, 209, 214, 215, 216, 218, 225, 227, 231, 236, 237, 238, 239, 240, 241, 244, 245, 248, 249, 250, 251, 256, 264, 267, 276, 280, 281, 285, 286, 294, 302, 304, 310, 316, 317, 321, 324

Christ of Faith, 292, 293, 295

Church, Catholic, 20, 26, 70, 107, 108, 109, 117, 219, 247, 248, 249, 256, 281, 288, 289, 300, 304, 324

Cicero, 166

Circumcellions, 107, 108, 109, 110, 114

Cistercians, 174, 176, 193

Clarke, Catherine, 299

Clement IX, Pope, 269

Clement XI, Pope, 271, 272

Clementine Peace, 269, 270, 274

236, 237, 245, 252, 268, 279, 280, 281, 292, 294

Second Vatican Council, *see* Vatican, second ecumenical council of

Segarelli, Gerard (of Parma), 188

Semi-Arianism, *see also* Arianism, 93

Semi-Pelagianism, *see also* Pelagianism, 119, 120, 121

Semi-Quietism, *see also* Quietism, 277

Sergius, Patriarch of Constantinople, 143, 144, 145

Sethians, 46

Sigismund, Holy Roman Emperor, 199, 200, 201

Simon of Cyrene, 45

Simon of Montfort, 177

Sin, *see also* Original sin, 68, 69, 73, 102, 111, 119, 132, 203, 207, 208, 209, 210, 211, 212, 214, 215, 216, 231, 276, 310

Slaves of the Immaculate Heart of Mary, 301

Sola Scriptura, 216, 218

Sophronius, Patriarch of Jerusalem, 143

Spirituals, 188

Steenhoven, Cornelius, 272

Stephen I, Pope, 71, 73

Still River, Mass., 302

Stoics, 17

Strasbourg, 241, 244, 246

Subordinationism, 51, 52, 57, 58, 76

Substance (Eucharist, Trinity) , 83, 97, 99, 132, 165, 167, 168, 318

Sylvester I, Pope, 80

Sylvester II (Gerbert of Rheims), Pope, 166

Tetzel, Johannes, 210, 211, 213, 214

Theoctistus, 156

Theodore of Mopsuestia, 123, 124, 127, 137, 138, 140

Theodoret of Cyrrhus, 129, 131, 138

Theodosius I, Emperor, 98, 114

Theodosius II, Emperor, 125

Theology of the Body, 321

Theology of the Family, 321

Theophilus, Emperor, 156

Third Lateran Council, 181

Thomas Aquinas, *see* Aquinas, Thomas, St.

Thomas the Slav, 156

Thomistic synthesis, *see also* Aquinas, Thomas, St., 316, 317, 318, 322

Three Chapters, 78, 137, 138, 139, 140, 141, 142

Tirol, 228, 240

Titus, 19

Toland, John, 280

Tome of St. Leo, 130, 131, 132, 135, 136, 137

Tradition, 21, 22, 23, 24, 46, 56, 68, 90, 124, 128, 134, 136, 147, 148, 151, 163, 166, 168, 169, 171, 182, 230, 231, 235, 261, 274, 296

Traditores, 105, 106

Transubstantiation, 225

Trier, 86

Trinity, 20, 26, 27, 29, 47, 48, 51, 52, 57, 59, 76, 77, 78, 80, 83, 98, 99, 117, 127, 133, 134, 154, 161, 280, 282, 285, 286, 310, 317, 320

Tritheism, 134

Tyrell, George, 294, 295, 296, 297

T

Taborites, 201

Tarasius, Patriarch of Constantinople, 152

Tertullian, 54, 55, 67, 68, 71, 83, 105, 107

U

Ulfilas, 99

Utraquists, 201

Utrecht, 272, 288, 290

Our Sunday Visitor. . .
Your Source for Discovering
the Riches of the Catholic Faith

Our Sunday Visitor has an extensive line of materials for young children, teens, and adults. Our books, Bibles, booklets, CD-ROMs, audios, and videos are available in bookstores worldwide.

To receive a FREE full-line catalog or for more information, call **Our Sunday Visitor** at **1-800-348-2440**. Or write, **Our Sunday Visitor** / 200 Noll Plaza / Huntington, IN 46750.

- -

Please send me: ___A catalog
Please send me materials on:
___Apologetics and catechetics   ___Reference works
___Prayer books   ___Heritage and the saints
___The family   ___The parish
Name_____
Address_____Apt._____
City_____State_____Zip_____
Telephone (   ) _____

A13BBABP

- -

Please send a friend: ___A catalog
Please send a friend materials on:
___Apologetics and catechetics   ___Reference works
___Prayer books   ___Heritage and the saints
___The family   ___The parish
Name_____
Address_____Apt._____
City_____State_____Zip_____
Telephone (   ) _____

A13BBABP

- -

Our Sunday Visitor
200 Noll Plaza
Huntington, IN 46750
Toll free: 1-800-348-2440
E-mail: osvbooks@osv.com
Website: www.osv.com

Your Source for Discovering the Riches of the Catholic Faith